Reuben's Fall

Sheri L.Leafgren

International Institute for Qualitative Methodology Series

Series Editor: Lisa Given, University of Alberta

The International Institute for Qualitative Methodology, under the auspices of the Faculty of Nursing at the University of Alberta, was founded in 1998 to facilitate the development of qualitative research methods across a wide variety of academic disciplines through research, publications, conferences and workshops. The series consists of volumes that received the Dissertation Award of the Institute, then were revised for publication.

Reuben's Fall

A Rhizomatic Analysis of
Disobedience in Kindergarten

Sheri L.Leafgren

Routledge

Taylor & Francis Group

LONDON AND NEW YORK

First published 2009 by Left Coast Press, Inc.
First paperback edition 2011.

Published 2016 by Routledge
2 Park Square, Milton Park, Abingdon, Oxon OX14 4RN
711 Third Avenue, New York, NY 10017, USA

Routledge is an imprint of the Taylor & Francis Group, an informa business

Library of Congress Cataloging-in-Publication Data

Leafgren, Sheri.
Reuben's fall : a rhizomatic analysis of disobedience in kindergarten / Sheri Leafgren.
    p. cm.—(International Institute for Qualitative Methodology series)
  Includes bibliographical references and index.
  ISBN 978-1-59874-494-1 (hardcover : alk. paper)— ISBN 978-1-59874-495-8 (paperback : alk. paper)
  —ISBN 978-1-59874-737-9 (eISBN)

1. Kindergarten—United States. 2. School discipline—United States. 3. Behavior
    modification—United States. I. Title.
  LB1205.L34 2009
  372.15—dc22

Cover design by Hannah Jennings
Cover photograph by Kerry Merriman

ISBN 978-1-59874-494-1 hardcover
ISBN 978-1-59874-495-8 paperback

Contents

*This book is dedicated to Julian and disobedient
children and teachers everywhere.*

*And to my own disobedient children
and grandchildren, with love.*

Foreword

Sheri Leafgren's study is a work of intellectual passion; and in the words of Anita Roddick, British businesswoman, human rights activist and environmental campaigner, "passion persuades." A penetrating critical examination of what it means to be a "good" student and a "good" teacher, Dr. Leafgren's beautifully written book is an elegant synthesis of Elliot Eisner's *educational criticism* and Gilles Deleuze's *rhizoanalysis*. She integrates these two complex concepts into a deeply insightful and multi-layered study resulting in a deep exploration of the ontological and ethical dimensions of educational practice. We're particularly impressed with her penetrating and fluid examination of "the spiritual, democratic, moral and joyful possibilities in the moments of children's disobediences."

Research on classroom misbehavior or disobedience has traditionally focused on "fixing" the problem of children's noncompliance. Dr. Leafgren suggests a differing, possibly disruptive, perspective or teacher stance. Advancing a more nuanced understanding of "disobedience", she promotes the idea that teachers should "view with fresh eyes the ways that children negotiate the context, complexity, constraints and freedoms of kindergarten classrooms as represented through moments of disobedience." Dr. Leafgren's "reality" is not conventional wisdom. When problematizing children's disobedience, her reality becomes embedded in the "spirituality" of children rather than societal developmental norms and expectations.

With the ability to connect multiple visions of schooling, Dr. Leafgren has represented children and teachers throughout her study by focusing upon two kindergarten classrooms in two different districts—one where she was a student and one where she was an elementary school teacher. In regards to schooling, she carefully explains the purpose of her book: "Given the compelling moral, social, spiritual and ethical motives for further exploration of the politics and philosophies underlying the constraints of school morality, this book seeks to provide particular insights into moments of disobedience through direct observations of kindergarten children as they acted on moral opportunities during the real time daily activities and routines of a kindergarten classroom." In effect, she has focused upon daily schooling interactions that when carefully considered offer more than simplistic analysis and understanding, but rather opportunities for viewing the often paradoxical "moments of disobedience" regularly occurring in classrooms.

Dr. Leafgren contends that children's socialization in schools occurs and recurs in "moments" of social interaction with the assumption that accumulated moments, over time, result in "swaddled children." According to Dr. Leafgren, children risk becoming morally, socially and spiritually "swaddled" and" constrained" via "adult dominance" and "preemptive school procedures and rules" that result in prescribed means for safety, security and predictability that often interfere with "children's potential to act on spiritual-moral opportunities." Her carefully constructed examples of such moments are both plentiful and thought provoking. They encourage the reader to increase one's awareness of possibility for further wondering about such opportunities within the context of educational purposes.

Through her writing, Dr. Leafgren communicates her understanding that teaching and the profession of teachers involves moral activity and moral agency to promote the betterment of the lives of children. She explores children's hidden wholeness, vulnerability, and wonder through naturally occurring classroom interactions that are full of connections and possibilities of commitment rather than compliance through "mutual bindings to shared values, traditions, ideas and ideals" (p. 61) as Sergiovanni (1994) has suggested.

When considering teachers, Dr. Leafgren promotes the idea of "softening" the lens of teaching through teachers' understanding of their practices and their understanding of children. She questions, "In what ways are kindergartners' moments of disobedience representations and enactments of something more than merely disobedience?" Through this "softening" or "fresh lens" metaphor, it would appear that teachers would necessarily embody a set of dispositions that are aptly summarized by Barell (1991): "They are open to others' ideas. They cooperate with others in solving problems. They listen. They are empathic. They tolerate ambiguity and complexity.... They are open to many different solutions and evidence that may contradict favored points of view.... They are curious and wonder about the world. They ask 'good questions'" (p. 34).

Teachers, embodying such dispositions, work with serious deliberation and thoughtful action regarding moral foundations of teaching and promote moral potential and capacity for children and themselves. Hansen (2001) furthers this conception and contends that, "The moral quality of knowledge lies not in its possession, but in how it can foster a widening consciousness and mindfulness. This moral cast of mind...embodies commitments to (i.e., habits of mind): straightforwardness, simplicity, naivete, open-mindedness, integrity of purpose, responsibility, and seriousness" (p. 59).

Carl Rogers, writing in the late 1960s, noted that education faced "incredible challenges." Dr. Leafgren, through her writing, considers one such incredible challenge, among others, existing today—alternative "consideration of 'truths,' understandings, and questions regarding children's disobediences"—and asks the reader to contemplate, through small moments of classroom social interactions, opportunities for big ideas and possibilities for action—ideas and action involving "the potential of children's classroom disobedience: potential not only in responding to others in caring, ethical ways, but also the potential in acting out the possibilities that a 'spiritual' childhood provides." Through the vehicle of her study, she provokes thoughtful consideration of children's and teachers' ways of being—with intellectual passion that persuades.

Overall, Dr. Leafgren's study is a fascinating and unusually mature account of how dedicated educators can "fold" moral imagination into curriculum deliberations and classroom transactions. Our use of *fold* refers to a Deleuzian folding, unfolding, and refolding that occurs when "exteriority becomes reversed into interiority... Thinking coincides with Being" (Badiou 2000, 89). From its opening pages, Dr. Leafgren's book is an embodiment of the artistry of this folding, unfolding and refolding. Through her subtle, multilayered, critical analysis of "Reuben's fall," she practices a holistic fluidity that integrates being, knowing, feeling and doing in the context of a "broad conception of mind...[and] multiple conception of meaning" (Eisner 1994, 89). Ultimately, this is her "methodology"; and

through this disciplined artistry, she documents the vital importance of "ethical fidelity" (Badiou 2001) in even the most prosaic
moments in a school day.

As Dr. Leafgren's dissertation co-advisors, we are extremely
proud of what she has accomplished. Her research is more than a
thoughtful critical analysis of the meaning of "disobedience" in education; it is a beautiful, soul-searching meditation on how a "love
of wisdom" is embodied and enacted in daily educational events.
"The devil is in the details" is a common expression in our culture.
In the case of Dr. Leafgren's research, it would be more appropriate
to say, "The moral universe is in the moment."

Richard Ambrose
James Henderson
Kent State University

Acknowledgements

One of the most valuable lessons I have learned in the process of completing this book is how extraordinarily lucky I am in having the support of family, friends, and colleagues. Here I would like to acknowledge and *thank* the people whose regard and care I so value.

Not so long ago, this book was my doctoral dissertation. I am deeply grateful to my friends and dissertation chairs, James Henderson and Richard Ambrose of Kent State University, for sticking with me through a long and, I am sure, confusing process, and for the inspiration of their own scholarship and ethical commitment. I offer a special note of appreciation to Rich, who has been a friend and active supporter for more than 20 years, and whose belief in my work I hope I can live up to. I also wish to thank the committee members Wendy Sherman-Heckler and Walter Davis for their support, insights, and for the challenges they posed throughout the process of completing the "big paper" (as Rich calls it). And to the final member of the committee, Francis Broadway, I thank you for all of the above and for years of true and genuine friendship.

I profusely thank the teachers and the children in the kindergartens at Andrews and Shadow Lake Elementary Schools. What generosity you demonstrated in offering me a chance to share in your kindergarten experience! I loved it.

Along the way, many caring friends generously contributed insights, encouragement and moral support, and I thank them: Deb Bruce, Terri Cardy, Dan Castner, Laurel Chehayl, Kim Cole, Diane Craig, Gen Davis, Richard Emch (especially for emails that made me laugh so hard, other things happened; and for all the times you said, *you can do it.*), Andy Gilbert (for sometimes *scaring* me into action. You know what I mean.), Sally Hodge, Eunny Hyun, Nida'a Makki, Michael O'Malley, Roger Pryor, Gloria Sanders, Brian Schultz, Shane' Williams, and friends I cited, Tommy Trantino and Kent den Heyer. As well, I appreciate the wise influence of Edwin George, Dona Greene, and the Council of Elders—Baba Fred Johnson, Ayubu Mahdi and Jumanne Mwuesi.

I am thankful to Carol Bersani and Terri Cardy of Kent State University's Child Development Center for the use of Terri's *lovely* classroom for the book cover. What a *child*space Terri has made for her students!

To the folks associated with Left Coast Press, Mitch Allen, Jennifer Collier and Hannah and Michael Jennings, thank you not only for your time, effort, and expertise—but for the *care* you took. Publishing with a heart!

I am deeply grateful to (and for) my caring and supportive children—Monica, Aaron, Kerry and Sylvia—who, through their own strength and independence, gave me the space and confidence to make this work. (Monica, "Julian" is for you.) Also thanks and love to my mother, Patricia Simmons, for her support and unconditional love. My brother Steve I thank for being my brother and my earliest creative inspiration.

And to every child I have met and every one I *will* meet, thank you for your energy, joy, curiosity, presence, and indomitable spirit. And for disobeying.

Chapter 1

Introduction:
Troubling Reuben's Fall

The moral universe rests on the breath of schoolchildren.

~ Rabbi Yehuda Nisiah (in Paley 1999)

Background Narrative: Reuben's Fall

Reuben fell. My professional life defined itself eighteen years ago when Reuben fell on the hard school-linoleum floor outside my classroom door. I was a young(er) person and a more naïve teacher at the time, blithely enjoying my lively class of kindergartners, covertly noticing some of the more interesting children in the kindergarten class down the hall, and on that morning, fully engaged in minding the interactions of the children in my own classroom when I heard the hard smack and muffled grunt signaling Reuben's fall. When I went to the door to see what had happened to disturb the commonplace silent, gender-based, double-lined trek connecting Mrs. Buttercup's kindergarten class to the restrooms at the end of the hall, I witnessed a significant event.

In the aftermath of Reuben's fall, Julian—one of those spirited, full-of-verve, curious, "bad" children whom I had coveted for my own classroom—had left his place in the back of the line to reach Reuben where he had fallen near the front of the boys' line and, as I arrived at the door, was helping him off the floor, asking, "Reuben, are you okay?"

As the other children steadfastly maintained their places in their straight, silent, boy and girl lines, Mrs. Buttercup shook her head, held up two fingers, and said to Julian: "That's two, Julian. You are out of line and you are talking. You're on the wall at recess." Going "on the wall" is a common punishment in grade school. It means the child must spend all or part of recess standing against the wall of the school building watching the other children play. I had observed that Julian, a lively child, spent most recesses "on the wall" for various infractions of the rules of order in his kindergarten classroom. A kindergartner falling down is not a rare event. The fact that most classmates would watch without response is also commonplace. And a child being reprimanded and/or punished for breaking a rule of order, regardless of the reason, is not at all unusual. I know this because I have been a participant of school as a pupil, teacher and observer for many years and have witnessed countless similar events before and since Reuben's fall.

However, this moment was a critical one for me. I saw clearly that Julian's actions were "good"—demonstrating care, empathy, courage, and kindness—and yet, he was punished. For good is also defined by teachers and children in school as order, silence, and stillness—in other words, compliance. In fact, *dictionary.reference.com* offers as their eighteenth listing for good: "well-behaved; obedient: a *good* child." In this case, Julian had not complied with the school and classroom rules—*No talking* and *Stay in your place in line*—as he moved to help Reuben and inquire into his well-being. As witness to the event, I was struck by the concomitantly good and bad nature of Julian's action.

This experience of the unexpected and cognitively chaotic counts as what Lozinsky and Collinson (1999) refer to as the "epistemological shudder" (and which Strong and Fuller [2000] describe as "alive moments"), an "affective response to an encounter with things *marvellous*." The term "marvellous" here makes reference to concepts of "difference," "out of the ordinary," and "unexpected" (in MacNaughton 2005, 111); and the "epistemological shudder" occurs when one's preferred representations do not allow one to make sense of what is seen, heard, or experienced and lead one to feel "uncomfortable, displaced, and in a sense almost paralysed, not knowing where to place this information" (Giugni 2006, 101).

As a witness to this event, I shuddered as I experienced a "fragmentation of contextual understanding" (MacNaughton 2005, 116), which has since led to a series of aporia as I trouble—"recall, rethink and retheorise" (p. 117)—the event of Reuben's fall. I wondered about the effect on the children of seeing kindness so devalued. I wondered what the children thought of Julian's act. While I did not ask at the time, I believe that most of the children, had they been asked if Julian was good, would have said, "No. No, Julian isn't good. He got out of line." Or, "Julian is bad. He had to go on the wall." For, certainly, we learn from the cradle that goodness most closely approximates compliance; if we don't learn it then, it is a hard lesson in the schoolroom.

Upton Sinclair (1922) addressed such schoolroom lessons in *Goose Step: A Study in American Education*, a scathing account of the field of education that chronicles years of study of America's institutions of higher education. Sinclair's findings documented the vapidity of those involved in the highest of educational pursuits and exposed the narrow and often unethical attitudes and practices of administrators and faculty. Recognizing the naissance of this state of affairs, Sinclair began his report in this way:

> Once upon a time there was a little boy; a little boy unusually eager, and curious about the world he lived in.... Every morning this little boy's mother saw to his scrubbing, with special attention to his ears, both inside and back, and put a clean white collar on him, and packed his lunch-box with two sandwiches and a piece of cake and an apple, and started him off to school.
>
> The school was a vast building—or so it seemed to the little boy. It had stone staircases with iron railings, and big rooms with rows of little desks, blackboards, maps of Abraham Lincoln and Aurora driving her chariot. Everywhere you went in this school you formed in line and marched; you talked in chorus, everybody saying the same thing as nearly at the same instant as could be contrived. The little boy found that a delightful arrangement, for he liked other boys, and the more of them there were, the better. He kept step happily and sat with glee in the assembly room, and clapped when the others clapped, and laughed when they laughed....
>
> The rest of the day the little boy sat in a crowded classroom, learning things. The first thing he learned was that you must be quiet.... Another thing you learned was that you must raise your hand if you wanted to speak. Maybe these things were necessary, but the little boy did not learn why they were necessary; in school all you learned was that things were so.... [I]f you asked the reason for it, the teacher would be apt to answer in a way that caused the other little boys to laugh at you—something which is very painful...

you had a sense of triumph over other little boys who were stupid. You enjoyed this triumph, because no one ever suggested to you that it was cruel to laugh at your weaker fellows. In fact, the system appeared to be designed to bring out your superiority, and to increase the humiliation of the others. (Sinclair 1922, 1–2)

Consider what Julian and his classmates might have learned from the event of Reuben's fall. They might have learned that such things as keeping silent and staying in line were "necessary," but not why they were so. The children in the lines may have learned that they were good and so superior to Julian, which would have confirmed that this lively child was bad and that each of them demonstrated their own goodness as they remained quiet and still even when confronted with Reuben's need for care.

I wonder about the role of school in a child's construction of his or her own sense of goodness. I wonder about the opportunities children have in the context of school to make real moral decisions regarding their own choices for good action, how they act on those and how their spiritual nature is represented in those decisions. I wonder, are kindergartners empowered to make decisions using their intellect for generous and generative purposes, or are their moral decisions based on coercion and habit (Dewey 1932/1985, J. Henderson 2001b)? I further wonder what we steal from children as we make them believe that being good excludes much of what is childlike, and as we communicate to children that their "childishness" is something to be derided and discarded, devalued even while the playfulness, verve, and intense awareness of the child—the "complete abandon, and whole-hearted faith" (Quinn 2001, 1)—are the very qualities that many would align with those of the most spiritual of beings. Indeed, spirituality has been closely linked to children's complexity, sense of wonder, and especially their joyful forays into ambiguity and uncertainty (i.e., Hay and Nye 1998). I wonder if this is what we have in mind when we teach children that their goodness is contingent on their orderly obedience.

I am drawn to this work because of to my deep interest and investment in children while troubling how they might reconcile their "child-spirit" self (Hart 1999/2003) with their "schooled-child" self in regard to their interactions with other children, adults, and the kindergarten environment. I wish to understand children better as they negotiate the context, complexity, constraints, and freedoms of a kindergarten classroom as represented through acts of obedience and disobedience. I enter this work believing that as children confront the complexities of the very human morality of "ends" and the more cultural morality of laws (Dewey 1929/1984, Zinn 1968), their disobediences might be related to a spiritual awareness unique to children that allows them to disrupt the universe in ways that may lead to joy.

Purpose of the Book

After initial reviews of the literature regarding disobedient behaviors of young children in the classroom, I identified five lines of inquiry. The majority of work by writers, theorists, and researchers in the area of classroom disobedience is directed toward the teacher and classroom along the lines of the following topics:

1. Disobedience (and childhood itself) as a form of deficiency (developmental, moral/religious, social, and behavioral) and/or as problems to be solved.

2. The need for a particular type of order and control in schools and the means of achieving child compliance—and, as a result, "a positive, productive classroom atmosphere conducive to learning" (Barbetta, Leong-Norona and Bicard 2005).

3. The teacher's perspective and role in children's moral and social behaviors, and the complexity of child compliance. Often discussed from a constructivist perspective in comparison to the more behaviorist approaches in the two prior categories, the goal here, however, is the same—to assert the authority of the teacher, but as a moral authority instead of a coercive one.

4. The political, philosophical, and spiritual constraints of school morality. Within this category are researchers who study the state of school itself and authors who, with a more philosophical bent, write about the ideals of school(ing) in contrast to what they perceive as the state of school.

5. The value of dissent and noncompliance toward an authentic democratic good life, reflecting Ralph Waldo Emerson's caution: "your goodness must have some edge to it—else it is none" (1940, 149, in Goodman 2001, 351).

My discussion of this literature in chapter 2 offers examples of findings and conclusions that may be helpful in gaining a fuller sense of school, schooling, and the discourse on classroom disobedience. While the first two categories of literature listed above provide many examples of discussions on children's disobedience—generally toward an authoritarian purpose—and while the authors in the final three categories raise moral, social, spiritual and ethical reasons for exploring further the moral complexity and ambiguity of schools, none of these discussions of disobedience offer opportunities to engage in the complexities and possibilities of the acts of the children as they disobey and comply in their kindergarten classrooms.

Given the compelling moral, social, spiritual, and ethical motives for further exploration of the politics and philosophies underlying the constraints of school morality, this book provides particular insights into moments of disobedience through direct observations of kindergarten children as they act on moral opportunities during the real-time, daily activities and routines of a kindergarten classroom.

My research is unique in that it does not focus on documenting classroom management styles or on solving "problems" related to noncompliance, nor does it focus on the teacher's perspective and actions in the classroom. Rather, the descriptions of observations made in real-time in a kindergarten classroom provide real-life moments of children's disobedience and resistance, as well as opportunities to explore connecting texts "that provide new entry points to ways of making sense of child observations" (MacNaughton 2005, 133) and critically challenge "compliancism" (Leafgren 2006) in a kindergarten classroom context. As the children translate the messages of "kindergartenness" into action through interactions with one another and the adults in the classroom, they negotiate the conflicting goodnesses as described by Goodman and Lesnick (2001) and as represented by the event of Reuben's fall.

This book describes the potential of children's classroom disobedience—potential not only to respond to others in caring, ethical ways, but also potential to act out the possibilities that a "spiritual" childhood provides. For it is in the nature of the spiritual child—fully present, wide awake, spiritually awake, mindful, completely engaged with what-is-there, totally abandoned, eyes wide open, deeply encountering—that such possibilities may be found (as described, for instance, in Buber 1958/1970, Greene 1981, Hanh 1998, Hart 1999, Jardine 1998, Kesson 1999, Noddings 1993, Purpel 2001, Quinn 2001, Steiner 1995).

Here, I apply methods of qualitative inquiry (Eisner 1998) to school and teacher traditions and to observations of kindergarten children in the context of their kindergarten classroom. This provides opportunities to orient "rhizomatic logic" to the readings of the children in order to "build complex and diverse pictures of 'the child', of 'observation,' and of 'research'[and offers] a tool for critically reflecting on how meaning is produced through the choices we make about what we use to map" the readings of children's texts (MacNaughton 2005, 144–145).

This book also provides a unique perspective on children's negotiation of spiritual-moral opportunities in the schoolroom. "To know what schools are like… we need to be able to see what occurs in them, and we need to be able to tell others what we have seen in ways that are vivid and insightful" claimed Eisner (1998, 5–6), for schools

> have moods, and they too display scenes of high drama that those who make policy and those who seek to improve practice should know…. The means through which such knowledge is made possible are the enlightened eye—the scene is seen—and the ability to craft text so that what the observer has experienced can be shared by those who were not there. (p. 22, 30)

I do not claim an "enlightened eye." I do not contend that my view is more sophisticated or more informed than others' views. Rather, I offer an "enquiring eye." This research does not serve to answer questions or solve problems from a position of specialized knowledge, but instead serves to complicate understanding and so to open minds and hearts to possibilities in moments of disobedience in the context of a kindergarten classroom. The application of rhizomatic analysis to the pictures/texts of the children "observed" allows for multiple meanings and literary, political, spiritual and social possibilities. The mapping of these readings "is open and connectable in all of its dimensions; it is detachable, reversible, susceptible to constant modification. It can be torn, reversed, adapted to any kind of mounting, reworked by an individual, group or social formation" (Deleuze and Guattari 1987, 12).

Problem Statement and Questions

While this book looks carefully at children in school as they define themselves and act as kindergartners, maybe even as "good" kindergartners, it also works to acknowledge the complexity of each child. Each child comes to school, potentially, as son, daughter, T-ball player, pest, grandbaby, Pookie-Bear, fast runner, big sister, pizza-lover, drama queen, tough guy, choir singer, video game player, Sponge-Bob fan, little brother, chore doer, bed-wetter, ballerina, and/or hip-hopper. Each child enters kindergarten each day after oversleeping or staying up all night; eating too much or too little; an argument with a sister or a kiss and hug from a dad; watching cartoons or listening to music; a wet, cold walk or a noisy bus-ride; a scrubbing "with special attention to the ears inside and back" or a roll out of bed and into yesterday's clothes; and also pre-equipped with a five to six year history of cultural, emotional, familial, media, relational, experiential, and spiritual influences.

In these ways, identities grow and shift rhizomatically. And so, ways of researching with children also need to be rhizomatic— overlapping, multi-focal and shifting with time. Rhizoanalysis challenges the idea that one moment in a child's life may be "caused" by his/her stage of child development, his/her gender, his/her teacher or by what another child said or did. Scientific findings of research using the representational "tree logic" of cause and effect are difficult to implement in education because humans in schools are embedded in complex and changing networks of being and social interaction. As each participant in every interaction has variable power to affect one another from day to day, and in the ordinary events of life, the generalizability of these educational research findings is greatly limited (Berliner 2002, MacNaughton 2003). The non-representational lateral logic of rhizoanalysis serves to create tensions related to "changeability, diversity, 'noisiness' (complexity)" and so highlights the complex and shifting links between, for instance, gender, cognition, class, race, culture, obedience, and compliance as the links shoot in unpredictable ways into a particular moment in a child's life (MacNaughton 2003, Smith 2003).

What all of the children involved in this book do share is the particular time of a study in the context of two particular kindergarten classrooms. They are all working out who they are as their kindergarten selves, and they all face on a daily basis interactions and opportunities in the kindergarten classrooms in which their moral lives are to be conjointly constructed and personally interpreted. Therefore, this particular study is designed to pursue understanding regarding the following three questions:

1. In what ways do these kindergarten children disobey in the context of the kindergarten classroom?

2. In what ways are these kindergartners' moments of disobedience representations and enactments of something more than merely disobedience?

3. In what ways are these kindergartners' moments of disobedience opportunities for responding to others in caring, ethical ways and acting out the possibilities that a spiritual childhood provides—such as reverence, awe, wonder, reflection, imagination, and purpose, and the sensitivities in awareness sensing, mystery sensing, and value sensing (Hay and Nye 1998).

For each of the questions above, efforts were made to generate and interrogate texts of the child (via videotaped observations of the kindergarten classrooms) in order to seek surprises toward "disrupt[ing] the familiar and obvious" (MacNaughton 2004) in what is known and so to form a new logic about what is happening in the text while building new understandings of its relationships to other texts. "Rhizomes are about mapping new or unknown lines and entry points, not tracing which records old lines or patterns" (Deleuze and Guattari 1987, 134–135). This research is an opportunity to "encounter to experience something we did not know before," to allow true inquiry into "the humbling phenomena of difference and what might be" (Greene 2001, 82).

Description and Discussion of Terms

The terms described here serve as a starting place to begin to consider the concepts represented by the language. I discuss here how each of the following terms is to be considered in the context of this book. By naming this section *Description and Discussion of Terms* rather than the traditional *Definition of Terms*, I deliberately contest the notion of defining via language.

As did Hwu (2004), I hope to lay out an interpretation of ideas in ways that are "unsayable," "undecidable," and "diagonal." As Deleuze (1987, in Hwu 2004) wrote: "Language has invented the dualism; therefore, we must pass through dualism because it is in language. In other words, to pass through dualisms is not to get rid of them, but rather to fight against language, to invent 'stammering'— AND... AND...AND..." (p. 182).

The decision to stammer and stutter through the terms in this paper is fitting because the intention of the work is to create uncertainty and space for each reader to make "subtle adjustments and re-adjustments" as the text "activates certain elements" in the reader's experience and understanding and, in this way, meaning may emerge (Rosenblatt 1994, 10–12). In fact, this same stuttering and stammering in describing the terms within this book reflects the method and intention of the work: to complicate the safe spaces of what we "know." As Rorty (1986, in St. Pierre 1997) posited: "We only know the world and ourselves under a description and perhaps *we just happened on that description*. If we entertain the possibility that all might not be what we have been led to believe—there might be worlds [and words] other than this" (p. 176).

Thus, each of the following terms is purposely blurred and contested—within this work and beyond it. Representative of the complexity of the nature of terms is the question posed by Letts and Sears (1999), "How does [a term such as] 'normal' get defined through the curriculum, and how can we change what it means?" (p. 95). In broad strokes, how is *any* concept or value defined through the curriculum of School—and how might we challenge these definitions? In the spirit of the lateral logic of the rhizome and of challenging the normality of compliance, the following descriptions of terms *are intended* to confound.

Good/Goodness

The use of the word good and/or goodness is represented here as contested and complex—as it must be for the purposes for which it is used in this study. While the word is defined in *The Reader's Digest Complete Oxford Word Finder* as that which indicates "competency, reliability, strength, thoroughness, expedience, freshness, worthiness, attractiveness, beneficial," etc., I focused on the two aspects of goodness that relate to goodness as the compliant and obedient *good* (as in good behavior) and as a kind, caring, and empathetic *good* (as in the moral good). Goodness "in man is not a mere passive quality, but the deliberate preference of right to wrong, the firm and persistent resistance of all moral evil, and the choosing and following of all moral good" (Romans 15:14, from *Easton's Bible Dictionary*).

Capra (1985) described the Zen-like paradox of good and bad. He challenged the application of values to moments of interaction by naming them as good and bad, and suggested that we recognize the truth hidden in the paradoxical nature of good and bad that cannot be solved by logical reasoning, but instead is understood in terms of "a new awareness" (p. 36). I propose this new awareness may be approximated via the lateral "logic" that undergirds the method of analysis used in this research project: *rhizoanalysis*. Through the application of lateral logic, as opposed to a linear logic, one may learn to engage in a new awareness within particular moments of children acting for the good as far as good feels as opposed to the objective good which has been defined, instructed, and directed by others.

In abandoning the linear, vertical tree logic which separates the *concept* good from the *lived* good, Deleuze noted Nietzsche's resistance to separations between the world of appearance and the world of essence of reality in flipping the "vertical axis of objective truth" sideways toward a "horizontal axis of values" (Deleuze 1983, Nietzsche 1966).

McCadden (1996) troubled the notions of the good child and the good kindergarten student as he compared moving from the profane to the sacred when entering a temple to the "portal rites" at the kindergarten door, "separating outside (child) behavior from inside (student) behavior and constructing the former as 'bad' within the context of the roles and responsibilities of 'students'" (p. 27). In these schooled-notions of the good and the bad, children can find goodness in their own encounters with the world, but also in adult responses to actions. Vivian Paley, who has made a life's work of seeking to transcend the adult perspective in her many books about young children, notes about Wally, the protagonist in her lovely book *Wally's Stories,* "Before he goes home he'll ask me if he was good. He has to tell his mother, and he is never sure" (Paley 1981, 6).

Goodness is a highly conflicted term within this document, and the nature of its conflict underlies much of the work of this book: the work of finding the goodness in being bad and the badness of being good.

Obey/Obedience, Comply/Compliance

Obedience and compliance imply doing what one is told, usually without evaluating the request, in order to bow to authority, to rules (stated and unstated), to potential rewards and punishments (direct and implied), and to tradition, in order to avoid disapproval, rejection, abandonment or some other negative, hurtful or punitive outcome. The essence of obedience is that one begins to view oneself as an instrument of another's wishes, and therefore no longer responsible for one's own actions. Obedience is often described in morality-laden terms (loyalty, duty, discipline) that refer not only to the goodness of the person but also to how well he fulfills his socially defined role (Bluestein 2004, Milgram 1974). Historians of religion have indicated a

> persistence across time and space with which cultures insist on defining what is sacred and what is profane...what is beyond the boundaries of acceptable behavior, of a line between what is permissible and what is not...[often] speak[ing] to the essentially middle-class nature of organized religion which serves to legitimate and sustain mainstream American culture. (Purpel 1989, 74–75)

Disobedience

In this book, I analyze moments of disobedience. Disobedience, in this work, describes an action or interaction that appears to disregard or defy structured expectations of a particular situation, place or person. For the purpose of this research, the classroom expectations might be explicitly stated (verbally or textually), or they might be implicitly expressed via the physical arrangement of school, by a variety of normalizing procedures and rituals, and/or by something as simple as a glance from another child. Determining moments of disobedience for this research requires that I compare a child's action/interaction against what is expected or directed as determined by a combination of cues.

For instance, in the case of Julian in the event of Reuben's fall described earlier, the most obvious cue of his disobedience was his teacher's response: "That's two, Julian…" However, there were other indicators of Julian's disobedience. For instance, the behavior of the other children that indicated that there was a norm in place that Julian disregarded, my own knowledge of typical kindergarten expectations of line behavior, what I knew about that particular class's history of walking in the hall past my door, and my having seen Julian and other children reprimanded and/or punished on prior occasions for similar infractions. Other cues may have included stated (written or verbal) school or classroom rules posted on walls, included in the school's handbook, or discussed in class.

Resistance

While resistance, here, is not used in the broadest of social justice themes as in the work of Giroux (1983a, 1983b) or Freire (1970), there is a relationship to those emancipatory works. Giroux(1983b) discussed the "hidden curriculum of public schools" as "located in a range of norms, decisions and social practices that tacitly structure school experience in the interest of social and class control" (p. 59), and represented resistance as "an oppositional act undertaken by those who wish to emancipate themselves from the structures of power that immobilize them" (p. 110–111).

In this book, the children's resistance, via moments of disobedience, pushes against the norms and practices that immobilize or "swaddle" them (Leafgren and Ambrose 2005), but doesn't do so intentionally for great social purpose. The resistance on this very small, local scale is, in Freire's (1970) terms, *a humanizing practice*. He wrote, "Humanization is thwarted by injustice, exploitation, oppression and the violence of the oppressors; it is affirmed by the yearning of the oppressed for freedom and justice and by their struggle to recover their lost humanity" (p. 45). In this book, I considered that the children resisted the constraining structures of kindergarten because they had not "lost their humanity."

Moral/Morality

Dewey distinguished between customary and reflective morality. Customary morality issues "definite precepts, rules, definitive injunctions and prohibitions," while reflective morality "grows out of conflict between ends, responsibilities, rights and duties" (in Gouinlock 1994, 21–22). In this study, it is the children's negotiation of customary and reflective moralities as they engaged in the moral opportunities within the kindergarten classroom that are documented in order to consider children's understandings regarding the inherent complexity of moral situations. McCadden (1998) discusses the moral complexity of a kindergarten classroom in his book, *It's Hard to be Good*, and describes his understanding of morality as

> socially constructed over time. Morality exists but there is no static morality. We, individually, collectively, and historically create, maintain and adhere to and modify it. Our individual understanding of a situation as moral is based on our experiences and our settled-upon understandings of what counts as moral....Yet as individual and collective social actors, what counts as moral to us is contingent on the roles we play in society. (p. 13)

The child's understanding of morality surely emerges in part from a spiritual nature and full engagement with the "other" in an act of *inclusion* that "makes it possible to meet and know *the other* [emphasis mine] in his [sic] concrete uniqueness and not just as a content of one's experience" (Buber 1956, xv). Here, I suggest that as children engage with what is outside of themselves, they perceive *the other* as having a unity of being and so engage in a mutual and reciprocal relationship rather than detachment or objectification. For as Buber (1958/1970) has further written about such engagement, "Spirit is not in the I but between I and You...and [it is] solely by virtue of his power to relate that man [sic] is able to live in the spirit" (p. 89).

Spiritual/Spirituality

Perhaps the most contested term in this list, spirituality signifies/is many things to many people. It carries historical, cultural, religious, social, emotional, relational, political, biological, and myriad other connections, and it intersects with each as a category of thinking, being, and conceptualizing the world and the moments in it.

Hadot (1995) struggled with the term *spiritual* in his introduction to the "wisdom" exercises practiced by philosophers. He noted

that the term is "a bit disconcerting" and out of fashion and described how he tried on other adjectives: "'psychic,' 'moral,' 'ethical,'
intellectual,' 'of thought,' [and] 'of the soul'" (p. 81)—but none captured the real dimensions of the exercises. In the case of this book,
the process of considering the term *spiritual* was similar to Hadot's
struggle as I sought the term/idea/concept most representative of
the studied moments in the children's lives. I, too, tried "moral,"
and "ethical"—as well as "spirited," "soulful," and "empathetic"—
but while related, no other word captured the dimension as truly
as does spiritual.

Strong and Fuller's (2000) discussion of spirituality and the
spiritual begins to approach the multi-faceted complexity of this
term. They identified three general themes:

> connection with others, connection with the universe, and spiri-
> tual space. Connection with others...being responsible as a human
> being...so that anything I do makes me a better person; better, you
> know, not with rules...but from being kind to others. Connection
> with the universe was typified...as moving beyond the world as we
> know it...[be]cause everything else with you is always tied to some
> part of us...emotionally, physically, psychologically...the spiritu-
> al connection or that spiritual part of us [and] finally, 'spiritual
> space' referred to a context where thinking and feeling things of
> spiritual significance was possible (e.g., 'I wasn't sure of where I
> was but I could be comfortable there'). (np)

In their exploration of spiritual sensitivity in children, Hay
and Nye (1998) developed three categories of sensitivity: awareness sensing; mystery sensing, and value sensing—all requiring a
state of being fully present, wide-awake, spiritually awake, mindful,
completely engaged with what-is-there, completely abandoned, eyes
wide-opened, and deeply encountering.

It is also important to discuss what spirituality *is not* in this book.
For our purposes, spirituality is not framed in the religious, the oth-
erworldly, or the mystical. It is not God-talk, not transcendence, not
a scientific measurement of a spiritual kind of development. Nor is
it the kind of spirituality in which people become like angels—"pure
spirits *without* bodies....From this point of view, spiritual life could
be lived only by withdrawing from the world...[denying the body]...

and remaining untouched by the messiness of material things"
(Harris 1989, 65).

Rather, the children's spirituality in this work is evidenced by
their grounded and intently sentient—even corporeal—engagement
and deeply-encountering connection *with* the world. For instance,
as I revised these pages I was sitting on the bank of a tiny river under a train trestle. As I wrote, families stopped, stood by the edge
of the river in front of me—and almost invariably, each child (every
boy and most of the girls) would stoop to pick up a stone to toss into
the water. They stood and watched the splash and the ripples that
the stones made, and then tossed some more. One boy stood gazing
at the river; but as he bent to pick up a stone, he was stopped by his
mother. "No, that's dirty!" she said and took his hand. As she turned
to walk away, the boy, still holding her hand, leaned away from her,
scooped up a stone and quickly tossed it into the water. He was
disobedient—perhaps even naughty; he may have gotten dirty; and
he most certainly engaged in a sentient encounter with "the other"
as his fully-present spiritual self. The boy disobeyed his mother, but
he also obeyed the stone and the stream. I saw all of these truths
within this moment—one value not more true than the other.

In this study, spirituality is not considered transcendent in the
sense that one becomes removed from (above) what is grounded
and solid. Rather, spirituality is transcendent in the sense that it
involves a way of being in the world where one is connected to other
beings (which includes one's community, people, and other parts of
creation), and a way of being that allows one to move from inward
to outward action and to seek that which lies beyond oneself. In this
vein, Phenix (1974, in Kimes-Myers 1997) described spirit as the
"property of limitless going beyond" (p. 13).

Exploring spirituality in this book is also not an exercise in
pointing out which children were "spiritual" and which were not,
nor was it a measure of how spiritual or spirited some children
might be. Kimes-Myers (1997) quoted Phenix to explain:

> It is phenomenologically not the case that some persons, called
> 'religious' or 'spiritual' types, experience [transcendence] and oth-
> ers do not...all human consciousness is rooted in transcendence'....
> When [children] are said to have 'spirit', this means that they ex-
> press 'perennial discontent and dissatisfaction with any and every

finite realization'....'Spirit' is what allows [a child] to 'giggle with delight' as she pulls herself upright. (p. 13)

Spirit is what allowed the rock to speak to the stream through the child; it's what insists that arbitrarily drawn boundaries designed to keep children apart do not keep them apart; and it's what "begins with our cultivating the inner eye that sees everything capable of [becoming]" (Harris 1989, 65).

Harris did not end her quote as I did. She wrote, "begins with our cultivating the inner eye that sees everything capable of *being God*." I chose to use most of her words because the idea of "cultivating the inner eye that sees everything..." speaks to what is apparent to me as I observe young children. We are all engaged in becoming, and I believe children have not forgotten this. When encountering the world spiritually, they see everything as potential for *becoming*, too. However, I left off "God" because another explanation of what spirituality is not in this particular research project is a product of a higher power. However, Harris's connections between spirituality and sensing/seeing characterizes well the ways children are spiritually in the world. Harris explained, "Initially, spirituality is seeing. This means not just looking but seeing what is actually there and entering the deep places and centers of things" (p. 65). As a similar notion of a grounded, sentient spirituality as a means to re-humanize education, Kathleen Kesson (2005) passionately declared:

So yes, let us bring all the power we can muster be it occult or political, to influence and inspire others to resist the dehumanization of education [and cautioned w]e need not buy into supernatural ideas in order to engage with such discourses. We need only to consider the notion that there is a self that is both more complex and more purposeful than a deterministic social construction theory can account for; that this self acts as an organizing center for and maker of meaning of experience; that this self experiences desire, which provides the momentum for human activity; and that desire is dynamically linked to inquiry as the foundation for authentic engagement with the world. This constellation of ideas forms, I believe, in the crux of the relationship between education and spirituality. If we were to take it seriously, we would of necessity, radically rethink the aims, structures, content, and processes of education, in order to make possible unfettered connections

between the self, desire, purpose, intent, will, wonder, awe, imagination, creativity, and responsiveness to other selves—signifiers
that are largely missing from the dominant techno/managerial/
standard discourses. (p. 43–44)

Kesson's discussion may lead one to consider ways in which to
make "unfettered connections." Therefore, in looking closely and
rhizomatically at moments of children's disobedience in the classroom, some texts laid against the observational texts are of a spiritual sort. As Kimes-Myers (1997) asserted, "assuredness, strength,
and spiritedness can be discerned in children everywhere when it is
not squelched, nullified, neglected, or in other ways repudiated or
overlooked" (p. 3). Rendon (2007) was also troubled by the fleeting
nature of our spiritual selves, writing that "the natural state of the
human being is whole and connected and somewhere along the line,
we're segmented—we break apart (mind, body, soul; into thought,
feeling, joy...)" (np). While some aspects of schooling may squelch,
nullify, neglect, repudiate, and break apart the spiritual nature of
children, in this particular study, the spiritual is *not* overlooked.

I contend that the spirituality present in all of us is more readily
apparent in young children than in most adults. Perhaps because
"somewhere along the line" (Rendon 2007) hasn't happened yet, and
the children haven't "broken apart"; or perhaps because children's
worldly experience is connected to their senses and their desire to
reach out, as opposed to adults' worldly experience of abstractions.
As Jerome Berryman (1985, in Kimes-Myers 1997) suggested, young
children "live at the limit of their experiences most of the time" (p.
13), which is an artifact, I suggest, of their engrossment (Noddings
2002) and intense awareness (Hay and Nye 1998). As Hart (2006)
wrote about children's spirituality, it may "exist apart from adult
rational and linguistic conceptions and from knowledge about religion. Although children may not be able to conceptualize a religious concept, their presence—their mode of being and knowing in
the world—may be distinctly spiritual" (p. 164).

Children's spirituality, as evidenced by their sensing, relating,
caring, hoping, and deeply encountering actions and interactions,
suggests a "way of being, way of knowing, and way of doing" as rooted in an ancient practice of "spiritual discipline" (Hadot 1995, in
Henderson and Slattery 2007) or "spiritual praxis" (Shahjahan 2007,

np). If so, those who care for children might engage with children in "disciplined inquiry, dialogue and self-examination" (Henderson and Slattery 2007) in a pedagogy of what Riyad Shahjahan (2007) calls "audacious hope in action," centering spirituality in curriculum, nurturing possibilities, "embodying the anti-oppressive pedagogy of interconnection" (np). Laura Rendon (2008) names this the *sentipensante*, a sensing/thinking pedagogy—educating for wholeness and social justice, rooted in ancient wisdom, and promoting nonduality, wholeness, and completeness.

Becker (1994, in Kimes-Myers 1997) named spirituality as a "code word for the depth dimension of human existence" (p. 257). In considering this dimension, especially in the human existence of young children, I discuss facets of spirituality that include:

1. Spirituality as sensing and sensuality (Corbett 1991, Hay and Nye 1998, Keleman 1981, Pillow, 1997, Rendon 2008, Tobin 1997);

2. Spirituality grounded in social justice, as inspiring hope and affirming action (Hanh 1990, hooks 1993, Shahjahan 2006);

3. Spirituality that connotes a fully-present, deeply encountering self (Greene 1981, Hanh 1998, Kimes-Myers 1997, Noddings 1993).

Spiritual/Moral/Civil Disobedience

In considering the potential value of children's acts of disobedience, some thought must be tendered to the spiritual-moral conflict that may have given rise to such acts. Zinn (1968) discussed civil disobedience as "the deliberate, discriminate, violation of law for a vital social purpose...its aim is always to close the gap between law and justice, as an infinite process in the development of democracy" (p. 119). And Linn (1989) discussed moral disobedience as what might be considered deviant behavior used as a coping strategy in the face of overwhelming moral dilemmas. Given the likely tension between the child-reflective morality and the institutional-customary morality, moments of disobedience may occur that are purposeful. For instance, when Reuben fell, Julian experienced his need for help and comfort and—even while knowing the rule, even while knowing that breaking the rule would likely lead to punishment—chose to transgress the order of the line in order to go to Reuben's aid. This is not only evidence of a nascent sort of civil disobedience, but bears weight as a disobedience of a moral and spiritual sort—as related to Julian's engagement with an other.

Democratic/Democracy

According to Dewey (1985), each of us is best served by a democracy created to maximize the common good. He described democracy as follows:

> Democracy is simultaneously a way of life, an ethical ideal, and a personal commitment. Specifically, it is a way of life in which individuals are presumed to be self-directing and able to pursue their own goals and projects. No society that maintains order through constant supervision and/or coercion can be rightly called democratic. Further, individual benefit and the common good are mutually enhancing in a democracy. (p. 349)

In considering the future and the state of democracy, Counts (1932) claimed that democracy can only be the "intended offspring of the union of human reason, purpose and will" (p. 37), and reminded that democracy is not a political institution, but is a

> sentiment with respect to the moral equality of men: it is an aspiration towards a society...fashioned in harmony with an American democratic tradition [which would] combat all forces tending to produce social distinctions and classes, repress every form of privilege and economic parasitism; manifest a tender regard for the weak, the ignorant, and the unfortunate; place the heavier and more onerous burden on the backs of the strong; glory in every triumph of man in his timeless urge to express himself and to make the world more habitable; exalt human labor of hand and brain as the creator of all wealth and culture; provide adequate material and spiritual rewards for every kind of socially useful work; strive for genuine equality of opportunity among all races, sects, and occupations; regard as paramount the abiding interests of the great masses of people; direct the powers of government to the elevation and the refinement of the life of the common man; transform or destroy all conventions, institutions and special groups inimical to the underlying principles of democracy; and finally be prepared as

a last resort, in either the defense of or realization to this purpose, to follow the method of revolution. (p. 37–38)

Or as Dewey would have said, a means "to maximize the common good."

Dewey (1960) described a relationship between freedom and experienced resistance. He believed that people do not think about, or go in search of, freedom "unless they run during action against conditions that resist their original impulses" (p. 286). He did not go on to define freedom as the release of all such "original impulses" or to conceive of education as an affair primarily of impulse. Rather, his concern was to encourage "free and informed choosing...'in the open air of public discussion and communication'...this, in turn, would happen only if persons were able to test their own capacities, to use their minds" (in Greene 1988, 6). In this way, the moments of disobedience and resistance explored in this book are not exclusively moments of impulse or mere naughtiness, but are moments representative of the child's spiritual nature from which goodness can be derived.

Moral Swaddling/Spiritual Swaddling

As adults wrap or bind babies in swaddling cloths, they do so for multiple purposes. One swaddles a baby to protect the infant and to keep it close. Women in many cultures carefully swaddle their infants in order to keep the child safe, secure and as close as possible, sharing warmth, breath and heartbeat. Swaddling in this manner allows the child to participate in the day-to-day doings of the mother—to observe what she does, and to feel cared for in the most fundamental sense.

Swaddling is also a means to restrain and control the child. Mead (1951) described the swaddled Russian child: "Hands that were tightly bound inside the swaddling bands could not explore... experiencing but never touching the teeming, vivid, highly charged world around it, being in it, but not of it" (np).

In this book, the term *moral swaddling* (Leafgren and Ambrose 2005) or *spiritual swaddling* is used to represent the constraints placed on children via "a range of norms, decisions and social practices" (Giroux 1983b 59) and adult dominance and pre-emptive school procedures and rules—constraints that not only protect the children from harm and offer security and predictability, but also prohibit fully "vivid and highly charged" interactions with other children and their environment, and so interfere with children's potential to act on spiritual-moral opportunities. Buber wrote extensively of the relational nature of the human spirit and cautioned that nurturing the spirit-self is not passive or restrained, but that the "human child...gains his world by seeing, listening, feeling, forming. It is in encounter that the creation reveals its formhood; it does not pour itself into senses that are waiting but deigns to meet those *that are reaching out*" [emphasis mine] (Buber 1958/1970, 76).

Reaching out implies the freedom to do so. Spiritual-moral swaddling operates in conflicted complexity. It is a metaphor used not to reduce uncertainty, but to complicate and so possibly enhance understanding.

Rhizoanalysis/Rhizomatic Analysis

Rhizoanalysis builds from the philosophical and cultural theories of Gilles Deleuze and Feliz Guattari (1987). In developing a comparison between a rhizome and a tree as a metaphor of the contrast between two forms of logic, they name the tree's linear structure—from roots through the trunk, to the branches—as a metaphor of the fixed, determining and linear logic that explains things in terms of cause-and-effect relationships. In contrast, "the rhizome's contrasting 'lateral' structure—a collection of mutually dependent 'roots' and 'shoots'—is a metaphor of a dynamic, flexible and 'lateral' logic that encompasses change, complexity and heterogeneity" (MacNaughton 2005, 120).

For the purpose of this book, the conceptual tools of rhizoanalysis, as described in chapter 3, allow me to explore the nuances and politics of the texts constituted of kindergarten observations in order to create new texts. These newly constructed texts explore "how it means; how it connects with things 'outside' of it, such as its author, its reader and its literary and non-literary contexts; and by exploring how it organizes meanings and power through offshoots, overlaps, conquests and expansions" (Deleuze and Guattari 1987, 21).

Significance of the Book

In this book, I seek to present an appreciation for the messiness and disobedience of authentic and spiritual childhood—a difficult task when in the context of school and in the broader social realm, "goodness" has become defined/enacted as obedience and compliance, often to the exclusion of empathy and advocacy among the children who live there. The book troubles school readiness as inevitably a part of a "normalizing practice which by its nature mistreats schoolchildren" (Foucault 1988, 18), and suggests that school instead might offer the trusting and appreciative ambiance where children might create "spaces of dialogue...where they can take initiatives and uncover humanizing possibilities" (Greene 1988, 13).

The book represents moments of disobedience in order to demonstrate that some of these "humanizing possibilities" may lie in conflict and moral decisions, even in forms of disobedience and challenge to authority. Purpel (2001) noted that we rarely read of "even an implied affirmation of the American tradition of revolutionary democracy as an expression of resistance to authoritarianism" (p. 93). This book seeks a view of the potential of goodness in "bad" behaviors—even while most of the moments of disobedience do not offer the clear vision of goodness that Julian's rule-breaking did. In similar fashion, then, perhaps teachers and other adults who work with young children will be prompted to seek those possibilities—even when not so glaringly clear as when Julian helped Reuben up from the hard schoolroom floor.

In Hostetler's (2005) article *What is "Good" Education Research?*, he laments the focus on the *methodological* good of educational research, sacrificing adequate attention to the question of what good comes from educational policies and practices, how do they or how do they not contribute to "a robust and justifiable conception of human well-being." Hostetler offers Nussbaum's vision metaphor: "The presumption is not that people err with regard to well-being because they are evil. We err because we overlook something, misperceive something. All of us have blind spots. But we can improve our vision" (p. 20).

This book is significant because it seeks to "improve our vision," to shine a fresh light on children's spiritual-moral sensibilities and abilities—especially as related to their spirit, their total presence in the moment, and their willingness to engage in surprise and contradiction. As noted by Henderson and Kesson (2004): "Many of the ancient wisdom traditions value paradox and understand it as an important aspect of spiritual development. To dwell comfortably with contradictions, to rest content with not knowing, to move ahead, mindfully, in the face of chaos, confusion, and uncertainty is to be spiritually awake and wise like a fool" (p. 48).

Ironically, the child who can embrace this foolish wisdom and wise foolishness is likely to be admonished to seek a more serious, ordered experience. By swaddling the children in our care with explicit and implicit demands, rules, structures and an imposed duty to be good, we inhibit their engagement in ambiguity and wonder and so block their path of awareness and responsiveness.

This book is significant because it offers a reminder of the complexity of "goodness." When teachers communicate to the children in their care that their positive regard is "conditional" (Rogers 1980) and swaddle them so tightly in their moral practice that they are compelled to remain steadfastly still in an orderly line (like the children in Mrs. Buttercup's line) even as their friend falls and cries out, then it appears that this complexity is being overlooked. While teachers may believe that demanding and coercing compliance is "for their own good," Miller (1983/1990) argued that such practice can be described as "poisonous pedagogy." Noddings (2002) explained that such pedagogy is "rigid and coercive; it seeks to substitute the will of the teacher for that of the student. Throughout the process of 'educating', teachers guilty of poisonous pedagogy take a highly moralistic tone, insisting that what they are demanding is right and that coercion and cruelty, if they are used, are necessary 'for the child's own good'" (p. 29).

This book is significant because it seeks to offer entry points into examining the "democratic good life" (which requires thoughtful and spiritual-moral disobedience) via moments of children's compliance and non-compliance. Henderson (2001a) described the morality of democratic living as a *wisdom challenge*, and celebrated the idea of what Zen practitioners call the beginner's mind, "which is truly open and fresh, willing to remain innocent and receptive to life, not attached to our knowledge. It is the willingness to be empty, and thus open to learning and growing" (Davidson 1998, 36–37, in J. Henderson 2001a, 19). These moments of entry invite an exploration of the freedom necessary in the school culture to allow children direct experience in the democratic way of living—as opposed to learning *about* it. As Dewey (1916) famously noted, "A democracy is more than a form of government; it is primarily a mode of associated living, of conjoint communicated experience" (p. 93).

This book is significant because, in the words of Howard Zinn (2005):

> I [don't] want ...to prepare [children] to take their obedient and accustomed places in the world so that they [will] then teach...their children to take their obedient and accustomed places in the world and then the world [will] continue as it always has been because unless people become disobedient and unless people step out of line, the world continues in its old ways. (np)

Chapter 2

Disobedience Texts and Contextual Literature

During air raid drills Miss Pearl stood at the front of the room with her arms folded across her vast breasts. "When we go outside, children, you will line up nicely, even if there is an atomic bomb."

~ Wenner (2004, 5)

When I visualize rhizoanalysis as a process, I see in front of me an expanse of soft, loamy soil containing the infinite number and variety of moments I might reap; I see my hand reaching through the loam to grasp a handful of humus-rich soil shot through with rhizomes. I peer at this handful of rich soil and realize that I could choose any shoot to follow and each would take me to different connections and each would tell a different story.

In the following, the soil is the moment of Reuben's fall and Julian's care, and the mapping of lines of flight as I reach my hand into that moment is one of the two functions of this chapter. Thus in the first section of this chapter, I enlist Reuben and Julian to frame a tale of disobedience and the possible texts that might disrupt our expected notions of disobedience. In the second portion of this chapter, I review a selection of background and contextual literature in the interest of setting the stage for this study of moments of children's disobedience.

This chapter is by no means an exhaustive review of the supporting literature for this work. Nor is it meant to offer one, for while an arbolic, tree-like account of this research of children's classroom disobedience would begin at the roots with a rationale and "the branches of theory and method would grow from the solid trunk of 'the literature' in order to feed the leaves, flowers and fruit of 'analysis, interpretation and conclusions'" (Clarke 1994, 4), this study purposely follows a less linear path. So, with no tree-roots with which to begin and no trunk to carefully trace the way to the proper leaves and flowers, how and where did I begin this task? As Derrida (1967/1974, in St. Pierre 2002) explains, "We begin, 'wherever we are,' in the middle of whatever project we're working on, in the middle of whatever seems so strange and squirrelly that we avoid talking about it with someone, in the spaces where the old concepts break down and simply aren't adequate to the task at hand" (p. 419).

Disobedience Texts: A Rhizoanalysis of Reuben's Fall

The moment I heard Reuben fall is a fitting place to begin this work because it was that particular event that made it irresistibly transparent to me the innate complexity of every moment of interaction. It has become nearly impossible since then for me to see any moment in a way that could be named as merely "good" or "bad" or by any name at all. It is, as Derrida would agree, the place to begin because it is where I am. Still.

Because I was unbound in that moment from the responsibility of naming Julian's act as good or bad and so not required to react accordingly (remember, I was a witness, not the teacher in this case), I realized that I was free to see it as unnameable—or given the moment's myriad possibilities—*re*-nameable.

As researcher, my role is free of conventions and customs of the teacher. I am unconstrained, and so compelled to follow the unpredictable, rhizomatic, meandering, decentralized, detachable, and reversible shoots of the "literature" and "rationale" and "analyses" in order to appear, disrupt, and "flower" (as in Clark 1994) throughout this first section of chapter 2. As I place texts from other sources—historical, heroic, religious, etc.—over, beside, and beneath the text describing the moment of Reuben's fall, the connecting literature (related to spirituality, moral swaddling, dissidence, and the democracy of disobedience) unfolds.

The Spirit and Wisdom of Childhood

'If a fool throws a stone into a water' goes an old saying 'even a hundred sages can't bring it back'...But an ingenuous child, who still thinks in pictures, might ask, 'Isn't the world full of stones—so why should a hundred clever people try so hard to get back this one? Why don't they look around? If they do, they might find all kinds of new treasures they can't see because they are so busy searching in vain in the water.'

~ Miller (1983, 11)

When Reuben fell, I heard it. Everyone there must have heard it. However, Julian *saw* it. Julian seemed to see everything. His engagement with the world was intense and sometimes inconvenient. In this case, however, his willingness/ability/choice not only to see Reuben and his fall, but to see and be aware of Reuben's *need* led him to kindness.

Hay and Nye (1998) discuss a spiritual awareness as a special kind of attention within a reflexive process—"being attentive to one's attention or 'being aware of one's awareness'" (p. 65)—a meta-awareness, perhaps. Sherblom (1997) discusses this kind of moral awareness by raising points made by Iris Murdoch that draw attention to an essential connection between attention and morality, indicating that moral action

> is not so much a matter of choice or values, but a matter of seeing the moral context clearly...that you can only choose within the world that you can perceive. This makes one's ability to perceive a foundational constraint on moral choice and a central aspect of moral experience.... She describes moral experience in terms of seeing and knowing people and moral contexts. She illustrates how moral sensitivities develop from continuous attention to the moral aspects of experience. (Murdoch 1970/1985, in Sherblom 1997)

This leads me to believe, then, that the spiritual awareness and sensibilities of Julian influenced his moral choices and actions—even when his choices could and did lead to retribution from one who only understood those choices as disobedience.

One text telling a similar tale of awareness and action comes from the field of psychiatry via the important work *Man's Search for Meaning*, written by neurologist/psychiatrist and existentialist Victor Frankl. In exploring a "will to meaning," Frankl (1984) recalled his experiences in a concentration camp. One story involved Frankl assisting another inmate:

> At one time, we had to carry some long, heavy girders over icy tracks. If one man slipped, he endangered not only himself but all the others who carried the same girder. An old friend of mine had a congenitally dislocated hip. He was glad to be capable of working in spite of it, since the physically disabled were almost certainly sent to death when a selection took place. He limped over the track with an especially heavy girder, and seemed about to fall and drag the others with him. As yet, I was not carrying a girder so I jumped to his assistance without stopping to think. I was immediately hit on the back, rudely reprimanded and ordered to return to my place. A few minutes previously, the same guard who struck me had told us deprecatingly that we 'pigs' lacked the spirit of comradeship. (p. 43)

Like Julian, Frankl stepped out of line, and like Julian, Frankl was punished for that transgression without reference to the cause of it. I also recognize another similarity in their choice—Frankl wrote, "I jumped to his assistance without stopping to think," and I understand Julian's action to be similar in nature. While I believe Julian knew he would likely be punished, I do not believe he weighed that possibility in his decision to act. I do not believe that either Frankl or Julian chose their action as an opposition to their particular regimes of oppression. They saw another's need, perceived the moral context within that need as described by Murdoch (1970/1985), and responded to it.

Literary texts play on the theme of acting based on a moral context. H.G. Wells made a dire prediction regarding human progress in *The Time Machine* (1895/1986) as the time traveler enters a time 800,000 years in the future. The human race by this time has evolved in ways so separated from one another that there is no attention paid to another's need. Wells's time traveler told of his arrival in this time and of watching in horror as one female nearly drowned while those who watched with slight interest offered no aid:

> That day, too, I made a friend—of a sort. It happened that, as I was watching some of the little people bathing in a shallow, one of them was seized with cramp and began drifting downstream. The main current ran rather swiftly, but not too strongly for even a moderate

swimmer. It will give you an idea, therefore, of the strange deficiency in these creatures, when I tell you that none made the slightest attempt to rescue the weakly crying little thing which was drowning before their eyes. When I realized this, I hurriedly slipped off my clothes, and, wading in at a point lower down, I caught the poor mite and drew her safe to land. A little rubbing of the limbs soon brought her round, and I had the satisfaction of seeing she was all right before I left her. I had got to such a low estimate of her kind that I did not expect any gratitude from her. In that, however, I was wrong. (Wells 1895/1986, 53)

The time traveler goes on to tell of Weena's gratitude to him for her rescue. In this tale, there appeared no threat of punishment or even a sense of transgression from a particular order. However, the creatures sitting on the banks of the stream risked nothing, even wet clothing or a glimpse of concern, to offer help. It was as if they did not see. As if they could not see what Julian *would* have seen.

To me, there is a parallel spirit among children and ancients. I have often commented on my sense of children's eyes and hearts—that they seem to be more open than adults' eyes and hearts. It may be their spiritual awareness that I sense. I feel that the ancient wisdom traditions share much with the joyful spirit of childhood. The child's "complete abandon and whole-hearted faith" (M. Quinn 2001) allows her to act as sage, or as many mystic traditions would affirm: divine. In describing the "necessity of becoming a small child again, of rediscovering spiritual childhood in order to reinstate the divine," Erny (1973) wrote:

Man, resuscitated at the end of initiations, having become a child again, must display in his behavior the traits of his new personality, in particular, 'ignorance.' In the face of mystery, and its obscurity, the mind is 'silly,' 'idiot,' like a 'blind hippopotamus'.... A second personality trait will be his playful and jocular character, the overflowing of the joy of his soul. Real knowledge engenders joy, turns its possessor into a child, and gives him freedom of spirit again and the wisdom of childhood.... To reach a state of childhood again is to become capable of melting oneself in the divine, of transforming oneself in it...Lao-Tseu [*sic*] used to say, 'Man must rediscover the heart of the little child to give himself peacefully to the Tao.' (p. 86–89)

In a similar vein, Nietzsche, well known for his deep suspicions regarding the motives underlying moralities and religion, was inspired by the spirit of the child to enter into issues of spirituality of faith in *Thus Spoke Zarathustra* (1883/1982):

> What is the child but an image of faith? The child is the hope of the future, the fulfillment of the past and the blessing of the present...the child responds to the world, to being-in-the-world, with a grand 'amen'! The child is the pure affirmation of existence, the utterance of a sacred 'yes' to life, which is the substance of faith. (p. 26)

Joseph Pearce in the Foreword of Hart's (2003) *The Secret Spiritual World of Children* wondered if "the 'child-spirit' can be other than that of our 'species-spirit' as a whole since the child and its wondrous world embrace the whole of life from the beginning" (p. *ix*), and further wondered how renowned child developmentalists seem to have missed the child-spirit for so long. In contesting the notion of children's incompleteness and immaturity, Hart (2003) explained that

> developmental theorists typically tell us that children are self-centered and incapable of real empathy or compassion; they have not developed sufficiently to really put themselves in someone else's shoes. Indeed, children can be enormously selfish and self-centered, but they can also be deeply empathetic and compassionate. They do not have to wait until adulthood to act unselfishly, feel into another's pain or share their heart. Their openness allows them to experience deep interconnection with the world, and their compassion can arise very naturally. The capacities of separateness and connection, selfishness and compassion exist simultaneously. (p. 69)

Julian lifted Reuben from the floor in the spirit of connectedness and compassion. He reached out to Reuben as he experienced Buber's (1958/1970) "I-thou" encounter in engaging with Reuben's need for help and care.

Kesson (2005) and Kimes-Myers (1997) explain "I-thou" through stories of children fully engaged with others ("thous"). Earthworms and bumblebees can be thous. In each of these stories, a child encounters something an adult might view as mundane. As the little girl in Kimes-Myers's (1997) story came across some earthworms,

> she felt invited... they squirmed, she loosened her grasp and looked more closely...taking an even closer look....Earthworms were the subject of her perception and there was a dialogue between the child and the worms. But her own feelings were also the subjects of her perception about her experience with earthworms and about being in her grandmother's garden with those of us who were also engaged in dialogue with her, each other, the world and with our own growing edges. (p. 23)

Kesson (2005) tells of joining her young granddaughter, Anika, who has "no appointments to keep," on a stroll through the neighborhood—a stroll which "involves prolonged moments of stillness." She describes Anika as "full of wonder, curiosity, and appreciation as she literally incorporates—takes into her bodymind—the world," a world which includes lavender bushes to smell, bristly seedpods to explore with "tiny fingertips," shocking pink petunias to rub "ever so gently," and black bumblebees at eye level with which to share the pleasure of black-eyed Susans and lavender bushes (p. 43).

One can find many who similarly reference the spirited and spiritual nature of the child as he or she embraces the whole of life in freedom, joy, wisdom, hope, and playfulness joined together in the body and spirit of the child. Recall Hay and Nye's (1998) categories of spiritual sensitivity: awareness sensing; mystery sensing, and value sensing, all of which require a state of being one might describe as being fully present, wide-awake, spiritually awake, mindful, completely engaged with what-is-there, completely abandoned, eyes wide-opened, and deeply encountering.

It is the qualities of sensitivity and mindfulness that speak to the "spiritual discipline" described by Hadot (1995). Ambrose (2005) referred to a kind of spiritual discipline applied by children as they engage with one another in classrooms as relational spirituality:

> Thinking, feeling and acting [very much like the 'way of being, way of knowing, and way of doing' of spiritual discipline] become spiritual when young children's consideration for each other enables them to select paths for interacting that provide possibilities of classroom community that reflect ethical and moral judgment.

What is right? What is fair? How can we determine how we will play, learn and 'breathe' (from the Latin, *spiritus*, 'of breathing, of the spirit') together in this shared time and space? (p. 93)

As Shahjahan (2007) enjoined us, the spiritual path is not an "individual path, but a communal one." Children's state of intense awareness and wide-awakeness engages them in what Kimes-Myers (1997) named a "spirituality of caring," a fully present way of being, knowing and acting which includes a relational, dialogical connection in which things become other body subjects, rather than just objects of perception. Buber (1958/1970) referred to this as an "I-thou relationship" in contrast with an "I-it" relationship in which the other has no "subjectiveness" and exists only as an object.

Hart (2004, in Ambrose 2005) described Buber's "between the I and you" as "a relational understanding of spirituality in which the spiritual is lived out at the intersection of our lives, in the 'between'... as a 'spirituality' that develops between one and others communally" (p. 94). As Buber wrote, "Spirit is not in the I but between the I and you. It is not like the blood that circulates in you, but like the air in which you breathe" (1958/1970). Hart (2004) suggested that relationships developed in early childhood classrooms are in fact spiritual and that the "air in which you breathe can become the community in which you share lived experiences" (in Ambrose 2005, 94).

Chapter 5 will detail texts representing moments of disobedience and children as spirited-moral actors within the context of Hay and Nye's (1998) spiritual categories of awareness-, mystery- and value-sensing. For in considering each of these spiritual expressions, I believe that those of us who care for, watch over, and learn from the child enjoy many opportunities to observe these instances of spiritual sensitivity—if we are willing to see them.

To foreground those moments from the research, and to foreground the process of laying texts over the text representing the moments of disobedience, the following sections describe lines of flight in re-theorizing, rethinking and reliving the moment of Reuben's fall. The connections and permutations of this particular moment include discussions related to moral and spiritual swaddling, dissent and dissonants, and the democratic nature of disobedience.

Moral/Spiritual Swaddling: A Function of the Schoolroom

'Did we miss something? He wasn't a troublemaker. He didn't even talk in line.' A teacher discussing Elias, the seven-year-old boy who shot a little girl on the school playground in a television episode of Law and Order.

~ DeNoon and Peterson (2000)

Now, the rules are listed on the walls,
So there's no need to repeat them,
We all agree, your parents and we,
That you just can't handle your freedom'

~ Morrison and Morrison (1999, 8–10)

Power comes when you make life predictable for people.

~ Howard Stevenson (in Wong and Wong 1998, 88)

I imagine that I reach into the rich soil of the moment of Reuben's fall and pull a shoot that led to a text of the children who stood in line: the ones who were good. How did I know they were good? Because they didn't have to go on the wall. They stayed in line. I did not ask them, but I wondered: did they see Reuben's fall, and so his need for care? I am sure they saw his fall. He was in front of the line, and it was a large, loud fall. But did they see his *need*?

When I spoke with pre-service early childhood teachers about this in later years, and asked them what Reuben may have thought/felt, many of them indicated that they believed he would have been embarrassed to have fallen down so largely and so loudly. They think everyone saw it. So, why did only Julian get out of line to offer his care? He was in the back of the line to begin with, so he was not the closest—others might have reached Reuben sooner. But no one moved. I call this swaddling. The children were wrapped so tightly in their commitment to the order of the line and blind obedience to the authority of the teacher that they did not fully see Reuben, and could not and did not reach out.

What follows are texts from film, psychiatry, anthropology and more to place next to the text of the children who remained in line. What the new texts do to the text of Reuben's fall to blur the value of compliance is mapped on texts discussing moral and spiritual swaddling.

A good friend of mine is a consultant. He specializes in cognitive science as related to human behavior and interaction. He has worked mostly in Texas, Pennsylvania, Ohio and California. His clients are exclusively school systems and prisons. Some may think that it is coincidence that those two institutions share a need for his expertise, but not me. In one of my classes for pre-service teachers, *Guidance of Young Children*, I use the movie *Instinct* (Turteltaub, 1999), set in a prison and based on Quinn's (1992) pivotal text *Ishmael*, to illustrate examples of constraint and surveillance that have parallels in the classroom. In one scene, the warden asked a guard if all were sticking to the schedule, and the guard replied, "Same thing every day, sir." Foucault (1979) followed these parallel and intersecting lines in his discussions of prison and law and order, and in this case, the logic of structured labor (tasks):

> It is a principle of order and regularity; through the demands it imposes, it conveys, imperceptibly, the forms of a rigorous power; it bends bodies to regular movements, it excludes agitation and distraction, it imposes hierarchy and a surveillance that are all the more accepted, and which will be inscribed all the more deeply in the behaviour of the convicts [students], in that they form part of its logic; with work 'the rule' is introduced into a prison [school], it reigns there without effort, without the use of any repressive and violent means. By occupying the convict [student], one gives him habits of order and obedience; one makes the idler that he was diligent and active... with time, he finds in the regular movements of the prison [school]... a certain remedy against the wanderings of his imagination. (p. 242–243)

The wandering of the imagination—the unexpected—is, by all means, to be avoided in schools as well as in prisons. For, according to some classroom experts, students want a well-managed classroom even more than the teachers do, "because a well-managed classroom gives students SECURITY. There are *no surprises* [emphasis mine], no yelling in a classroom where everyone, teacher and students, know what is happening. It comes from installing procedures and routines" (Wong and Wong 1998, 85). This example of Wong's extensive work in the field of classroom management is typical of the literature regarding obedience and disobedience in regard to the behaviors of young children in school, mostly focused on the need for order in schools and the means toward achieving child compliance

It appears that, in many schools, teachers seem to have joined in a consensus that the silencing, order and control of these spirited children will lead to greater success and proficiency. And yet, Keleman (1981) passionately decried this assumption regarding the academic benefits of controlling our children: "In the name of Knowledge, we dampen and channel aliveness....We cramp our children's bodies so that we can form their minds...learning becomes painful. Learning becomes a chore that requires discipline" (p. 28). Gatto (1992) called these disciplined chores "intellectual dependency":

> Good students wait for the teacher to tell them what to do. It is the most important lesson, that we must wait for other people, better trained than ourselves, to make the meanings of our lives...successful children do the thinking I assign them with a minimum of resistance and decent show of enthusiasm...Bad kids fight this, of course, even though they lack the concepts to know what they are fighting, struggling to make decisions for themselves...How will we allow that and survive as school teachers? Fortunately, there are tested procedures to break the will of those who resist. (p. 8)

Sadly, resistance is rare. After decades of being intellectually, morally and spiritually swaddled—a state experienced from one's earliest years—it is difficult to be aware of one's constrained state. Most people have learned from childhood to feel it normal, expected, right to wear masks of compliance and obedience:

> Orders are masks forced onto our existence from our earliest childhood until the day we die. That is why it so difficult to see through these masks or to remove them. Too many masks stuck to too many faces. As time passes, the masks become a straitjacket on our ability to create and live. These masks imprison our spirit. In time, we become what we surrender to. Or as Lucretius put it, 'we do all that force forces us to do.' (Trantino 2001, np)

Force or coercion does not need to be physical. The moral and spiritual swaddling of our children is not a literal wrapping of the limbs; it is in fact, as Foucault suggested, not necessary to constrain. In the name of "their own good" and in order to earn and keep the regard of their caregivers, children are admonished and driven to be good, to keep their hands to themselves, to mind their own business, to stay on task, to be still—ultimately to disengage from the world that envelops them. As Trantino (2001) worried, "we feel it right to be masked"—to be swaddled, and when the swaddling is "habitual and embodied in social institutions, it seems the normal and natural state of affairs...[the] experience is so restricted that they are not conscious of restriction" (Dewey 1937, in Gouinlock 1994, 265).

Alice Miller (1978, 1983, 1990, 2000) has written extensively about the cost of the suppression of children as their caregivers pursue fulfillment of their own conscious and unconscious wishes. Joined by Noddings (2002) in detailing the damage wrought by "poisonous pedagogy," Miller described a rigid and coercive pedagogy embraced by many teachers who insist righteously that their demands are right and good for the child.

And if it does feel right, one must ask Noddings's (2002) question: can coercion be a sign of caring? Is the coercion and force employed to "handle" their children "indeed a manifestation of caring" (p. 29)? Perhaps in terms of socializing the child to what is expected of him or her, and in terms of leading the child into the safety of compliance (as in the security and control proffered the swaddled infant), this is so. But at what cost? Even when enacted by well intentioned, caring teachers, what are the unintended consequences? If as Buber claimed (in Noddings 2003, 174), "all actual life is encounter," what are the consequences of wrapping the children in structures which inhibit the quantity and quality of their "encounter"? Just as the swaddled infant is denied the opportunity to tactically and kinesthetically interact with her environment when so constrained, the child is similarly deprived of real association with the world, and so the opportunity to enact the freedom, joy, wisdom, silliness, hope, abandon, faith, beginnings, playfulness, verve, whole-hearted faith and intense awareness that are the hallmarks of the child-spirit.

The Dissidents

'The fact is, Solomon,' he continued, as he roped the popcorn machine onto his cart, 'to cause a little trouble now and then is maybe good for a man.'

> ~ Mr. Jerusalem (All Kinds Junk Bought and Sold,
> in Jean Merrill's *The Pushcart War*, 1965)

How could we allow something like this without pumpin' our fists?

> ~Mosh (Eminem, 2004)

Our prophets were right— we should shake our fists, plenty of times we should. Our rabbi told us once to 'learn how to shake your fists.'... When should we shake our fists? At who[m]?

> ~ Coles (1990, 251)

Patty sat still and, to avoid their eyes,
She lowered her little-girl head.
But she heard their words and she felt their eyes
And this is what she said....
I don't mean to be rude: I want to be nice,
But I'd like to hang on to my freedom.
I know you are smart and I know that you think
You are doing what is best for me.
But if freedom is handled just your way
Then it's not my freedom or free'

> ~ Morrison and Morrison (1999, 12)

Like Jean Merrill's Mr. Jerusalem, Julian caused a little trouble now and then. Perhaps he didn't shake his fists. Like Toni Morrison's Patty, he was not rude; he was nice and not defiant in a way that deliberately challenged his teacher or even the rules. He was, however, resistant—resistant to the structures that constrained his total presence and the rules that prohibited his full-interaction with "thou." It is this resistance that makes Julian a dissident—one who dissents from the structured order, the order of the dominant—and so one who is always suspect.

The following are short tales of other child-dissidents—from history, from literature, from the Bible, from death row, and from a first-grade essay on triple-lined first-grade paper. Within each of these brief stories are rhizomatic connections to Julian's act of dissonance in the hallway immediately outside the boy's bathroom and across from my classroom. Maybe in some of these texts there is a little rudeness and a little bit of shaking of the fist. In all of them there are children seeking their freedom.

In his essay *The Condition of My Condition*, Trantino (1972) describes life in school in which the children "were being kept apart and we were keeping ourselves apart and we were all hurting like a motherfucker but no one was telling" (p. 23). However, listening closely enough, we realize that there are those who *do* tell. One function of this book is to attend to the voices of those who have become aware of the painful trauma resulting from the "poisonous pedagogy" (Miller 1983/1990) of their childhood and have found ways to call out. Here are texts of voices resisting the constraining nature of adult-child pedagogy; and in doing so, perhaps finding means to confront it. As the late James Macdonald (1995) avowed: freedom is our personal self-development project in life and the "only moral tenable goal" for education.

Fortunately for all of us, not all children come to compliance easily. Children can be aware of the injustice of authoritative impositions and rebel in their hearts and minds. From New Jersey's death row, Tommy Trantino wrote metaphorically of the cost of compliance in *Lock the Lock* (1972), using a six-year-old self to express the ache:

> I was in prison long ago and it was the first grade and I have to take a shit and even when you have to take a shit the law says you must first raise your hand and ask the teacher for permission so I obeyer of the lore of the lamb am therefore busy raising my hand to the fuehrer who says yes Thomas what is it? And I Thomas say I have to take a—I mean may I go to the bathroom please? Didn't you go to the bathroom yesterday Thomas she says and I say yes ma'am Mrs. Parsley sir but I have to go again today but she says NO and I say but Mrs. Parsley judge sir ma'am I gotta go make number two! Eh? she says and I say eh my goddamn ass I GOTTA TAKE A SHIT GODDAMIT and again she says NO but I go anyway except that it was not out but in my pants   that is to say right in my corduroy knickers goddamn...In bed later that night I thought about getting a big kitchen knife and stabbing up this goddamn teacher who shit

in my pants and made my mother wash it out but I said nah nah
that is also against the lore of the lamb   so I didn't do it   but
this kinda taught me something about prisons at a very early age
lets see now   I was about six years old at the time   and yes I
guess that even then I knew without cerebration that if one obeys
and follows orders and adheres to all the rules and regulations of
the lore of the lamb one is going to shit in one's pants   and one's
mother is going to have to clean up afterwards ya see? (p. 17)

From death row, first grade was remembered as a prison, a place
where permission must be granted in order to use the bathroom
and a place where shitting one's pants is preferable to disturbing
the order of the classroom. James Macdonald (in B. Macdonald
1995) suggested a consequence of School's basic assumption about
students—that they "will do the wrong thing (what you do not want
them to do) unless you make them do the right thing"—when he
paraphrased Friedenberg from his 1965 essay in *The Dignity of
Youth and Other Atavisms*:

> There is no difficulty in understanding why, under these condi-
> tions, a federal judge who, when he was in school, had needed a
> hall pass to go to the toilet until he was 17 would not hesitate to
> refuse the issuance of a passport to an American citizen who was
> a member of the Communist Party. (p. 38–39)

Another child who resented the constraints of first-grade and
expressed his discontent was Tiger T, a real first-grader whose
mother shared his tale with members of her graduate education
class. She shared his written assignment on first-grade handwriting
paper. Her son began his paper in demonstrated defiance by using
his preferred name "Tiger T," a title he had been forbidden to use
or answer to during the school year. His two-page, neatly printed
response to his teacher's assignment to write about what he would
remember about first grade read as follows: "I will remember first
grade because I'm sick and tired of it. When Mrs. M says crack,
crack, crack, me gonna crack I'm glad she is retireing. But I hate J.
because in reading group she will not leave alone. I didn't get any
corn dog. At next picnic you get me one or you dead meat."

Tiger's mother intercepted this assignment before he took it
to school, and so his teacher will never read what Tiger *really* carried from his first grade experience. She will never realize he was

"sick and tired" of coercion via exclusion, withholding of privilege, intimidation, and invisibility. Instead she read a paper signed not "Tiger T" the forbidden name, but by the name on the boy's school record, and while his mother did not share the revised version, one can imagine well the content which would be deemed appropriate to turn in to The Teacher.

Herman Hesse (author of novels steeped in conflicted notions of body and mind, of orderly existences and chaotic worlds of sensuality, and of God, man and nature—novels such as *Demian, Steppenwolf,* and *Narcissus and Goldman*)—struggled through a childhood of resistance and dissonance. Alice Miller (1983/1990) tells the story of the difficulties of Hermann Hesse as a child who:

> Like so many gifted children, was so difficult for his parents to bear, not despite but because of his inner riches. Often a child's very gifts, his great intensity of feeling, depth of experience, curiosity, intelligence, quickness, and his ability to be critical, will confront his parents (and teachers) with conflicts that they have long sought to keep at bay with rules and regulations...all this can lead to the apparently paradoxical situation when parents who are proud of their gifted child and who even admire him are forced by their own distress to reject, suppress, or even punish what is best, because truest, in that child. Two of Hesse's mother's observations may illustrate how this work of destruction can be combined with loving care: 'Hermann is going to nursery school; his violent temperament causes us much distress' (when he was 3); and when he was 7: 'Things are going better with Hermann whose education causes us so much distress and trouble. From the 21st of January to the 5th of June, he lived wholly in the boys' house and only spent Sundays with us. He behaved well there but came home pale, thin and depressed. The effects are decidedly *good* and salutary. *He is much easier to manage now*' [emphasis mine]. (p. 120–121)

While young Hermann finally caved in to his isolation and depression, others found ways to quietly resist, such as Kozol's (1967) young Stephen as evidenced in his weekly interactions with the Art Teacher. While serving as a substitute teacher in the Boston Public Schools early in his career, Kozol was moved to despair as he witnessed children who had resigned themselves to their invisibility and the lack of regard by nearly all who should have cared for them, but he also bore witness to the moments of great and slight defiance. He described Stephen's failure to quit as follows:

> I think that much of his life, inwardly and outwardly, must have involved a steady and as it turned out, inwardly at least, a losing battle to survive. He battled for his existence and like many defenseless humans, he had to use whatever odd little weapons came to hand. Acting up in school was part of it. He was granted so little attention that he must have panicked repeatedly about the possibility that, with a few slight mistakes, he might simply stop existing or being seen at all. I imagine this is one reason why he seemed so often to invite or court a tongue-lashing or a whipping. Doing anything at all that would make a teacher mad at him, scream at him, strike at him, would also have been a kind of ratification, even if it was painful, that he was actually was there. (Kozol 1967, 5–6)

Stephen refused to be invisible.

Perhaps the ultimate dissident child derives from the Finnish epic *Kalewala,* in which we find the theme of *l'enfant terrible* who from the third day is struggling so hard he gets the swaddling clothes loose, then tears them and smashes his cradle. "Attempts are made to kill this baneful child, but no matter what death is prepared for him, whether through water or through fire, he overcomes it." In the Vogul epic songs, having become an orphan, the divine child appears as the "immortal avenger" (Erny 1973, 83).

Miller (1983/1990) discussed the dissidents as

> individuals who refuse to adapt to a totalitarian regime...not doing so out of a sense of duty or because of naïveté but because they cannot help but be true to themselves....[while] rejection, ostracism, loss of love and name calling will not fail to affect them; they will suffer as a result and will dread them, once they have found their authentic self, they will not want to lose it. And when they sense that something is being demanded of them to which their whole being says no, they cannot do it. They simply cannot. (p. 84–85)

Miller (2000) further offered the example of the Jesus Christ figure (our final dissident child) as a reason to "relinquish destructive models and to mistrust the principle of obedience." As she explained:

the figure of Jesus confounds all those principles of Poisonous Pedagogy still upheld by the Church, notably the use of punishment to make children obedient and the emotional blindness such treatment inevitably entails. Jesus was respected, admired, loved and protected, his parents saw themselves as his servants and it would never have occurred to them to lay a finger on him. Did that make him selfish, arrogant, covetous, high-handed or conceited? Quite the contrary. Jesus grew into a strong, aware, empathic and wise person able to experience and sustain strong emotions without being engulfed by them....We need children with open eyes and ears, children prepared to protest against injustice, stupidity and ignorance with arguments and constructive action. Jesus was able to do this when he was twelve years old and the scene in the temple demonstrates eloquently that he could refuse the obedience asked of him by his parents without hurting their feelings. (np)

In these examples of the resistant child taken from the literature is a taste of the possibilities of disobedience. In resisting the tight constraints of order and the silencing of their unique voices, these children made space for themselves to be children and so, spirited, alive and ever aware. Perhaps in these keenly attuned ears, the disobedient child ever hears the sound of the *shofar* (ram's horn):

A sound like no other, at once a plaintive cry and a shrill demand for alert attention...[representing] the demand that we overcome our very human tendency to resignation and passivity in the face of life.... To live life with awareness means to see oneself and others possessing the power of choice—to refuse, to question, to posit alternatives—to what is presented to us as permanent and unalterable.... Its enduring purpose is to awaken us from the tendency to 'sleep walk' through our lives. (Shapiro 2006, 23)

Unless the sound of the school bell drowns it out.

Seeking the Good in Being "Bad": The Democracy of Disobedience

Law never made men a whit more just; and, by means of their respect for it, even the well-disposed are daily made the agents of injustice.
~Thoreau (1848/1966)

Small things—the morning, perspective—can be lost in the
     bowels of the earth,
in tunnels where trains convey bodies, human beings with
     purposes,
human beings surviving.

~ Wenner (2004, 3)

I worry about small things being lost. This research seeks to document and shine light on those small things that may be lost in the shuffle of order, control and achievement. Small things, especially the small joys inherent in mischief, silliness and surprise, can be easily misplaced in the larger order of things as the child becomes wrapped securely in the swaddling clothes of the rules, procedures and surveillance of the schoolroom.

While concern for the public schools continues to be "centered on control and compliance...[with] a perpetual pedagogy of surveillance" (Reynolds 2004, 22), Dewey (in Gouinlock 1994) suggested that

> the foundation of democracy is faith in the capacities of human nature; faith in human intelligence and in the power of pooled and cooperative experience resisting the common autocratic and authoritarian scheme of social action [which] rests on a belief that the needed intelligence is confined to a superior few, who... are endowed with the ability and right to control the conduct of others. (p.266)

Realizing and trusting in these capacities may allow opportunities to further develop the moral and social intelligence necessary for democratic life and human well-being. If some of these "capacities of human nature" include the spiritual skills of awareness sensing, mystery sensing, and especially, value sensing (Hay and Nye 1998), then the children in our adult care already have a head start on the democratic good life. However, nurturing these capacities and skills calls for making space for the freedom to practice them.

Some researchers (Kohlberg and Lickona 1987, Piaget 1995, Turiel 2005) would claim that just as children construct and reconstruct their knowledge of the world as a result of interactions with the environment, morality is structured by concepts of harm, welfare, and fairness, and requires that one live and operate as a moral agent within a democratic community. If one considers how this might play into the event of Reuben's fall, one might wonder how—if given the chance—might the children in Julian's class have pooled their collective intelligence and experience to reconcile the collision of the moralities of compassion and convention.

Within that moment of conflicting "goods," there would have been opportunity to engage in concurrent considerations of compassion, focused on the well-being of others; and convention, which focuses on the adherence to social order and norms, via a framework of Turiel's (2005) "qualitatively differing forms of social experience" in order to begin to take meaning from Reuben's fall and Julian's kindness.

Counts (1932) had predicted a harshening of our regard for one another in lamenting one of the great lacks in our schools:

> Nothing really stirs us, unless it be that the bath water is cold, the toast burnt, or the elevator not running...we are moved by no great faiths; we are touched by no great passions. We can view a world order rushing rapidly towards collapse with no more concern than the outcome of a horse race; we can see injustice, crime and misery in their most terrible forms, all about us, and, if we are not directly affected, register the emotions of a scientist studying white rats in laboratory. And, in the name of freedom, objectivity, and the open mind, we would transmit this general attitude of futility to our children...this is a confession of complete moral and spiritual bankruptcy. (p. 19–20)

Evidence that an "attitude of futility" is being passed on to children is often found in places where children are particularly successful and good according to adult standards of success and goodness. One such place was the site of the 2004 National Spelling Bee. Unlike Reuben and Weena, a rescue was not in store for Akshay Buddiga. On the nationally televised (on ESPN) National Spelling Bee, Akshay, standing at the microphone during the finals, collapsed in a faint on the stage. While he managed in a short time to rise and even to spell *alopecoid* correctly, it was the response of the other children that was most striking.

Not one of the children who sat on stage—even those at whose feet Akshay fell— rose or even started to rise to assist him. One girl looked down as Akshay lay, his leg touching the toe of her shoe.

She carefully moved her foot from beneath him, and crossing her ankles, placed her feet beneath her chair. The spellers watched, perhaps fearing disqualification if they rose from their chair when it was not their turn to spell. Just as the citizens in H. G. Wells's future world and the children in Mrs. Buttercup's class maintained their places in the face of someone's need, so did the Scripps-Howard spellers. Can you spell *altruism*, boys and girls?

While generalizing about spelling bee competitions may be unwarranted, there appears to be a relationship of sorts among bee participation and dogmatic adherence to traditional and stringent cultural norms. It would not be a far reach to claim that these child-spellers were even more acculturated into the structured order of their event than were Mrs. Buttercup's children to their ordered line.

> Young children are frequently exposed to others' emotions, as bystanders and as causes. With few exceptions, research on conditions associated with children's responses of aiding and comforting in these two kinds of circumstances has generally proceeded along two different conceptual paths, depending on whether the child is a bystander or a cause of distress. Children's aiding and comforting in situations in which they are bystanders has traditionally been considered in the framework of altruism....The core moral behavior is the child's sense of concern and responsibility for the welfare of others. (Zahn-Waxler, Radke-Yarrow and King 1979, 319)

These moments of exposure to others' emotions and needs are opportunities for children to respond to what they see and feel in the context of that moment. As Frankl (1984) wrote:

> This is what being human is all about. We have to learn from his *sapienta cordis*, from the wisdom of his heart, that being human means being confronted continually with situations, each of which is at once a chance and a challenge, giving us a 'chance' to fulfill ourselves by meeting the 'challenge' to fulfill its meaning. Each situation is a call, first to listen and then to respond. (p. 71)

In the moment of Reuben's fall, Julian listened and responded with an exhibition of care and what Zahn-Waxler et al (1979) would call "altruism" toward his classmate. Just as Frankl and the time traveler did, Julian acted with care and concern even at the known risk of the consequences that would result from the disobedience necessary to respond to Reuben's call. In considering Julian's courage and kindness, I recall what I know of Julian—a boy who spent recesses on walls, and mornings in halls—and realized his noncompliance often seemed to be a result of his constantly engaged, fully-present, and spirited nature. As I have read and learned more about the "child-spirit" (i.e., Hart 2003), I have come to the conclusion that one of the reasons Julian so appealed to me—long before his act of heroism—was his spirited engagement with the world, his verve and curiosity and joy. I also believe that it was his attunement and relationship with the "other" (the "thou") that may have allowed him to see Reuben the way he needed to be seen. I have grown to believe that if we look carefully we may see these qualities within the day to day actions and interactions of young children, and that many of these qualities may be present in the context of acts of disobedience.

What might be learned when engaged in, and confronted with, acts of non-compliance? Nucci (2005) indicated that it is "only by engaging in moral wrongs and experiencing the effects of such wrongs on others and on one's self that genuine moral growth is possible" (p. xii), echoing a similar argument (in Baumrind 2005) that the development of competence and character in children requires the cultivation of the ability to responsibly dissent and accept unpleasant consequences, as well as to constructively comply with some authoritative directives. However, beyond the benefits that these authors claim for conflicts and disobedience, this study seeks to look past the happy endings and re-direct the intentionality into the middle of the acts themselves, for as children live out the "constructive tension that is necessary for growth" (King 1963, 67), they simultaneously live the spirit of the moment.

A Complicated Conversation

Recently I visited a local artist—native Cherokee, Edwin George—and he showed me a tomahawk, the stone blade that he had found in the forest and the carved wooden pipe that he had crafted himself. I admired the beautiful feel and look of his work and marveled over the smooth density of stone head of the tomahawk. And I said,

"Wow, this really *would* hurt!" Edwin seemed surprised at my reaction and corrected me. "No," he said, "it's not to hurt. It is a symbol of peace." He explained how the tomahawk had traditionally been used to represent peacemaking in Cherokee culture. A tomahawk would have been present during talks of war. If the talks went well, the pipe of the tomahawk would be smoked and passed as a symbol of peace, then taken out and buried. When I—raised on Roy Rogers and John Wayne and once owning *and wearing* a full Dale Evans cowgirl outfit in red (even the boots)—looked at the tomahawk, I saw a weapon. When Edwin looked at the tomahawk, he saw an opportunity for peace and resolve.

My vision was impaired, offering only an incomplete picture. I did not see the object fully and allowed myself to see it through a cloud of beliefs based on media, cultural ignorance, and assumption. Edwin's understanding complicated my understanding. Conversations should be complicated—"extraordinarily" so. There must be room for complexities and multiple realities in "complicated conversation across and within culture, class and place" (Pinar 2004, 157).

In Butler's (1998) work with children attending an inner city school, she was initially disturbed by what she perceived as the "fictitious" or "inconsistent" nature of the children's stories. However, she embraced the complicated conversations and began to interrogate her own investments in facts and consistency. She used her discomfort with these stories as a way to

> enter into the realities of the children...[and] interpreted these inconsistencies as deriving from the contradictions embedded in their everyday realities, dominant media images and their parent's dichotomous admonitions about 'bad' behavior, which aimed to protect the children... all of which led the children to endless conundrums: Why were the police violent and unreasonable when the messages from TV kept saying the police are there for protection and safety? How come people who sell and use drugs are 'bad' when some of the people they love most in the world sell and use drugs? How come drugs are 'bad' when the money from them is what provides food and clothes? (p. 103, in Saukko 2001, 88)

These contradictions do complicate things, but they also offer an opportunity to engage joyfully in paradox like the Taoists and

Buddhists as they use *koans* to embrace rather than attempt to conceal contradiction. A *koan* is a story, question, or statement in Zen history and lore, generally inaccessible to rational understanding, yet that may be accessible to intuition. When Zen teachers warn *not to confuse the pointing finger with the moon*, they indicate that awakening is the desire, not the ability to interpret. They caution their students to the danger of confusing the interpretation of a koan with the realization of a koan.

Barone (2001) described a similar goal in educational inquiry:

> In abandoning an obsessive quest for certain and total knowledge that transcends a fallible, human perspective, [we] opt for an epistemology of ambiguity that seeks out and celebrates meanings that are partial, tentative, incomplete, sometimes even contradictory, and originating from multiple vantage points. Such an epistemological stance seems appropriate to a project of educational inquiry whose role or purpose is the enhancement of meaning, rather than a reduction of uncertainty. (p. 152–153)

This study seeks, in koan-like fashion, to display the complexity of each selected moment, exposing the paradoxical nature of goodness instead of concealing: "never separated—facing each other even though we have not met" (Capra 1985, 35).

Breaking the Waves (Asmussen, von Trier and Pirie 1996) is a wonderfully complex film that serves to disrupt our understanding of this particular paradox of "the good." The film offers viewers a destabilizing experience in ambiguity as well as a model of how text can serve such a challenging role—a model for my own research. Makarushka (1998) discussed the film, and especially the character of Bess, exploring

> von Trier's meditation on competing notions of goodness and the cultural assumptions that inform them...[and] how Bess negotiates the moral landscape within which she lives as daughter, sister-in-law, member of a religious community, and wife. The church elders and Bess represent von Trier's vision of the two extremes of the contested notion of the 'good'...For instance, where to be 'good' means not to make waves, not to destabilize the 'natural' order of things, not to express deeply felt emotions, not to experience pleasure, the character, Bess, is undeniably the 'other'...her otherness is interpreted as a flaw, an emotional deficit.

[Makarushka takes on the Nietzschian/Deleuzian resistance to an objective good]: To inquire whether Bess is a 'good' girl is misleading, if not misguided. It assumes an external reference against which all choices and behaviors can be measured and assessed. In the end, what matters is not whether Bess is a 'good' girl. Rather, her goodness matters: a goodness that allows for vulnerability, that takes risks, that crosses from the familiar to the unknown. If the 'good' is a static moral category that assumes compliance, goodness is dynamic, transgressing, and, therefore, dangerous. (np)

The rich and rhizomatic analysis of moments of Bess's goodness in the film begins to get at the complexity and beauty of the spirit of goodness—which is what I seek to express in the analysis of moments of children's disobedience and goodness in this book.

Contextual Literature: Disobedience

The purpose of the following discussions on disobedience in the context of school is to provide:

- an overview of categories of research and other writings related to disobedience;

- background information regarding the school setting, for in order to discuss disobedience—a disregarding or defiance of the structured expectations of a particular situation, place or person—a discussion of the background of those structured expectations is necessary;

- a sampling of examples of what is available for teachers and parents to read about discipline—and thus, some of what is included here in the contextual literature is not "research" per se, but instead, is the type of book or article a teacher would read who is, herself, wondering about "disobedience": what would she likely be reading;

- and finally, an additional framework in order to discuss the significance and purpose of the book.

Later chapters (4 and 6) provide discussion of additional literature related to disobedience and kindergarten classrooms.

After initial reviews of the literature regarding disobedience concerning the behaviors of young children in school, I identified five lines of inquiry. The majority of authors focus on: (1) disobedience as deficiencies; (2) a need for order and control and how to achieve such order and control; (3) teacher perspective and role; (4) political, philosophical, and spiritual constraints of school morality; and (5) dissent and the democratic good life.

Disobedience as Deficiency

In the field of classroom behavior, many researchers discuss forms of disobedience (and childhood itself) as deficiencies—developmental, moral/religious, social, behavioral, or of character—and as problems to be solved. Because there are so many ways in which children can be deficient, and because there are so many fields of study devoted to solving the problem of childhood, there is no shortage of research in this category of disobedience study (for instance, in Burnard 1998, Colvin Sugai and Patching 1993, Debruyn and Larson 1984, Duke and Jones 1984, Eisenberg and Hand 1979, Everston and Harris 1992, Freiberg 1999, Kohlberg 1981, McGoey, Prodan and Condit 2007, Piaget 1932, Pittman 1985, Turner and Watson 1999, Wang 1993, Weinstein, Tomlinson-Clarke and Curran 2004, Wheldal 1992).

A glance at the literature offers many solutions for dealing with children's deficiencies in the classroom setting: time-out, notes home, pre-correction, and Discipline as an educational specialty emphasize solving the problem of disruptive and undeveloped children (i.e., Duke and Jones 1984, McGoey, Prodan, and Condit 2007, Turner and Watson 1999), while others claim you can change the classroom management paradigm, manage any classroom, develop children's behavior and "handle them all" (Debruyn and Larson 1984, Freiberg 1999) in spite of the children's many deficiencies.

To illustrate this claim, Debruyn and Larson (1984) list 117 "deficiencies" in their book for teachers and parents: *You Can Handle Them All: A Discipline Model for Handling Over One Hundred Different Misbehaviors at School and at Home.* Suggestions are provided for "handling" such problem children as "The Agitator," "The Crier" [there are two Criers, one "who claims foul" and the other "who sheds tears"], "The Influencer," "The Blabbermouth," "The Petty Rules Breaker," "The Procrastinator," "The Rebel," "The Repeater" "The Immature," "The Interrupter," "The Lazy," "The Dreamer," "The

Sidetracker," "The Questioner," "The Snotty," "The Satisfied with Second Place," "The Pest," and "The Troublemaker," with the purpose of providing step-by-step approaches for changing them—for making them better at being "good" students.

For each of the 117 deficient characters, Debruyn and Larson offer a description. For instance, the description of The Questioner:

> Asks an abnormal number of questions...has his/her hand up in the air continually... asks questions even when he/she seems to know the answers... [having effects such as] "proceedings are interrupted...teacher and classmates are annoyed...time is stolen from other students because the questioner requires 'double instruction'...teacher is diverted from following lesson plan...teacher may feel this student is attempting to 'trap' him or her." (p. 227)

And another, The Influencer:

> Has power to influence... delights in 'trapping' teacher or making schoolwork seem insignificant...may even make rules that conflict with classroom or school rules... encourages others to speak out, complain about an assignment, or refuse to comply with teacher requests [with effects such as] 'teacher experiences an uneasy feeling in class... teacher is embarrassed... authority of teacher is undermined... teacher may become frustrated or angry... neither followers nor the influencer is learning... followers of the influencer as well as other students are distracted.' (p. 158)

The above descriptions of children imply that children are deficient in character and moral development. More and more schools have adopted (purchased) programs designed to "teach character to children." While Lickona (1997) ostensibly advocated caring relationships and moral feeling, he named good character as "virtues." Virtues such as: "prudence, justice, temperance and fortitude" (p. 46)—virtues that can then be taught per week or month. He noted this example of a teacher who combined "high expectations and high support," the kind of teacher who "believes every child can learn." Lickona told of visiting the classroom of such a teacher and noting the list of classroom rules, "writ large and posted in the front. The first rule was 'Always do your best in everything.'" On further examination of the room, he notes a sign on the wall reading "A PERSON WILL SELF-DESTRUCT WITHOUGH A GOAL."

And he saw featured on the bulletin board the value of the month, "AMBITION, defined as 'hard work directed toward a worthwhile goal'" (Lickona 1997, 55).

This recalls the words of President George W. Bush in a speech given in Santa Clara, California, on May 1, 2002. He stated that the public education system in America "is one of the most important foundations of our democracy. After all, it is where children from all over America learn to be responsible citizens, and learn to have the skills necessary to take advantage of our fantastic opportunistic society" (in Weisberg 2002, 64).

Indeed, *if* the purpose of bringing all of our children together to learn and practice the highest ideals of our culture were to nurture ambition and to develop "opportunistic" skills, then the constraining structures that serve to keep children apart from one another (physically and emotionally) *would* serve that purpose. However, Gay (1997), in response to Lickona's body of work on character education, represented the relationship between multiculturalism and character education, and posed the question, "Honesty, truth and responsibility about what, when and for whom?" thus simultaneously challenging President Bush's statement and Lickona's body of work, noting that character education is often centered in "individual attributes and actions," often neglecting the "social and collective" (p. 98).

Also included in this group of authors and theorists are those who view children's disobedience as a symptom of their early development, placing children at the lowest levels of moral and behavioral development (for instance, Kohlberg 1981 and Piaget 1932). As Hart (2003) explained, "Developmental theorists typically tell us that children are self-centered and incapable of real empathy or compassion" (p. 69). Hart (1996) earlier noted that "children have been generally seen as developmentally immature, without sufficient intellectual growth to manifest anything that might not be understood as meaningfully reflective and/or spiritual" (p. 164). Hart additionally noted that Wilber (1996) had described children's ways of thinking and feeling as being merely "instinctual, impulsive, libidinous, id-ish, animal and apelike," likely guided by Piaget's 1968 stage model in which children are viewed as "largely incapable of meaningful reflection" (in Hart 2006, 164). Considering the vast quantities of research naming and then seeking to squelch all of the problems children bring, it is no wonder that "the emphasis on children's social incompetence and irresponsibility means ... children need to be brought to a state of socialibility through the continued surveillance and control of a *benevolent* authority" [emphasis mine] (Thomas 2002, 91).

Duke and Jones (1984) noted that for decades, discipline writers have split between theories relying on punishment and those relying on "communication between teacher and student" (p. 27). However, neither side seems to be considering what the child is learning about authority, democracy, or her role in the larger culture; rather, both seem to seek merely to adjust the child to the classroom, coercively or by winning the child's assent—which is also coercive, but less obviously so (see *Figure 1*).

In Figure 1 below, Groening's cartoon (1997) illustrates cogently and comically the doubled nature of coercion: one overtly constrained with ropes and a gag; the other less obviously constrained with the promise of a reward—and yet still tied and under surveillance. What is notable is that the ice cream serves to distract the character from its state. In complying, and so gaining reward, the character is privileged, and yet, concurrently, is not any more free than the character so explicitly under-privileged.

Krieg (2006), in her paper about "unbelievable children," found that when early childhood teachers discuss their students, any "difference" (as "constructed through processes of normalization") is understood as a deficit. The teachers in her study discussed "children and families who did not 'fit' their ideas of what 'should be'" (p. 11). These deficits—described as "very, very active," and "aggressive" and ADHD-identified—are pedagogically addressed in order to make the children "different" from what they were (and so, better). Krieg noted that the teacher "sees 'rescuing' children from their abnormal levels of 'activity' and 'aggression' as an important aspect of her work" (p. 11).

These authors and theorists offer diverse conclusions and implications to teachers and parents—from Kohlberg's "just community schools" and Piaget's (1932) cooperative decision-making and problem-solving among children to the series of sanctions recommended by Burnard's (1998) or Pittman's (1985) quantification of a first-grade teacher's management routines. In each of these conclusions, there is a quality of looking down at the children in this research as opposed

Figure 1: "Look How Much Easier Your Life Could Be." © 1991 Matt Groening. Reprinted from The Huge Book Of Hell, © 1997 Penguin Books.

to gazing/looking *at* and *with* them. Whether supporting "development" or coercing and coaxing certain behaviors, the implication in this work is that children must be moved from where they are to where they should be.

A Need for Order and Control in Schools

A large body of research is devoted to discussing the need for order and control and the means toward achieving child obedience. While there is some overlap between this and the previous category—and many of these writers discuss children and their deficiencies—the focus here is on the school and the teacher and the importance of, and means to attain/maintain, an orderly, disciplined, well-managed, quiet, predictable, safe, and efficient classroom (to be found, for instance, in Dreikurs 1982, Jones 1978 , McDaniel 1994, Pittman 1985, Rinne 1997, Roffey and O'Reirdan 2001, Rogovin 2004, Schwartz and Pugh 1981, Tanner 1980, Weiner 1980, Wragg 2001, Wynne and Ryan 1993).

In the tradition of Bentham (1787/1995) and his Panopticon—a "principle of construction applicable to any sort of establishment, in which persons of any description are to be kept under inspection; and in particular to penitentiary-houses, prisons, houses of industry, work-houses, poor-houses, lazarettos, manufactories, hospitals, mad-houses, and schools" (p. 29)—these researchers and authors who study various means of controlling children generally base their inquiry on determining what structures and actions schools and teachers should undertake to best survey and normalize children and their behavior.

Much of this work explores the means by which teachers can, with efficiency and minimal effort, achieve total control over the children in their care, all while appearing to be just and fair. As Dreikurs (1982) indicated in *Maintaining Sanity in the Classroom* (and we may easily surmise to whose sanity he refers), "It is autocratic to use force, but democratic to induce compliance" (p. 67). In the case of this category of the literature, the authors are not looking down at the child, but seem to not be looking at her at all—which may seem somewhat ironic given the panoptical notion of the work.

Rogovin (2004) described the importance of control via surveillance and the role scanning the room plays in enforcing the rules:

> Rules must be enforced. The teacher is the enforcer when the children are not following the rules....Remember, you are trying to prevent inappropriate behavior and you are trying to implement and enforce the guidelines. My friend...always tells her student teachers to 'Scan the room'. For her, that means her furniture is low enough so that, no matter where you are sitting or standing, you can see every child. It means that if you are working with one or two children, you look up occasionally and scan the room. The more the children have internalized the positive behavior, the

more you can focus on the academic activities, and the less fre-
quently you have to scan the room. (p. 19–20)

These writings communicate a kind of battle, telling of teachers
"trapped" by the children as described by Debruyn in the previous
section and of the insurrectors and "buddies who will teach you
a lesson," described here by Welker (1976), McDaniel (1994) and
Gray (1976). The first author (Welker 1976), states clearly in the abstract of his article, "The author does not attempt to promote any
educational philosophy; but, rather, stresses the need for classroom
control in all environments" (p. 238), and then warns teachers to
prepare for the worst:

> Right from the beginning of the school year, be well-organized and
> prepared to teach on the first vibration of the late bell. Many nov-
> ice teachers have been told by their supervisors—'Don't smile until
> after Christmas'. Of course, this is a bit crass; nonetheless, there
> is some wisdom to be found here. If you start with the attitude of
> being 'buddy-buddy' with your students, you may find that your
> buddies have decided to teach you a few of their lessons. (p. 239)

Some authors argue against less authoritarian means of "managing the classroom" through not-so-veiled intimations of a chaotic,
lawless society, noting that a teacher knows that "an orderly society is
dependent upon students who have learned the rule of law, one of the
major values in a democratic society" (McDaniel 1994), and that

> from the moment he signs a contract the teacher shares with the
> public school a tacit obligation to society. In the main, we al-
> low ourselves to be governed by duly elected persons and their
> representatives. This is the only way our society can function in
> an *orderly* way [emphasis mine]. It is not good, therefore, that
> our young people become adept at insurrection. The teacher
> who allows students to victimize him in his classroom indirect-
> ly encourages them to victimize the man at the newsstand, the
> stranger in the park and the cop on his beat. (Gray 1967, 1)

It is not unusual to read these dire notions of child-as-threat.
Throughout the classroom management and discipline writings (as
will be explored in chapter 4), the relationship between the children
and their teachers is presented as antagonistic— the teachers must

predict and prevent any unexpected, unwanted, unordered act in order to win the battle and, so, the war.

Toward this victory, there are dozens and dozens of books and articles (for instance, Canter and Canter 1992, Jones 1978, Roffey and O'Reirdan 2001, Weiner 1980, and Wong and Wong 1998) that can be easily accessed by teachers online, at popular bookstores, in community libraries, on *Amazon*, *half.com*, and at yard sales. In one of these (Rinne 1997), upon opening to the Table of Contents, we can see that there is help to be found in:

- Managing space, location and grouping;
- Managing non-verbal experiences;
- Managing time;
- Monitoring student attention
  - teacher eyes
  - teacher location
  - 'withitness';
  - overlapping;
- Controlling distractions and catastrophes;
- Giving encouragement and criticism;
- Controlling games students play;
- Training students in self-control; and
- Anticipating and planning.

As Thomas (2002) warned, the role of the school has become a "means of control and regulation of school children," and a weak teacher (the "buddy," the "victim") might have only "an inadequate and dangerous control of children whose social incompetence could lead to a threat to the social order" (p. 92). With the social order at stake—a social order dependent on children who know and unquestioningly follow the rules and laws—the conversation about what is possible among the people sharing a classroom becomes narrow indeed. In fact, school is nothing special is it? Wrote Bowd (1982) in defending the need for order and control in schools, "Schools, like businesses, church congregations, and trade union locals are social organizations. The behavior of their individual members is restricted and constrained by their rules and traditions" (p. 13).

There are several important lessons to be learned from this category of the literature: (a) teachers have easy and relatively varied access to books, journals and web links that promote and validate the ideal of the "order of the dominant"; (b) these readings provide a plethora of advice, techniques, and strategies to attain and maintain order in the classroom; (c) the discussions include not only how-tos, but also stress that this order is vital to society; and (d) an awareness of what teachers may be reading or discussing in their lounges, staff meetings and workshops may allow a means to create dissonance regarding both the method and the intent of this predominant literature in the field.

Teacher Perspective and Role

Within the discussion of what occurs in classrooms related to disobedience and classroom management, some authors, theorists and researchers focus their inquiry on the teacher's perspective and role in children's moral and social behaviors and the complexity of child compliance. The group of writers (Buzzelli 1993, DeVries and Zan 1994, Hansen 1995, Jackson, Boostrom and Hansen 1993, Johnston and Buzzelli 2002, McCadden 1998, Noddings 2002, Sheets, 1996, Solomon, Watson and Battistich 2001, Watson 2003, Weinstein et al. 2004) in this body of the literature differ from the prior two in both intent and the methods that categorize it. The focus is on collegial relationships between the children and their teacher rather than adversarial ones; and generally speaking, order and efficiency are not the first priorities in the discussion. At least ostensibly.

In this category of literature, the authors again focus on the teacher, but on his or her role and choices in relation to the children. For instance, in two studies (Sheets 1996, Weinstein et al. 2004) looking carefully at teachers' actions in response to their regard for the students' cultural identity, the researchers found those teachers who demonstrated care and concern for the children as they are developed "caring classroom communities" because the children "were convinced those teachers cared for and believed in them" (in Weinstein et al, 33). This discussion of the reciprocal integrated and negotiated relationship of the child and the teacher is representative of the work in this category of the literature. Also common in this work is the inclusion of discussion of the confounding effects of constraints on teacher-student relationships. For instance, Watson's (2003) research and work with a classroom teacher and her class using "developmental discipline" is based on the tenets of attachment theory, which examines the effects of children's prior relationships on their ability to form new ones.

In further considering how to engage children in building and maintaining positive, productive relationships in the classroom, Buzzelli (1993) discussed two types of discourses that teachers use with children, *univocal* and *dialogic*, as having "moral implications for children's development and learning...one representing an epistilogical world of knowledge acquired as bits of information and another epistemological world in which knowledge is constructed through 'social experiences.'" He compared the dogma of "being told" (a high-priority in the previous sets of literature, and as explored further in chapter 4) to "the rich possibilities of empathic thinking and responding to the internal sense of 'right or wrong'" (Buzzelli 1993, 383–385).

However, the structural constraints of school confound the relational basis of this work. While some teachers may recognize the value of caring relationships, they perceive their role as classroom managers as separate from, and of higher priority to, their role as *carer*. McCadden's (1998) study detailed the impact of these conflicting roles, and discussed findings that as teachers struggle to balance their management role with their relational role, managing often becomes the way to care. On close examination, however, the care and the management are not easily distinguished, as, ultimately, the end goal of the good relationship is often toward gently coercing children to agree to comply, with little examination of what we are asking them to comply to. Even in this kinder, gentler space, the child is considered as the object of a teacher/child relationship, not as a subject of it.

Political, Philosophical and Spiritual Constraints of School Morality

The political, philosophical, and spiritual constraints of school morality motivate the conversation in some circles, and this may be the space for the examination of what we are asking them to comply with. However, generally these discussions take place in the field of curriculum and among academicians. Casual observation and extended associations with schools and teachers informs me that this literature rarely reaches the classroom. Those theorists and writers (for example, Ayers 2001, Foucault 1988, Gatto 1992, Greene 1988, hooks 1994, D. Jardine 1998, D. Jardine, Clifford and Friesen 2003, Kesson 1999, Kohn 1993/1999, Macdonald 1995, Noddings 1993, Paley 1999, Purpel 2001) who discuss the political, philosophical, and spiritual constraints of the order of school typically engage in writing passionate texts with few practical notions to appeal to teachers and little in the way of real research to appeal to scholars. Even so, it is this literature that most appeals to me because I believe deeply that it is passion that moves us—more so than the careful rigor of research or the precise dogma of the method-writers.

I am particularly moved by Purpel (1989) as he lamented the limiting nature of the schoolroom when "indeed, the essence of education can be seen as critical, in that its purpose is to help us see, hear and experience the world more clearly, more completely, and with more understanding...creativity and imagination" (p. 26–27), all toward enabling us to re-make our world for the purpose of human freedom.

This lies in direct contrast against McDaniel's (1994) provision for freedom via education. He set a series of prerequisites prior to engaging in seeing, hearing, and experiencing the world:

> Once teachers are accepted by their students as leaders, as competent instructors, as firm-but-fair disciplinarians who establish clear rules and reasonable structure, then a basis for learning, and for *freedom within limits* exists [emphases mine]. Defiance, disruption, and 'games students play' become rarities rather than every-day, escalating, eroding misadventures. Then, and only then, can teachers begin refining and humanizing their techniques of discipline. Then, and only then, can teachers begin extending to students an opportunity for shared planning, for negotiating contracts, for full participation in rule setting and student courts. Then, and only then, can teachers begin the important and meaningful task of democratizing the classroom. (p. 3–4)

As Toni Morrison phrased it in her lovely poetry quoted at the head of this section, "But if freedom is handled just your way, then it's not my freedom or free."

John Gatto, a winner of national teaching awards, wrote a book devoted to reviewing the lack of freedom in schools with earthy directness and with some righteous ire as well. The following is one excerpt from his 1992 book *Dumbing Us Down: The Hidden Curriculum Compulsory Schooling:*

> Schools are intended to produce, through the application of formulas, formulaic human beings whose behavior can be predicted and controlled...to a very great extent schools succeed in doing this, but...the products of schooling are, as I've said irrelevant. Well-schooled people are irrelevant. They can...push paper and talk on telephones or sit mindlessly before a flickering computer terminal, but as human beings they are useless...it is absurd and anti-life to be part of a system that compels you to sit in confinement with people of exactly the same age and social class. That system effectively cuts you off from the immense diversity of life and synergy of variety; indeed it cuts you off from your own past and future...it is absurd and anti-life to move from cell to cell at the sound of a gong for every day of your natural youth in an institution that allows you no privacy. (p. 27)

It is in this category of literature that the most committed advocacy for children—or the *idea* of children—can be found. Because of this, many of these sources are featured in chapter 6 and throughout the book. However, the voice and view of real children is rare in this group of writers...so the role of this literature will be to provide the social structure and the *so what* of the research to come.

Dissent and the Democratic Good Life

Butchart (1995) provides an overview of the history of classroom management:

> Since the fifties, disciplinary literature has fallen silent on the long-term social objectives of school discipline, stressing the immediate control of students. The emphasis has shifted from ends to means and strategies. Rather than developing philosophies of discipline linked to visions of a preferred social order, writers have developed systems and models whose only criterion for success is their short-term goal of classroom order. Many of the models rely heavily on

behaviorism, attempting to deploy rewards and penalties effectively in the service of authoritarian control. Others attempt to be more constructivist and humane. Few develop any clear conception of democratic social life, either as a short-term goal or a long-term objective. Both the behaviorist and constructivist approaches attempt to reassert the authority of teachers. (p. 179)

Butchart nailed it.

In all of the lines of research and writings above there is missing any discussion of the fundamental relationship between what we do in schools and what we claim is our most basic objective: democracy and freedom. As caring adults, are we asking what impact walking in lines for six years has on a child's willingness to walk other than the beaten-path? Are we asking what is the impact of relationships built on contingencies, rewards and punishments? Are we wondering what is the relationship between uncritical compliance and real democracy? Some are.

Discussion regarding the value of dissent and disobedience toward an authentic democratic good life involves researchers and writers (for instance, Ayers 2005, Baumrind 2005, Bluestein 2004, Cannella 1999, Chomsky 2004, Dewey 1932, Foucault 1980, Garrison 1997, Goodman 2001, Lightfoot 2000, McCadden 1996, Miller 1983/1990, J. Miller 2000, Nucci 2005, Oser 2005, Oser and Spychiger 2004, Purpel 1989, Zinn 2001) who seek, in examining disobedience, to reflect Ralph Waldo Emerson's caution: "your goodness must have some edge to it—else it is none" (1940, 149, in Goodman 2001, 351). Recall Dewey's words from chapter 1 regarding democracy as: "simultaneously a way of life, an ethical ideal, and a personal commitment. Specifically, it is a way of life in which individuals are presumed to be self-directing and able to pursue their own goals and projects. No society that maintains order through constant supervision and/or coercion can be rightly called democratic" (1985, 349).

I lay this against McDaniel's text which claimed that only as a result of supervision and coercion, then and only then can a classroom even consider becoming "democratized." Dewey (1960) also described a relationship between freedom and experienced resistance. He believed that people do not think about, or go in search of, freedom "unless they run during action against conditions that resist their original impulses" (p. 286); and so, it becomes vital that opportunities for conflict and error occur. This would conflict with the notions in the first few groups of researchers/writers, where much of the intent is to prevent and preempt such opportunities.

Nucci (2005) raised similar points in his discussion of moral development and character education. As described in other sections in this chapter, researchers/writers (Bennett 1993, Kohlberg, Levine and Hewer 1983, Lickona 1991, Piaget 1932, Wynne and Ryan 1997) who promote moral education often present a picture of moral growth and education that conforms to the general notion that children should get morally "better" as they develop and that moral education entails either a process of gradually building up virtue through socialization into one's cultural norms or movement toward a more adequate (better) form of moral reasoning. Nucci (2005) troubled this picture of moral improvement—a picture that "belies the role of resistance, conflict and contrarian elements in both the course of individual moral development and moral 'progress' at the societal level" (p. vii). Oser (2005) confirms Nucci's notion, noting the positive role of resisting via "engaging in moral wrongs and experiencing the effects of such wrongs on others as... the basis for genuine moral discourse" (p. vii).

In engaging in democracy, such discourse is necessary. As Martin Luther King (1963) wrote, "We know through painful experience that freedom is never voluntarily given by the oppressor; it must be demanded by the oppressed." Conflict and tension can serve positive moral and democratic ends. As King elaborated, "I have earnestly worked and preached against violent tension, but there is a type of constructive tension that is necessary for growth...to create the kind of tension in society that will help men to rise" (p. 67). As disobediences work to create these certain kinds of "tensions," chapter 6 will offer further discussion of this particular theme in the complexities inherent in moments of children's disobedience.

While there is no shortage of research, authorship and sales in the area of disobedience in the classroom—especially related to how to beat it—there is comparatively little that engages in study of disobedience in its complexity, and even less that studies the child's choices and meaning-making rather than the teacher's. While the content of the research and writings included in this chapter have informed and do inform our understanding of discipline, school and, to a degree, disobedience, this book's purpose is also to disrupt and destabilize what is dominant in the research and writings. In some cases, by sharing it—which is a focus of chapter 4—and in others, by offering stories of children engaging with and in the "structured expectations" of the classroom. As Butchart (1995) suggested:

> First, we need to extend our critique of classroom practice to embrace classroom discipline and management as the necessary groundwork toward articulating more ethically and politically defensible classroom practices. Second, we need to provide insight into disciplinary structures—that is, the structures, rituals, practices, and procedures that have become embedded in schools... that extend disciplinary power and...limit or constrain the intellectual and political aims of teaching." (p. 168)

Chapter 3

The Method: Rhizoanalysis, Qualitative Inquiry, and a Twist of Lather

As kids, we were border crossers and had to learn to negotiate the power, violence, and cruelty of the dominant culture through our own lived histories, restricted languages, and narrow cultural experiences.

~ Giroux (1996, 9)

Negotiations sometimes last so long you don't know whether they're still part of the war or the beginning of peace. And philosophy's always caught between an anger with the way things are and the serenity it brings ....Not being a power, philosophy can't battle with the powers that be, but it fights a war without battles, a guerrilla campaign against them. And it can't converse with them, it's got nothing to tell them, nothing to communicate, and can only negotiate. Since the powers aren't just external things, but permeate each of us, philosophy throws us all into constant negotiations with, and a guerrilla campaign against, ourselves.

~ Deleuze (1995, frontpiece)

Introduction

As indicated in the previous chapters, issues surrounding young children's disobedience in the context of the classroom have been the subject of much consternation, discussion and publication for decades. The bulk of this discussion has concerned combating—in ways proactive and reactive—the disobedient behaviors and promoting the compliant. A lesser share of the discussion has included themes exploring the constraints of school morality and the value of dissent and disobedience toward an authentic democratic good.

81

However, there is little in this discussion that includes the dis-obedient child herself or the close, careful looks at the moments of disobedience that might direct discussion toward the range of the possibilities inherent in those moments—possibilities that might serve to challenge what is assumed about children's compliance and disobedience. Obviously, there have been close and careful looks at children's obedient and disobedient classroom behaviors. But these have been offered as means of categorizing, fixing and working with and around toward other ends—ends identified by Foucault (1979) as "notions of classification, and classification as a means to con-trol efficiently" (p. 144). Even those studies that serve to describe the life of children in their classrooms (Jackson, Boostrom and Hansen 1993, McCadden 1998, Mehan 1979, Solomon, Watson and Battistich 2001) do so in order to understand what is in place in the classroom as a moral and intellectual space to act, not to disrupt.

However, the purpose of this particular study is to disrupt and resist the assumed and known. As Greene (1991) advocated, we must refuse to function compliantly, "like Kafkaesque clerks" (p. 8). As well, Foucault believed what we hold to be true (known) about, for instance, child development or managing children within a classroom is "a fiction created through 'truth games' that express the politics of knowledge of the time and place" (in MacNaughton 2005, 5).

Kathleen Kesson (2006) discussed this research project as a means to disrupt, wondering how might this study work to "jar us out of our taken-for-granted, socially conditioned assumptions about childhood, and insist that we take a much closer look at the forms of consciousness embodied in young people... and to apply these insights to our own lives, and perhaps even learn something from young people about how to live in the world" (np).

Toward this end, one might adopt a spiritual approach to education in which one would encounter the "indwelling spirit" (Macdonald 1995) of the people we teach. Such an approach would require that teachers be "open and vulnerable ourselves in the pres-ence of those we teach...to focus on the development of habits of mind that many consider central to a spiritual presence in the world: reverence, respect, awe, wonder, reflection, vision, commitment and purpose" (Henderson and Kesson 1999, 98).

Within such a spiritual approach to education and research, I view these habits of mind as essential to a rhizomatic viewing of children's moments and so was particularly drawn to this method of analysis as a natural fit with rich potential to "to lay bare the questions that have been hidden by certain implicit taken-for-granted answers about education and inquiry; to foster 'brooding about the issues involved in telling [schoolpeople's] stories'" (Lather 1997, 234); and most certainly, to reduce the "commonsensical certainty" (Barone 2001, 155) about good (where good = compliant) children and disobedient (and so, bad) children.

In this way, teachers and other adults may, in interrogating their comfortable and entrenched responses to children in the classroom, begin to frame responses that might allow for potential democratic notions of disobedience. As sharing the stories of disobedient, resilient, and spirited children may lead the researcher and readers to consider more fully the complexity inherent in children's acts of disobedience and to dismantle and disrupt "compliancism." The method itself works toward an expression of this resistance. In the tradition of Eisner and Dewey, the method joins the content in expressing spiritual, resistant, and disobedient themes reflected in childhood.

The stories emerge from moments of children's disobedience in two kindergarten classrooms in their literal state through carefully contextualized and detailed text. Observation and recording of real time daily activities and routines of children in these classrooms provide the moments of entry into the following inquiries:

1. In what ways do the kindergarten children disobey in the context of the kindergarten classroom?

2. In what ways are the kindergartners' moments of disobedience representations and enactments of something more than merely disobedience?

3. In what ways are the kindergartners' moments of disobedience opportunities for responding to others in caring, ethical ways and for acting out the possibilities that a spiritual childhood provides, such as reverence, awe, wonder, reflection, vision, commitment and purpose; and the sensitivities in awareness sensing, mystery sensing, and value sensing (Hay and Nye 1998)?

For each of the questions above, efforts were made to generate and interrogate texts of the child, to seek surprises in order to "disrupt the familiar and obvious" (MacNaughton 2004) in what is known, and so, to form a new logic about what is happening in the text via building new understandings of its relationships to other texts.

Therefore, this study combines qualitative inquiry as presented in Eisner's (1998) *The Enlightened Eye: Qualitative Inquiry and the Enhancement of Educational Practice* and the method of rhizo-analysis as adapted, with the assistance of MacNaughton (2004, 2005), from Deleuze and Guattari's (1987) discussion of rhizomes in *A Thousand Plateaus: Capitalism and Schizophrenia*, toward presenting an appreciation for the possibilities within the messiness and disobedience of authentic and spirited childhood.

Rationale for Conducting Qualitative Inquiry and Rhizoanalysis

> *Functioning simultaneously and autonomously, we are a rhizomatic entity...*
>
> *Our potential is the potential to dismantle.*
>
> ~ Nelson (2004))

Qualitative Inquiry

"To see is to experience qualities. [Qualitative inquiry]...is about the perception of qualities, those that pervade intimate social relations and those that constitute complex social institutions, such as schools. It is also about the meaning of those qualities and the value we assign to them" (Eisner 1998, 1). Eisner further discusses qualitative inquiry via the experience of quality, explaining that while the sensory system is the instrument through which we experience the qualities that constitute our environment, the ability to truly experience these qualities requires more than merely their presence—it requires action. "Experience is a form of human achievement, and as such it depends on an act of mind...we learn to see, hear and feel. This process depends on perceptual differentiation...the ability to see what is subtle but significant is crucial" (p. 21). Becoming knowledgeable and wise about qualitative matters requires that one experience or create qualities worth experiencing.

This book seeks to see through experienced and concurrently fresh eyes qualities worth experiencing in a kindergarten classroom and to express these qualities via what Eisner (1998) described as criticism, "an art of saying useful things about complex and subtle objects and events so that others can see and understand what they did not see and understand before" (p. 3). This will not come about because I, the researcher, know more, but because I seek to *see* more in the qualities present in the typical daily kindergarten experience.

In a twist on what might be considered the knowledgeable expertise of what Eisner (1998) termed "the connoisseur," prior experiences, the body of information, the broader contexts and personal values and priorities are tempered with uncertainty. At times, critical perception can follow only after one abandons what one thinks one knows. As Ellsworth (1992) reminded: "all knowings are partial... there are fundamental things each of us cannot know" (p. 101).

The two kindergarten classrooms selected for the study represent the typical social context of the daily activities and routines of American kindergarten classrooms. The direct observations used in this research captured children's disobedient actions often taken for granted without being considered in a wide range of possibilities. The process of capturing the moments of the kindergartner's interactions with and within the social context was designed to respect the qualities of those experiences and to perceive what is "subtle but significant."

Eisner (1998, 33–40) describes six features of qualitative inquiry that served to guide the process of inquiry in this study. The features—field-focused, self as instrument, interpretative character, use of expressive language, attention to particulars, and criteria for success—are presented in *Table 1*, along with a brief explanation of the application proposed for this research.

One purpose of this research is to provide a perspective on children's moments of disobedience in the schoolroom via what Eisner termed the enlightened eye of qualitative inquiry through which "the scene is seen." Qualitative inquiry was selected as a means of study because it supports direct observation of the actual actions and interactions of and between the children and their teacher during the daily activities and routines of a kindergarten classroom. As Eisner (1998) has claimed, "To know what schools are like...we need to be able to see what occurs in them, and we need to be able to tell others what we have seen in ways that are vivid and insightful" (p. 22).

Table 1: Features of Qualitative Inquiry and Applications in Study

Features	Applications
Field Focused Takes place in setting(s) of interest. Observe, interview, record, describe, interpret and appraise settings as they are ("naturalistic") (from Lincoln and Guba 1985). Includes humans interacting, but also inanimate objects such as architecture, room arrangement, textbooks, locations of particular items, posters, displays, etc.) (Eisner 1998).	**Field Focused** In addition to the videotape of the children enacting their kindergarten day, descriptions of room arrangement, schedule, texts (teacher talk, child talk, posters, readings, codes, classroom and school rules as posted, etc.), school contexts, and other particulars of the field which contributed to the mood and aesthetics of meaning were included contextually and in the context of the moments of entry to analysis.
Self as Instrument Being able to see what "counts." Combining sensibility, perceptivity, sense-making, and use of schema toward unique insights as sources of meaning. "Sensibility alerts us to nuanced qualities and the schema relevant to a domain, the significance of what to seek and see" (Eisner 1998, 34).	**Self as Instrument** My experience as a kindergarten teacher allowed me to claim a degree of expertise in recognizing the typical schema of a kindergarten classroom. As a researcher, I also claim an open mind, a willingness to embrace possibilities, and, in seeking to learn more about the process of research, as well as more about children as compliant and non-compliant beings, a questioning spirit. While this project interrogated "disobedience," the *way* it was questioned was flexible and emergent and responsive to what was observed.
Interpretive Character One meaning of interpretation relates to accounting for or explaining reasons for what one has observed. Why? The other role of interpretation relates to meaning, penetrating the surface, and in Geertz's (1973) words, "thick description." Meanings such as these are influenced by the conceptual tools used by the researcher and by antecedent factors that serve as background (Eisner 1998).	**Interpretive Character** It is not my intent in this study to reduce uncertainty but instead to "seek out and celebrate meanings that are partial, tentative, incomplete, sometimes even contradictory, and originating from multiple vantage points" (Barone 2001, 153). The conceptual tools of rhizoanalysis allowed me to explore the nuances and politics of the text constituting the kindergarten observations in order to create new texts. These newly constructed texts explored "how it means; how it connects with things 'outside' of it, such as its author, its reader and its literary and non-literary contexts; and by exploring how it organizes meanings and power through offshoots, overlaps, conquests and expansions" (Deleuze and Guattari 1987, 21).

Features	Applications
Use of Expressive Language The presence of voice in the text is vital in the development of understanding as it relates to empathy, emotion, and vicarious feeling. "Why take the heart out of situations we are trying to help readers understand?" (Eisner 1998, 37).	**Use of Expressive Language** Dewey (1934) made the distinction between stating meaning and expressing meaning. While the data gathered here is initially "stated" as transcribed, the quality of meaning is derived as much from the aesthetic (as opposed to anesthetic) nature of the text itself as from the content of it. In Dewey's words: "The expression as distinct from statement, does something different from leading to an experience. It constitutes one" (p. 84, in Eisner 1998, 31).
Attention to Particulars Maintains the flavor of particular events, people and objects and so maintains the uniqueness of each case. "Revelation of the particular situation requires, first, awareness of its distinctiveness...but beyond that, the ability to render those distinctive features through text is required" (Eisner 1998, 38).	**Attention to Particulars** While the identity of the children and their teachers remained confidential, their "selves" are not to be lost to generalizations or abstractions. This quality is highly pertinent to the purpose of the study, requiring that particular attention be paid to the unique nature of what some would characterize as the most mundane of situations. The process of expressing the distinctive qualities included meticulous attention to detail (and so the reason for videotaping), full inclusion of contextual support, and carefully constructed descriptive text.
Criteria for Success (Coherence, Insight, and Instrumental Utility) Acknowledges the role of persuasion in qualitative research..."seeing things in a way that satisfies, or is useful for the purposes we embrace" (Eisner 1998, 39). Evidence toward persuasion derives from weight and fit, and then ultimately what counts is a matter of judgment.	**Criteria for Success (Coherence, Insight, and Instrumental Utility)** Schopenhauer (in Hart, 2003) noted that in research, the "task is not so much to see what no one yet has seen, but to think what nobody yet thought about that which everybody sees" (p. 110). Part of my task, then, was to ensure the reader recognizes school, kindergartners, and the events of the kindergarten day. The role of insights via the analysis led to the potential instrumental utility to be derived from the research.

Beyond the vivid and insightful, I hoped to tell what I have seen in ways that are also disruptive. As MacNaughton (2005) cautioned:

> The everyday language, ethics, routines, rituals, practices, expectations, ideas, documents and invocations of quality in early childhood services are formed through and motivated by very particular understandings of children and how best to educate them. Over time, some of this knowledge has settled so firmly into the fabric of early childhood studies that its familiarity makes it just 'right', 'best' and 'ethical'. (p. 1)

If such knowledge is agreed upon as "right," to challenge and disrupt it smacks of disobedience and begs non-compliance to the normalized familiar. It was my intention that this research and its methodology would thus enact the complexity of disobedience even while learning about it from the children.

Qualitative inquiry into moments of children's disobedience selected from observations of kindergarten children in the context of their kindergarten classroom provided opportunities to orient rhizomatic logic to the readings of the children in order to "build complex and diverse pictures of 'the child', of 'observation' and of 'research'...[and offered] a tool for critically reflecting on how meaning is produced through the choices we make about what we use to map" our readings of the children (MacNaughton 2005, 144–145). These readings require the best of my (the researcher's) ability to, as qualitative inquiry requires, "experience or create qualities worth experiencing."

Rhizomatic Thought

Rhizoanalysis builds from the philosophical and cultural theories of Gilles Deleuze and Feliz Guattari. They used the contrast between rhizome (rhizomatic) and tree (arborescent) as a metaphor of the contrast between two forms of logic. In challenging the dominant structure of thought as "tree logic," Deleuze and Guattari (1987) applied a metaphorical description of the tree's structure—from roots through the trunk to the branches—to a "fixed, determining and linear" logic used to explain in terms of cause-and-effect relationships. In contrast, the lateral structure of the rhizome's collection of mutually dependent roots and shoots is a metaphor of a more flexible and dynamic logic that "encompasses change, complexity and heterogeneity" (p. 120). *Table 2*, adapted from Rosenberg's 1994 discussion of rhizomatic and arbolic logic, provides a simplified (ironically, binary) overview of the contrasting characteristics of the two metaphors of logic. Even while examining the contrast between the two forms of logic, it is important to recall Deleuze and Guattari's caution regarding their intersection, for this is "no dualism, no ontological dualism between here and there, no axiological dualism between good and bad, no blend or American synthesis. There are knots of arborescence in rhizomes, and rhizomatic offshoots in roots" (Deleuze and Guattari 1987, 20).

Table 2: Deleuze and Guattari's Rhizomatic and Arbolic Logic

Rhizomatic	Arbolic
Non-linear	Linear
Anarchic	Hierarchic
Nomadic	Sedentary
Smooth	Striated
Deterritorialized	Territorialized
Multiplicitous	Unitary and binary
Minor science	Major science
Heterogeneity	Homogeneity

"The 'arborescent' model of thought designates the epistemology that informs all of Western thought, from botany to information sciences to theology" (Best and Kellner 1991, 98). Arbolic thought is represented by the tree-like structure of genealogy, branches that continue to subdivide into smaller and lesser categories, and is said to be "linear, hierarchic, sedentary, and full of segmentation and striation....Arbolic thought is vertical and stiff" (Best and Kellner 1991, 98).

According to Best and Kellner, arbolic thought is State philosophy (p. 98); by contrast, rhizomatic thought is nomadic. Rhizomatic thought is non-linear, anarchic and "radically horizontal" (Lechte 1994, 102). Rhizomes create smooth space, and cut across—even permeate—boundaries imposed by vertical lines of hierarchies and order. "Rhizomatic thought is multiplicitous, moving in many directions and connected to many other lines of thinking, acting, and being. Rhizomatic thinking deterrorializes arbolic striated spaces and ways of being. Rhizomes are networks...build[ing] links between pre-existing gaps between nodes that are separated by categories and order of segmented thinking" (Deleuze and Guattari 1987, 7). In like fashion, both the Buddhists and Taoists speak of a "network of words" or a "net of concepts," thus extending the idea of the interconnected web to the realm of the intellect (Capra 1985).

The merit of rhizoanalysis as the analytic perspective for this study is in Deleuze and Guattari's notion of the nomad and rhizome as *"articulated tactics of resistance to domination"* (in Rosenberg 1994, 288). In applying rhizomatic principles to this research in order to study children's resistance to domination, I purposely seek to promote resistance to the underlying structures that tend to be unexamined.

Thoreau (1848/1966) warned, "The State never intentionally confronts a man's sense, intellectual or moral, but only his body, his senses" (p. 236). Foucault (1979) described four techniques (enclosure, partitioning, spatial designation, and ranking) in which power creates "docile bodies" out of its subjects (p. 141–145). In similar fashion, Deleuze and Guattari (1987, in Rosenberg 1994) described a micropolitical field of struggle

> located between the 'zone of indiscernibility'—representing the ways in which the mind and body of a person is 'dominated' or determined by systems of cultural signification that remain invisible to that subject—and the 'zone of impotence,' in which the person is unconstrained by those systems, and so 'can thrive in a space of creative resistance to domination.'" (p. 272)

Children's living, breathing disobedience—their "resistance to domination"—implies a rhizomatic, deterritorializing interaction with, within and without the enclosed and partitioned structures of the classroom space and interactions, and therefore manifests a nomadic penchant for resisting the restrictive techniques of power as described by Foucault. The sedentary, partitioned and designated spaces of the dominant culture's (adult's/teacher's) classroom environment are challenged, disrupted and reimagined by children as "malleable, living, permeable, and ambiguous micro-spaces and spaces" (Patton 1996, 288). There is a fit here: rhizoanalysis resists.

Rhizoanalysis: Principles

Deleuze and Guattari describe six principles of rhizomes that directed the method of rhizoanalysis in the course of this study. A brief overview of each of these principles (connectivity, heterogeneity, multiplicity, asignifying rupture, cartography, and decalcomania), and a description of the vital (for this research) concept of nomadic thought follow:

Connectivity and heterogeneity. The first two principles are those of connection and heterogeneity that specify: "any point of a rhizome can be connected to anything other, and must be" (Deleuze and Guattari 1987, 7). However, the rhizome is also anti-hierarchical, so no point comes before another, and no specific point must be connected to another particular point. These two principles recall the Chinese tern *li,* which can be roughly translated as "the innumerable vein-like patterns in the Tao...signifying the pattern of jade or fibers in muscle....*Li* is a natural and unescapable law of affairs and things.... In the Eastern view, then, as in the view of modern physics, everything in the universe is connected to everything else and no part of it is fundamental" (Capra 1985, 280).

In applying the principles of connectivity and heterogeneity to this research, I considered the Derridian notion of beginning "wherever I am" and then not only following the texts into other texts, but also purposely connecting unexpected texts in order to create surprises and so, potentially, new understandings of those texts.

Multiplicity. Third is the principle of multiplicity. A rhizomatic system is comprised of a multiplicity of lines and connections. "There are no points or positions in a rhizome, such as those found in a structure, tree, or root. There are only lines" Deleuze and Guattari 1987, 8). Multiplicity celebrates the many and the plurality in contradistinction to "unitary, binary, and totalizing models of Western thought, thus affirming the principles excluded from Western thought and reinterprets reality as dynamic, heterogeneous, and non-dichotomous" (Best and Kellner 1991, 99).

I interpreted the principle of multiplicity as an opportunity to confront the if/then notions of classroom disobedience (e.g., *if* you talk out of turn, *then* you miss recess); and to complicate perceptions of what is good and bad in the kindergarten.

Asignifying rupture. Fourth is the principle of an asignifying rupture. "A rhizome may be broken, shattered at a given spot, but it will start up again on one of its old lines, or on new lines" (Deleuze and Guattari 1987, 9). In a recuperative nature of the rhizome, movements and flows can and should be re-routed around disruptions; and severed sections will regenerate and continue to grow, forming new lines and pathways.

In following lines of flight related to the selected moments of disobedience, there were breaks and ruptures related to unexpected detours and incoming lines of possibility. Given the purpose of the study as a disruptive and complicating provocation to the reader *and* to me, the researcher, these breaks and interruptions were welcome intrusions. As detailed in chapter 5, the ruptures often led to multiple layers of text laid over the texts of the moments of disobedience.

Cartography and decalcomania. The fifth and sixth principles. Rhizomes are about mapping new or unknown lines and entry points, not tracing old lines or patterns (Alvermann 2001, Deleuze and Guattari 1987). "A rhizome is not amenable to any structural or generative model" (Deleuze and Guattari 1987, 12). In cartography, Deleuze and Guattari distinguish between maps and tracings. "A tracing is genetic; it evolves and reproduces from earlier forms and replicates existing structures. It is arborescent. All tree logic is a logic of tracing and reproduction" (p. 12). In contrast to tracings, maps are open systems with no starting or ending points.

One means of mapping new or unknown entry points is to lay or fold one map or text over another. Laying a text over another as a "decal" allows for viewing points in new places and through other points. In this study, entering at various points with moments of disobedience, in combination with laying various texts over the texts of the moments, served the disruptive intent of rhizomatic logic and led to surprises.

Nomadic Thought and Resistance.

Apart from rhizomatics, nomadology and nomadic thought emerge from *A Thousand Plateaus* as an idea vital to this research. As described by Bey (1991), the rhizome and the nomad are "inseparable in the sense that the rhizome is the path that the nomad follows" (p. 101). While it is clear that rhizomatic pathways and lines of flight are structures through which nomadic movement can take place, the two terms, "rhizome" and "nomad" are linked in other ways, too. "Rhizomatics is a form of 'nomadic thought' opposed to the 'State thought' that tries to discipline rhizomatic movement both in theory (e.g. totalizing forms of philosophy) and practice (e.g. police and bureaucratic organizations)" (Best and Kellner 1991, 102). The disruptive intent of this particular study requires confrontation of State thought. According to Massumi (1992):

> Deleuze and Guattari consider nomadic thought to be the minor science or minor language that constantly becomes colonized by major science, the arbolic State. These State side philosophers and scientists operate in closed systems; while nomadology functions in open ones....The space of nomad thought is qualitatively different from State space. Air against earth. State space is 'striated,' or gridded. Movement in it is confined as by gravity to a horizontal plane, and limited by the order of that plane to preset paths between fixed and identifiable points. Nomad space like the rhizomatic surface is 'smooth' or open-ended. (p. 6)

Recently, when traveling from the United States to Finland, I noticed that when flying over rural areas in the U.S., the land appeared gridded—fields sharply marked in straight, squared, evenly-sized sections of green, brown and yellow—seemingly imposing ruled order on the land; while the fields in Sweden were curved and variably shaped and sized—as if respecting and following the natural bends and fluctuations of the land. While I do not know much about the Swedes other than what my grandfather told me, I wonder about their nomadic nature. I included the theme of nomadic thought here with the more well-known principles of rhizomatics in order to acknowledge and commit to the value of creating a smooth, open-ended surface on which to write the stories that will emerge from moments and fragments of text.

It is these stories or texts that allow us (the reader and the researcher) entry onto lines of flight. "For all of the human history that we know of, we have made stories to tell ourselves—stories of our origins, our purposes, our struggles, and our passions—and for centuries these stories have been 'the curriculum...and transmitted the values and ethics that bind communities together'" (Henderson and Kesson 1999, 91–92). By engaging in the "astoundingly liberating an act of story sharing can be" (Barone 2001, 180), I weave the moments of children's disobedience with the rhizomatic links and connections in order to "playfully explore what understandings and meanings the story makes possible" (Jardine 1992, 56).

Rhizoanalysis transforms our focus on the interpretation as a stable text to be read and interprets it as "a constantly moving configuration that is ripe with potential for divergent movements. The [moment] has no organizing center, frame, single meaning, or static pivot, but rather evolves and splinters in multiple directions" (Leander and Rowe 2006, 13). Barone (2001) contrasted the function of the epic as an unambiguous text that may serve to reduce uncertainty with the function of the story that in its "novelness" may serve to promote a dialogue with no set of voices privileged over another. In a Bakhtinian (1981) sense, these sorts of exchanges "serve as constant reminders of otherness in speech, as they celebrate a diversity of voices offering varied interpretations of phenomena... and so entice readers to revolt, to break the silence, to dismantle the textual illusion for their own purposes" (p 157). Further, only when a reader is self-doubting can she "be persuaded to question her own perspective and engage in the kind of dialogue that may lead to a textual event with what certain pragmatist philosophers call critical utility...[causing her] to question certain values previously considered beyond questioning" (p. 176). Barone (2001) cautioned us that reading a text such as the ones that derive from this research "requires an ultimate suspension of mutual mistrust in favor of an opening sharing of ideas and ideals toward a future that is both desirable and possible" (p. 179).

Reuben's fall was striking in its effect on me in seeing the good and the bad in all their complexity and nuanced richness. The power of this aporia is what led me to ask the questions asked in this book. Barone (2001) discussed critical utility—the moment of

Reuben's fall is what led me to self-doubt and to become persuaded to question my own perspective and engage in what certain pragmatist philosophers call critical utility, to "question certain values previously considered beyond questioning" (p. 176).

As I troubled my inquiry, I came to the conclusion that I did not seek to see only more examples such as Julian's courage and kindness while breaking classroom rules, but moments of child disobedience that co-exist with other qualities and selves and values—ones that are not so glaringly representative of Julian's paradoxical behavior. For there is more to goodness than the altruism of helping (see Kohn 1990). There is also the goodness of joy, of awareness, of wonder, of sensuality and sensing, of valuing and of mystery and awe, of I-thou relationalism, of engagement and belonging.

Classroom Rhizomatics

I wrote in chapter 1 of witnessing the moment of Reuben's fall as an "experience of the unexpected and cognitively chaotic," as an "epistemological shudder," a "marvelous" moment that led me to "recall, rethink and retheorise" what I had known before. However, it can certainly be understood that the events of Reuben's fall and Julian's punishment are not at all, in themselves, unfamiliar or "marvelous." Anyone spending time in school would witness similar events on a regular basis. The unexpected derived from seeing the moment as an occasion to recall, rethink, retheorise, and disrupt.

In my mind, the classroom now begins to become the rhizomatic map: "The rhizome pertains to a map that must be produced, constructed, a map that is always detachable, connectable, reversible, modifiable, and has multiple entryways and exits and its own lines of flight" (Deleuze and Guattari 1987, 21). It is possible that due to the transpiercing of rhizome and map, the classroom becomes a rhizome itself through the children who live there and, concurrently, through this research. The kindergartners' methods and modes of breathing, moving in and through, wondering, and engaging the space of "classroom" pose a manner in which a researcher (and the children) may, while re-reading the idea of a classroom as a connective whole, be re-writing the classroom as a range of social, moral and spiritual possibilities.

Here the mapping of classroom space accomplished by kindergartners and the concept of "map" that Deleuze and Guattari articulate are not only complementary, but essentially identical. The rhizome and the map intersect, overlap, and form each other. The classroom becomes a rhizomatic map; it becomes a rhizome-structure when it is restructured as a map instead of a tracing.

> From a 'rhizomatic' perspective, we can never 'be'...in a fixed and final way; instead, we are always 'becoming'...as fashions, expectations, experiences, values, beliefs, opportunities and desires change over time and between cultures and geographies. From a 'rhizomatic' perspective, the development of...young children requires more complex explanations than the cause-and-effect relationships between, for example, parent expectations and children's behaviour. The 'lateral' logic of rhizoanalysis challenges the idea that one act causes another and that one idea or meaning inevitably leads to another. It highlights instead how relationships and meanings link in complex and shifting ways in our 'becoming.' (MacNaughton 2005, 121)

My budding exploration of rhizomatic logic in research analysis leads me to wonder how using it might challenge early childhood research(ers) to look much more carefully and openly at children's (and adults') discourse for its possibilities rather than merely reporting how it works.

As MacNaughton (2005) challenges: "To engage with the politics of our reporting the child is to go beyond merely reporting. To do so requires some simple moves towards rhizomatic logic" (p. 131). She suggested the following:

- Generate texts of the child (via observation in this study). MacNaughton called these "data fragments—observations or sections of an observation that differ in terms of who was observed, when, where how, why and by whom" (2005, 123). I refer to these data fragments as "moments."

- Interrogate the generated texts. Ask who is heard and how? Which are the texts one would *usually* defer to for answers? How might observations be used to offer space for children whose voices struggle to be heard?

- "Be 'nomadic' and find texts beyond the expected ones. Break boundaries from early childhood: The choices you make about what texts to layer into the meanings of your observations will link to the rhizome you aim to build—to your political intent.

The aim in rhizomatic logic is to link meanings (semiotic chains)" (MacNaughton 2005, 131). In the words of Deleuze and Guattari (1987): "A rhizome ceaselessly establishes connections between semiotic chains, organizations of power, and circumstances relative to the arts, sciences and social struggles" (p. 7).

• "Place these other texts in the middle of one's own texts [in this book, the selected moments of disobedience] and see what they do to each other that surprises." Ask what is in the middle of the text by placing other texts in the middle of it. What do they do to each other? Reinforce? Rupture? Connect? Overlap? Point to the same direction? Call on same discourses? "Seek surprises in this work in order to disrupt the familiar and obvious in what is known. Building new logic about what is happening in the text is about building new understandings of its relationships to other texts" (MacNaughton 2005, 133).

• Use the surprises as points from which to practice new routes to freedom, well-being, and moral wisdom. For "rhizomatic logic can orient you towards new lines for action, new ways to understand the child and ways in which dominant discourses of [disobedience]... twist in on each other in the daily lives of early childhood" (p. 134).

Participants and Setting

Participants

As the purpose of the study was to describe moments of children's disobedience in the context of a "typical" kindergarten, the participants included all of the children in two public school kindergarten classes and their teachers. The classrooms were selected on a basis of convenience. There was no prerequisite for participation other than that the classrooms were public school kindergartens considered typical, that the sites were located within thirty minutes of the university, and that consent be granted by and/or for all those involved.

The selection of participating classrooms was influenced by the likelihood of gaining permission to conduct research at the sites. The original plan had been to implement the study in only one classroom. However, my concern regarding school system approval in

Andrews Elementary's large urban district was significant enough to approach another teacher (Mr. Scott) in a smaller system where approval was granted immediately. Additionally, each child's participation was contingent on parental and personal (the kindergartner's verbal) consent. The teachers I selected have a reputation for having positive relationships with families of their students, and so I knew I could enlist the teachers' assistance in gaining parental consent for each child. This plan was successful, and every child in both classrooms—the morning kindergarten at suburban Shadow Lake Elementary and the all-day kindergarten at urban Andrews Elementary—participated with consent. Each participant chose the pseudonym to be used for the purpose of the study. It is important to note that some of the children named themselves in potentially confusing ways: as non-children (Mr. Johnson), as a profession (Fireman, Mr. Policeman), as characters like The Mummy or Flash, and even a vegetable (Corn-on-the-Cob).

Kindergarten Children

Typically, children entering kindergarten are five to six years old (although some children will enter at four and turn five during the first month of kindergarten). Many will have had prior school-type experiences, such as preschool, daycare, Head Start or a children's program related to the family's religion (such as Sunday school). For some children entering kindergarten, though, this will serve as their first transition into a group environment away from the home and family. Most children enter kindergarten with some school skills: academic skills, such as recognizing one's name, naming colors and shapes, counting, some reading; social skills, such as waiting for a turn, lining up, following simple directions; emotional skills, such as separating from a caregiver; and physical skills, such as using the restroom independently. However, as every kindergarten teacher knows, this is not true for all children.

In observing the children of Andrews Elementary and Shadow Lake Elementary, these commonly accepted characteristics of a kindergartner held true. Most of the children had school knowledge and skills as described above. And I learned that another source of school knowledge and skills came from older siblings—this from observations of children from both classrooms ("My brother told me that when you forget your gym shoes, it's bad"—from Ariel, crying, on gym day); and from statements made during a lesson ("Oh, I know that song! My sister sings that song every day!").

Teachers

The teachers in this study were selected based on prior relationships and convenience. Katie Krinkle and Michael Scott, the kindergarten teachers involved in this study, opened their classrooms to the process of this study and assisted in gaining consent from the families of the children in their respective classes.

As do all kindergarten teachers in public schools in this state, Mrs. Krinkle and Mr. Scott hold baccalaureate degrees from universities offering programs leading to a teaching license/certificate for the early childhood or elementary education field. In addition, Mrs. Krinkle holds a master's degree, and Mr. Scott was, at the time of this study, completing his master's thesis toward his own degree. Further details about kindergarten teachers in general, and about Mrs. Krinkle and Mr. Scott in particular, are presented in chapter 4.

Setting

The study was conducted in two local (midwestern) public school kindergarten classrooms, one set in a large city school district and the other in a neighboring suburban district. Mrs. Krinkle's kindergarten, set in the city district, was a full-day program with, variably, 20 to 23 children over the course of the study. Mr. Scott's kindergarten, set in the suburban district, was a half-day program, and there were 22 children.

The two schools were typical in their structures: each held grades K- 5, and each was partitioned accordingly. Each of the schools operates under State Department of Education mandates, using State Academic Content Standards as the content portion of the curriculum. At the time of this study, there was an overlap in the systems' adoption of texts to support those academic standards—each system choosing traditional texts published by familiar and highly successful (in a business/capitalist sense) publishing companies. Each is a neighborhood school, attracting the children who live in the neighborhood—usually less than a mile away from the site—rather than open enrollment children. Neither school is a magnet school nor an experimental school.

In these K-5 schools, the kindergarten is the entry into school. Traditionally, kindergarten is viewed as a place and time to prepare children for "real" school. If one were to enter a school and view classrooms while making one's way through the school, it would be easy to recognize the kindergarten room(s). Kindergarten classrooms generally share the following features: in place of individual desks for each child, a kindergarten room has tables with four-eight small chairs placed at each table, and instead of a place for the teacher to stand at the board or an overhead there is a carpeted area in front of a reading chair for the teacher. Sometimes the chair may even be a rocking chair. Typically, the carpet area will also have a chart board, a big book easel, and a bulletin board that will display a calendar. This is where the children are usually called to gather at the carpet for opening exercises, calendar work, to hear stories and books, to partake in whole-group lessons and classroom meetings, to practice whole-group activities related to developing reading and writing, and for closing exercises.

Centers are another component of the kindergarten classroom. In most kindergarten classrooms, one might still find a make-believe or housekeeping center consisting of kitchen-type furniture, dolls, pretend food and house-wares, and dress-up clothing. Other centers may include materials and activities related to science, pets, library, puppets, computers, blocks/building, math using 'manipulatives', water play and/or sand, musical instruments, and arts/crafts. While there is great variability in how teachers use such centers with their children, generally children will be permitted in centers at designated time(s) during the day, often on a rotating basis with prescribed conditions for numbers of children at each.

This description of typical kindergarten classroom culture is extended in chapter 4 in order to illustrate in what ways the classrooms used for the study might or might not be considered typical in terms of environment, daily activities, materials, and routines. This is followed by a more specific description of the classroom settings/contexts in which this study is set.

Procedures

Human Subject Considerations

As mandated, I complied with the conditions for consent required by the university's Institutional Review Board (IRB) and with the selected school systems' requirements for engaging in research in their schools. Before submitting applications for research, I spoke extensively with the two teachers to ensure that what I presented to the IRB and school administrations would be acceptable to the teachers.

Permission was granted by all three of those organizations, and the classroom teachers assisted me in contacting families and obtaining consent for all children within the classrooms to be videotaped. Because Mrs. Krinkle and Mr. Scott both have unusually close and trusting relationships with their school communities, I was not greatly concerned about getting consent from the parents—and my optimism was validated when each teacher delivered 100% consent from the families of their children. Actually, Mr. Scott delivered 100% from his morning kindergarten, but only 90% from his afternoon kindergarten (two families declined to allow consent). Because I was concerned about conducting this research in circumstances that would require me to "avoid" a child in a classroom, the refusals in the afternoon class released me from making a decision regarding which of Mr. Scott's two sections to choose. Mrs. Krinkle's class was an all-day kindergarten. In conducting the research in Mrs. Krinkle's classroom, I found I needed to gain additional consent from the other adult participants in the class. During fall semester, Mrs. Krinkle served as a mentor teacher for a field student from my university and for five students from a neighboring university. Each of the field students provided written consent. We also obtained consent from the mother of a four-year-old who often spent time in Mrs. Krinkle's room while the mother participated in PTA volunteer activities in the school.

Data Collection

During the second week of school, in September 2006, I began visiting Mr. Scott's classroom. I was still awaiting approval from Mrs. Krinkle's school system, and so planned to spend a month (averaging two visits per week for eight observations/six videotaped) in Mr. Scott's classroom and then a month (averaging two visits per week for eight observations/six videotaped) in Mrs. Krinkle's upon said approval. I received approval from the administrative offices in mid-September, and began my data collection in the city school in early October. There was no gap in weeks between the two sites. As soon as I completed my work in Mr. Scott's room in the first week of October 2006, I transitioned to Mrs. Krinkle's kindergarten classroom.

In order to become a familiar person to the children, to gain a sense of classroom routines and child interactions, and to introduce and practice videotaping procedures, I visited each classroom two times before actually videotaping the classes. During those visits, in addition to the aforementioned familiarity goals, I kept field notes of contextual data and took digital still-photos of the two classrooms (while empty) and of the school hallways and signage. These notes and still photos provided the details regarding the physical, structural and institutional characteristics of the two schools and the two kindergarten classrooms. It was from these data sources that much of the site-based contextual information in chapter 4 was derived.

I spent approximately three hours per visit in order to become acquainted with the classrooms, to develop context, compose context notes, and to plan the best times and places to videotape. In the case of Mr. Scott, this was the whole "day" for his morning kindergarten; for Mrs. Krinkle's class, I spent one day in the morning each week, and the other day I came in the afternoon. During this time, I wrote extensive field notes to capture the physical environment of the classrooms and schools, the daily "schedules," and various details related to procedures in place, ways the various areas of the classrooms tended to be used (or not), and details related to the children and teachers. This period of adjustment allowed the children and their teachers to become used to my presence and the use of the field notebook and camera. I took the camera with me from the beginning, and when introduced to the children by their teachers, I showed it to them and explained how I would be using it. It was also during these initial visits that I obtained verbal consent and pseudonyms from each of the children.

Data collection for the study took place during Fall 2006 from the first full week of September through the first week of November. The length of the data collection period was contingent on the "qualities of experience" (Eisner 1998) captured during the moments of observation and collection.

In addition to classroom visits, I met with and spoke with the two teachers on at least a weekly basis. We met for dinner two times during the month of data collection for each teacher, and once the three of us met together. Mrs. Krinkle and Mr. Scott had not known each other or met before the occasion of this dinner meeting. I used these meetings and phone conversations to gather details about the two of them and information about their respective sites, and to engage in conversations about observed classroom interactions. This allowed for an informal participant check and in many instances, informed this research as related to the school and classroom expectations regarding children's and teachers' roles in kindergarten. As disobedience as been described in chapter 1 as "an action or interaction that appears to disregard or defy structured expectations of a particular situation, place or person," it was vital to this research to gain an understanding of the structured expectations of each site.

My Role in Data Collection

In gathering data to represent the complexities of these kindergartens and of the children themselves, I was interested in looking closely at the small, the seemingly mundane. As I worry about small things being lost, I saw the mundane as fascinating.

In a continuum of detached observer through full-blown participant, I would place myself somewhere in the middle. While I deliberately refrained from engaging with the children in ways that would confirm authority, I did interact with them in naturalistic ways. I laughed, talked, tied shoes, helped when help was needed, made comments, explained my camera and presence, and was obviously "there". Privy to some of the benefits of participant observation—even a partial one—I concur with Lohman's (in Emerson 2001) suggestion that "the sympathies and identities established through a close familiarity [may] reveal meanings and insights denied the formal investigator" (p. 13). In my casual interactions as described above and as a past participant in kindergarten classrooms as a kindergarten teacher, I was able to call on the close familiarity described, and hopefully, the meanings and insights.

Because I wanted to observe the children as they interacted within the space of School as they were surveilled and not surveilled by authority, I made every attempt to distance myself from the role of teacher. The children, of course, viewed me as an adult, and so imbued with some authority... but as a subordinate adult. Out of courtesy—but also by design toward defusing my authority in the children's eyes—I deferred to Mrs. Krinkle and Mr. Scott, asking permission to place or move the camera, asking permission to come along when the children left the classroom, and asking them to introduce and explain my role to the children in my presence.

Concurrently with confounding an adult authority role, my work required that as I observed the children's interactions, I participate as an observer to see the child's moments of disobedience as an adult could/would/might. The purpose was not to understand the child's intentions or reasons—which is why I chose not to interview them or question their choices—but instead to see the actions/interactions as any observer, albeit a skilled observer, might, one who has participated, and continues to participate, in kindergarten/school outside of this study.

Data Analysis

"Fieldwork is seen as a deeply reflexive process in which 'findings' are inseparable from the methods used to generate them" (Emerson 2001, 2). In considering the analysis of these data at this embryonic state of my work, I attempted to weave together components of Eisner's qualitative inquiry and Deleuze and Guattari's rhizoanalysis. What follows are themes that influenced the process of analysis.

How Do We Know What We Know

Eisner (1998) asked, "How do you know what you know?" He responded by suggesting the following means of knowing with a *"reasonable* standard of credibility" (p. 110) [italics mine], that I further temper with Ellsworth's (1992) caution regarding the "partiality" of knowledge.

Structural Corroboration and Internal Coherence

Multiple types of data were related to each other to support or contradict the interpretation or evaluation of the study (e.g., environmental context, supporting documents such as posters, codes, etc.). I pursued a confluence of evidence to breed credibility. The following points regarding structural collaboration influenced my analysis (unless noted, quotes are from Eisner 1998):

- "In seeking structural corroboration, we look for recurrent behaviors or actions, those theme-like features of a situation that inspire confidence that the events interpreted and appraised are not aberrant or exceptional, but rather characteristic of the situation" (p. 110).

- "Because qualitative methods are vulnerable to effects [of one's vested interests or educational values], *it is especially important not only to use multiple types of data, but also to consider disconfirming evidence and contradictory interpretations or appraisals* [emphasis original]… when one presents one's own conclusions it is both prudent and important to consider those alternative interpretations and appraisals that one considers reasonably credible ….It does not mean relinquishing one's own view" (p. 111).

- "Structural corroboration requires a mustering of evidence. The weight of evidence becomes persuasive. It is compelling. In a sense, matters of weight and coherence appeal to aesthetic criteria. They are qualities felt as a result of what is revealed. The tight argument, the coherent case, the strength of evidence are terms that suggest rightness of fit" (p. 111).

- "In writing educational criticism, the critic can allude to the multiple data sources in order to provide warrant for interpretations and appraisals. The form through which such warrant is provided is left to the critic. Like criticism in the arts and humanities, the manner in which criticism is written should bear the signature of the writer" (p. 111).

- Geertz (1988) regarded the author's voice as one source of the work's authority (p. 112). As a former kindergarten teacher, my analysis would include this kind of "empathetic understanding."

In order to provide multiple types of data, I sought out not only credible and compelling data related to the children in the two kindergarten classrooms in this study, but also a body of evidence related to kindergarten classrooms, teachers, and schools writ large.

As educational criticism requires engaging in the complexities and subtleties of particular events, the discussion in chapter 4 of the two kindergartens in the context of Kindergarten, the two teachers in the context of Teachers, and the two schools in the context of School will serve to account for some of the complexities of children's interactions while engaging with their teachers, kindergartens and schools.

Referential Adequacy

Eisner (1998) named the primary aim of educational criticism as that of illuminating its subjects toward bringing about "more complex and sensitive human perception and understanding ....The work is referentially adequate when readers are able to see what they would have missed without the critic's observation" (p. 112-113). The following paragraphs discuss the importance of referential adequacy to this work.

Eisner and Barone's (1997) discussions of forms of texts clearly resonate with the quality of rhizoanalysis that allows for exploration of the politics of a text in order to create new texts. This serious work has a playful quality that further resonates with the study itself—that of discerning the possibilities inherent in the playful and serious disobedience of young children. As MacNaughton (2005) explained, "rhizoanalysis reconstructs a text by creating new and different understandings of it; and it does so by linking it with texts other than those we would normally use" (p. 120). For instance, one might use rhizoanalysis to re-plot the links between an observation of a child and a child development text or a political text and a popular culture text in order to reconstruct an understanding of disobedience in that observation. For instance, as one constructs a rhizome of disobedience meanings in the observation, one rethinks what it means to do disobedience at five years of age and how one might see and work with children's compliancism in kindergarten.

In selecting the fragments of texts to map over the moments of texts captured by the research, there is, by design, a pronounced deliberateness in this choosing. For purposes of considering "a robust and justifiable conception of human well-being" (Hostetler 2005), "a 'morality' of democratic living as a wisdom challenge" (Henderson 2001), and the potential freedom of authentic democracy (for instance, Greene 1988, MacDonald 1995, Purpel 2001), I sought to lay texts to engage with and disrupt how compliancism interests and circulates within and through discourses of well-being, morality, a wisdom challenge, and democracy. Randomly chosen or traditional texts, discourse, and theorists would not produce the same effects, but would merely remap the epistemology of the child. "The intent of rhizoanalysis is to use text, discourse and theory to 'cast a shadow' over mapped text to create tracings that disrupt and challenge what had been mapped" (MacNaughton 2005, 136).

In purposefully choosing and laying new texts next to the texts of moments of disobedience, I sought to educate, if education may be described as a practice of "organizing knowledge for a truth to break through" (Badiou 2000). I resist the concept of truth as it is normally known in the science of education, and so, adopt Badiou's (2000) notion that "truths consist of process rather than illumination. They emerge in a process instigated by an event which breaks through the 'state of situation' a person before the event took to be either natural or sufficient in its 'concerns, opinions and descriptions'" (p. 61). As Badiou noted later (2006), "a truth is solely constituted by rupturing with the order which supports it, never as an effect of that order," calling this rupture which opens up truths, "the event" (p. xii). This recalls an earlier description of the "epistemological shudder" which, according to Giugni (2006), occurs when one's "preferred representation of the known world prove[s] incapable of immediately making sense of the marvelous and may have a reaction that makes her feel uncomfortable, displaced, and in a sense almost paralysed, not knowing where to place this information" (p. 101).

In this research, I analyzed moments of disobedience. In order to "see" these moments, it was imperative that I recognize them as moments of disobedience and capture as much of the full context as I could. Given the "figured world" of the kindergarten in which "categories of expression and more tangible artifacts 'afford' ways of doing not only things but also people" (Holland, Lachicotte, Skinner and Cain 1998), I sought to identify a moment as one of disobedience by comparing a child's action/interaction against what is expected or directed using a combination of cues. These cues included:

- Others' response to the action/interaction (a headshake);
- Written, verbal or non-verbal expectations and rules ("blow a bubble, boys and girls");

- Responses to prior similar behaviors (a child looks to the teacher to check the teacher's response when another child steps out of line);
- Known typical actions (children in schools aren't allowed to talk when in line);
- The "normed" behaviors at that moment (what are the other children doing?).

Among the many moments of disobedience that occurred during my visits to the sites, I chose those moments to analyze which seemed to have the richest potential for "seeing" within the disobedient moment the child as his or her spiritual self—and so the moments rife with spiritual-moral and democratic possibilities. In the process of reviewing the film and beginning the transcription, the possibilities emerged in a rhizomatic fashion.

As Deleuze and Guattari (1987) have described, the rhizome is a map—a map with multiple entryways, a map that "is open and connectable in all to its dimensions; it is detachable, reversible, and susceptible to constant modification. It can be torn, reversed, adapted to any kind of mounting, reworked by an individual, group, or social formation. It can be drawn on a wall, conceived of as a work of art, constructed as a political action or as a meditation" (p. 11). Mapping the moments—the texts of the kindergarten classroom—served to constitute and re-constitute the "truth" about the child and the role disobedience plays.

Validity

Here I have replaced Eisner's *consensual validation* with a more poststructural discussion of validity. In Eisner's (1998) discussion of consensual validation, the focus is on consensus among "judges"—which Eisner de-emphasized as a means of validating educational criticism. He wrote: "Consensual validation in criticism is typically a consensus won from the readers who are persuaded by what the critic has to say, not by consensus among several critics" (p. 113). Given the disruptive nature of this study, a "consensual" type of validity would seem at cross-purposes. In seeking to "open up truths" (Badiou, 2006) as a result of disrupting the familiar order and structures, a consensual type of validation is not only unlikely, but is also not desired.

Therefore, I sought out other discussions of research validity. In keeping with the rhizomatic logic of the study, I determined that aspects of Lather's *catalytic validity* in addition to her translation of Deleuze and Guattari's rhizomatic validity were better matches to my intentions for this research.

Lather (1991) proposed a "more collaborative, praxis oriented" model for validating research in naming an emancipatory and advocacy model of validation: catalytic validity. Here the researcher is not neutral and acts on a purpose and a desire to engage people in self-understanding and self-determination. I also like the way Lather engages in struggles with the idea of other validities in poststructural research. She wrote about rhizomatic validity:

> A supple line, a flux, a 'line of flight…where thresholds attain a point of adjacency and rupture,' my ephemeral practices of validity after poststructuralism are 'an arrangement of desire and enunciation' rather than a general recipe. My intent has been to forge from a scattered testimony a methodology that is not so much prescription as 'curves of visibility and enunciation.' (Lather 1993, 686)

What she described is what I would like my work to do for teachers (and so for children). Not to offer a prescription or a recipe—but to complicate their roles and lives as they ride along unexpected lines of flight. Perhaps, instigated by an event such as a moment of disobedience, disrupted further by a rhizomatic twist, a teacher may engage in "the process of 'affirmative invention'…described as a trajectory no longer contained within the point of the situation [a line of flight]" (den Heyer 2009). As my intentions for this work do, rhizomes (metaphorically) "work against the constraints of authority, regularity, and commonsense, and open thought up to creative [and affirmative] constructions" (Lather 1993, 680).

Lather (1993) offered a further description of rhizomatic validity. It:

- Unsettles from within; taps underground;
- Generates new locally determined norms of understanding, proliferates open-ended and context-sensitive criteria, works against reinscription of some new regime, some new systematicity;
- Supplements and exceeds the stable and permanent;

- Works against constraints of authority via relay, multiple openings, networks, complexities of problematics;

- Puts conventional discursive procedures under erasure, breaches congealed discourses, critical as well as dominant. (p. 686–687)

This list of descriptors demonstrates the contrast of rhizomatic validity to consensual validity. As well, the content foregrounds what will occur in the discussion of the moments of disobedience in chapter 5. As described by Alvesson and Skoldberg (2000) in their book about reflexive methodologies:

> The 'truth' of the moment is, therefore, not abstract and otherworldly, but concrete, particular and sensuous—while at the same time being open, in an ongoing state of creation by the actors, transcending the boundaries between the ordinary and the fabulous… it is more related to Bakhtin's dialectic and paradoxical 'vulgar' poetics where joking and seriousness, high and low occur abruptly side by side. (p. 174)

The moments of disobedience—as represented by the texts in chapter 5 (and along with the rhizomatic texts to be laid next to them)—are their own event, and while the interpretation is mine, it is also the reader's. The validation will derive in this way from the reader's interaction with the text in the form of a "catalytic validity" (Lather 1991). The value of the work derives from the meaning made by the researcher and the reader from engaging with the rhizomatically laid texts.

Eisner (1998) discusses the relationship between qualitative inquiry and literary texts, connecting the value of these texts in what is fundamentally related to the disruptive quality of rhizoanalysis: "Texts can take different forms: literally written text can do what the figurative treatment of language cannot; poetry can say what prose cannot convey, and vice versa" (p. 22). Barone (2001) described narrative texts (especially fictional ones) as designed to "do what good art does so well. And what is that? According to the novelist James Baldwin (1962), the greatest achievement of art is the 'laying bare of questions which have been hidden by answers'" (in Barone 2001, 154).

Barone and Eisner (1997) analyzed deep structures of works of literature to determine the design elements that challenge and impact the reader. While they acknowledged that it is "nigh impossible to delineate them precisely and completely," they list: "the presence of expressive, contextualized, and vernacular forms of language; the promotion of empathetic participation in the lives of characters; the creation of a virtual reality; the presence of the author's personal signature; and perhaps most importantly, a degree of textual ambiguity" (p. 154).

In analyzing my own findings, I sought to include language that was contextualized as opposed to abstract, and vernacular rather than technical. As Barone (2001) describes his choice of language in relating the stories of one teacher's impact on the lives of his students, I, too, sought to use contextual language in order to "re-create the lived worlds of protagonists [children] and to encourage readers to dwell momentarily within those worlds" (p. 154). As someone who once titled a paper *The Joy of Not Knowing*, I anticipated that my personal signature would be expressed via a degree of textual ambiguity—but that remains to be seen by the reader.

The Function of Rhizoanalysis

Deleuze wrote in *Negotiations* (1995) about *Anti-Oedipus*:

> We're not writing for people who think psychoanalysis is doing fine and see the unconscious for what it is. We're writing for people who think it's pretty dull and sad as it burbles on about Oedipus, castration, the death instinct and so on. We're writing for the unconsciousnesses that have had enough. We're looking for allies. (p. 22)

I share intent similar to Deleuze's. I, too, imagine (about education, not psychoanalysis) "these allies are already out there... people who have had enough and are thinking, feeling and working in similar directions" (Deleuze 1995, 22). Moreover, I anticipate that there are texts in this work that will speak to those who share this unconsciousness—allies that are already out there, people who have had enough.

The experience of speaking to an unconsciousness is meaningful to me. I have experienced the effect of disrupting texts many times. Earlier, I described using the movie *Instinct* (Turteltaub, 1999) in my teaching because of the clear connection to be made between the constraining and surveilling natures of both school and prison. The moments that made this clear to me—that spoke to my unconsciousness—were these: As correctional officers were walking groups of prisoners from one place to another, one said gruffly, "Hands at your side." I recognized myself in that moment: as a kindergarten teacher, I had said the same thing to children as we moved from one place to another. "Hands at your side." Hearing it said like this—in this place of the prison, and by a person set to guard another—allowed me to hear myself saying and doing what I would hold abhorrent in anyone else. I never did it again. When the character played by Cuba Gooding, Jr., challenged the character of the prison's senior psychologist, played by Charles Durning, regarding a tradition in place in the prison gymnasium, Durning's character responded, "It works." And Gooding's character said, "It works *for us.*" This prompted another disruption which I laid against my unconsciousness and so "recalled, rethought and retheorised" every instance of reading and hearing "what works" in the context of school. And I realized who it nearly always works *for.*

It seems to me that in every school and classroom, decisions—funding, pedagogical, and curricular—must be justified by an explanation of how the decision will certainly result in some impact on some numbered measures of children. As my former principal required us to defend and rationalize by results, I recall thinking but not saying, "Who cares?" every single time. I meant it, but could not say it too often without sounding flip and so hobbled in my request. I felt it—my unconsciousness felt it—but could not articulate why.

But Jonathan Kozol could. I remember vividly the first time I saw *Children in America's Schools with Bill Moyers* (Hayden and Cauthen 1996). Kozol served on the discussion panel, and in the final five minutes of the two-hour program, he wondered aloud why we wouldn't provide beautiful places for our children to go to school *"even if it doesn't pay off* [italics mine]. Even if it isn't useful to America's competitive edge. Even if it isn't good for IBM or General Motors or Wall Street" (np.), and I was stunned. He articulated what I had long felt. My unconsciousness had held those ideas and did not "know" them until I heard them. After that, I was able to say "Who cares?" in response to the bottom-line results—question, mean it, and know why I meant it.

In this way, this research serves to inform my own understanding. By turning the "enquiring eye" on the moments of children's interactions with kindergarten to experience afresh their instances of obedience and disobedience, and laying texts over them to inform the possibilities within those moments, I sought to understand the disobedience in ways guided by engaging in new texts. Just as Kozol's passionate appeal refreshed my unconsciousness regarding the texts of results, so this project serves to lay fresh texts over the text of disobedience. I have had enough, and I believe others have too. I, too, am looking for allies.

Summary

Employing a qualitative inquiry approach, the purpose of the book is to present moments of kindergarten children's disobedience in order to more fully understand the complexity of each moment concerning children's interactions with other children, adults and the kindergarten environment. The intent is to better understand the phenomenon/function of how the spirited-child negotiates the context, complexity, constraints and freedoms of a kindergarten classroom as represented through moments of disobedience.

While typically past research has directed our attention to fixing the problems of disobedience and studying it to determine how it fits in the roles and relationships of children and teachers, the present study offers an opportunity to view these familiar actions through fresh lenses of possibilities. In order to openly seek lateral paths toward developing new understandings and questions regarding the non-compliant nature of children, rhizoanalysis is used to destabilize and challenge the known and given texts of children's disobedience. In employing rhizoanalysis, I seek to disrupt the assumptions often made regarding the actions and interactions of young children as bad or good and to provide examples of seeing each moment of interaction as many things—both-and-neither bad n/or good. To reiterate my intentions as articulated in chapter 1, I enter this work believing that as children confront the complexities of the very human "morality of ends" and the more cultural "morality of laws" (Dewey 1929/1984, Zinn 1968), their moments of disobedience might be related to an awareness unique to children that allows them to disrupt the universe in ways that may lead us into joy.

Chapter 4

S/schools, K/kindergartens, T/teachers

*A school should be the most beautiful place in every town
and village—so beautiful that the punishment for undutiful
children should be that they should be debarred [sic] from
going to school the following day.*

~from a local public school website, on the principal's page

*How can you say no child is left behind
We're not dumb and we're not blind
They're all sitting in your cells
While you pave the road to hell.*

~P!nk, *Dear Mr. President* (2006)

Introduction

This chapter includes discussions of S/school, K/kindergarten and
T/teachers, each topic first writ large, and then in specifics related
to the places and people involved in this study. Given the upcom-
ing analysis in chapter 5—laying texts over the texts describing
children's actual moments of disobedience in kindergarten classrooms—it is imperative to first provide contextual background regarding the schools, kindergartens, and teachers the children will
be interacting with/in.

Recall that for the purpose of this study, disobedience describes
an action or interaction that appears to disregard or defy structured
expectations of a particular situation, place or person. In order to
identify a particular event as a moment of disobedience, an understanding of the "structured expectations" of the institutions of
Schools, Kindergartens and Teachers is necessary. One function of
this chapter is to detail these expectations. Further, as mentioned
in chapter 2, a purpose of this study is to disrupt and destabilize
what is dominant in the highly accessible writings that serve to

influence those institutional expectations. This chapter brings into play sources of information from the public arena: teacher internet sites, public school websites, best-selling books and programs marketed to classroom teachers, and teacher preparation textbooks.

The means of sharing this overview of Schools, Kindergartens and Teachers—and of the particular schools, kindergartens and teachers involved in this study—approximates what Eisner (1998) describes as criticism: "an art of saying useful things about complex and subtle objects and events so that others can see and understand what they did not see and understand before" (p. 3).

This chapter includes criticism, description, interpretation, valuation and identification of dominant features of the pervasive qualities of School, Kindergarten and Teachers, especially as related to children's disobedience. Rather than engaging as a true "connoisseur" (Eisner, 1998), the discriminations and perceptions I provide are a combination of expertise (a result of my experience in kindergarten) and naiveté (a result of my willingness to bring fresh eyes to the page). However, true to the concept of connoisseurship, the function of this chapter is to reveal the complexities of the place of school, kindergarten and teachers as related to children—as well as to serve as catalyst of new ways of seeing and thinking about children's disobedience—but through a position of not knowing.

School

> *Living in school is an essentially inferior, vulgar, imitative, second-rate human experience because this is the kind of ecological press that surrounds us both in and out of school...a living embodiment of the very shoddiness that pervades our general social experience... a rather faithful replica of the whole.*
>
> ~Macdonald (1995, 51)

There is no dearth of talk about school. In the quote above, James Macdonald lamented the unfortunate reflection of the shoddy side of human society in the space and place of school. I have visited dozens of classrooms across several districts and states, and have sadly found that many children's experience in school is, indeed, a "second-rate human experience." Children's relationships with teachers and with the other children are reduced to a series of procedures and if/then conditionals as through "observation, surveillance, and normalized judgment in schools, the calculable child is formed [and] they become members of the classification schoolchildren" (Ehrensal 2003, 120).

Related to the concept of the "calculable" child is Krieg's (2006) discussion of the "institutionalized" child. In Krieg's study, she listened carefully to the way that early childhood teachers talked about children. In one excerpt, Krieg shares a teacher's discussion about how being positive with students gets results. Krieg noted that in Ray's talk, she presents

> a picture of the 'institutionalized' child. The child is listed ('I've a list of all my students'), labeled ('not very intelligent'), documented ('the past teachers have put comments on them'), identified ('this child low'), tested ('at the beginning of the year') and later, as age defined ('at that age...') [and further interprets Ray's story as one in which the child is quite passive]...according to Ray, the child 'doesn't think' and has 'come so far' and 'thrives'. (p. 5)

Krieg notes that teacher talk such as Ray's presents an understanding of the child as being done to, and presumes that this is as it should be since the child is associated with attributes of dependence, immaturity, pre-competence, development (as age appropriate) and compliance. Given evidence of such beliefs about the calculable and institutionalized child, it is not surprising that the adults in charge at school view their role as one that will direct these children into the order already determined by the more mature, developed and competent adult.

Alfie Kohn (in Watson 2003) suggests that "everything turns on the fundamental questions that drive classroom practice." He claims that some schools/school people determine actions based on the question, "How can we get these kids to obey?", while others base actions and decisions on the question, "What do these children need?" (p. xiii). As classroom teachers engage in classroom decision-making, they often consult experts—and experts in classroom management often frame their advice on meeting the needs of the adults in school or the needs of the school itself, and not so much around the needs of individual children in the moment of their need. While there are hundreds of books published for classroom teachers to meet their classroom management and/or discipline needs, Wong and Wong's 1998 *The First Days of School: How to be an Effective Teacher* is recognized by many (as evidenced by the number of books sold) as the preeminent book on classroom management and student achievement.

Teacher education programs adopt the book as a classroom management text. School systems purchase the books in bulk to distribute to new teachers. In fact, the two school systems that house the research sites of this study have—either currently or in past years—purchased copies of this book for all newly hired teachers— a practice common in the area. In addition, the Wongs are booked as speakers over two years in advance. The website *www.harrywong. com* reports that the Wongs have sold over 3.3 million copies of their seminal book *The First Days of School.* The website describes the book as the "preeminent book on classroom management and... the most basic book on how to teach [and that it is used] in thousands of school districts, in over 102 countries, and in over 2,017 college classrooms". Tom Larkin, owner of Lecture Management (www.lecturemanagement.com), says of Harry Wong, "For 30 years, he has been the preeminent speaker in education, speaking to over one million people internationally." This overwhelming popularity is indicative of how closely Wong has tapped into the zeitgeist of the classroom as a place where children are calculated as subjects of carefully structured procedures and where teachers hope to better calculate their most efficient interactions with children.

David Jardine (1998) tells of a time that he was dismayed by his student's lack of affect as he watched her teach a lesson to the children in her student teaching placement. He noted that "she seemed to be 'somewhere else' during the lesson, appearing vaguely unhappy, not 'there' somehow [and] suggested that this 'disconnectedness' might have been partially responsible for why the children seemed to stray" (p. 5). Jardine reported her "frightening, but also vaguely sad and almost poignantly humorous" response: "You mean you want me to smile more? Maybe I should have used more eye contact or something?" (p. 5). This student teacher may one day join the ranks of teachers who claim Wong's work as "lifesaving" if she were to read the two-page script explaining *how to smile* (see *Table 3*).

I emphasize here the extent of the Wongs' popularity with teachers and the extent of their work not because I wish to criticize their book, but because I wish to make clear that their work is so popular with the teaching public due to the notion of school as an ordered, disciplined, and predictable place. As school personnel enact this popular notion of School, the Wongs join other Classroom Management experts—and their number is legion—in providing the most effective, simple, convenient, and *easy* strategies with which to compel children into the straight and narrow spaces left for them.

Representing the field of classroom management, the Wongs' work resonates consistently with Foucault's (1979) description of how to produce "subjected and practiced bodies, 'docile bodies'" (p. 138). The use of techniques of subtle and constant coercion, "supervising the processes of the activity rather than its result and...exercised according to a codification that partitions as closely as possible time, space and movement" (p. 137), aligns closely with the Wongs' recommended techniques for being an effective teacher. The following table (*Table 3*) provides examples of techniques as described in Foucault's 1979 study of public institutions, *Discipline & Punish: The Birth of the Prison*. Aligned with this selection of Foucauldian techniques and concepts (enclosure and partitioning; timetables and minute control of activity; a precise system of command; surveillance; normalizing judgments; and the carceral) are a sampling of techniques from the Wongs' 1998 book, *The First Days of School*.

Wong and Wong's book is not the only classroom management book that could potentially be held to a similar comparison. However, I chose this book by virtue of its popularity—and thus, how it represents what a large number of educators believe is necessary in order to be better and more efficient teachers, and to more efficiently and *easily* control their students. This brief analysis is included in this overview of School because I believe it validates the heart-felt concern expressed by James Macdonald at the beginning of this section that "living in school is an essentially inferior, vulgar, imitative, second-rate human experience" (Macdonald 1995, 51); and that somehow, sadly and inexcusably, "children are no longer our kin, our kind; teaching is no longer an act of 'kindness' and generosity bespeaking a deep connectedness with children" (D. Jardine 1998, 5).

In dominant narratives of the good classroom, run by a good teacher, goodness is found in predictable, ordered, and controlled contexts. But I wonder, might a sort of goodness in the space and place of school derive from a commitment to what some call the "democratic good life"? According to Dewey (1985), democracy is

> simultaneously a way of life, an ethical ideal, and a personal commitment. Specifically, it is a way of life in which individuals are presumed to be self-directing and able to pursue their own goals and projects. No society that maintains order through constant supervision and/or coercion can be rightly called democratic. Further, individual benefit and the common good are mutually enhancing in a democracy. (p. 349)

Table 3. Foucault and Wong: Means of Control

Means **Enclosure, partitioning**

Where someone is indicates who and what he is. For instance, if he is on the wall at recess, he must be bad.

Foucault, 1979   *Discipline & Punish: The Birth of the Prison*

"Classrooms should be divided up into three parts: 'The most honourable for those who are learning Latin... it should be stressed that there are as many places at the tables as there will be writers, in order to avoid the confusion usually caused by the lazy'. In another, those who are learning to read: 'a bench for the rich and a bench for the poor' so that vermin will not be passed on. A third section for the newcomers: when their ability has been recognized, they will be given a place" (p. 314–315).

Wongs, 1998   *The First Days of School*

"Have a strategic location ready for students who need to be isolated from the rest of the class. Disruptive students must be separated from the class or at least from other problem students" (p. 95).

"Disruptive students must be placed close to the teacher. This is appropriate for distractible, dependent and occasionally resistant students" (p. 95).

Means **Timetables; minute control of activity**

Decisions are deferred to the clock and the schedule. There is no question of what to do now. The schedule knows.

Foucault, 1979   *Discipline & Punish: The Birth of the Prison*

"In the elementary schools, the division of time became increasingly minute...by orders that had to be obeyed immediately: 'At the last stroke of the hour, a pupil will ring the bell and at the first sound of the bell all pupils will kneel, with their arms crossed and their eyes lowered...the teacher will strike the signal once to indicate that the pupils should get up, a second time as a sign that they should salute Christ, and a third that they should sit down...9:00 the children go to their benches, 9:04 first slate, 9:08 end of dictation, 9:12 second slate, etc....an attempt is also made to assure quality of time used... the elimination of anything that might disturb or distract... it is expressly forbidden...to amuse one's companions by gestures, to play any game whatsoever, to eat, to sleep, to tell stories or comedies" (p. 151–152).

"In the correct use of the body, which makes possible a correct use of time, nothing must remain idle or useless…[for good handwriting, for example], the pupils must always hold their bodies erect, somewhat turned and free on the left side, slightly inclined, so that with the elbow placed on the table, the chin can be rested upon the hand, unless this were to interfere with the view; the left leg must be somewhat more forward under the table than the right. A distance of two fingers must be left between the body and the table for not only does one write with more alertness, but nothing is more harmful to the health than to acquire the habit of pressing one's stomach against the table…the right arm must be at five fingers from the table, on which is must rest lightly…. A disciplined body is the prerequisite of an efficient gesture" (p. 152).

"Writing exercise: 9: hands on the knees. This command is conveyed by one ring on the bell; 10. hands on the table, heads up; 11. clean the slates: everyone cleans his slate with a little saliva or better still with a piece of rag; 12 show the slates; 13 monitors, inspect. They inspect the slates with their assistants and then those of their own bench. The assistants inspect those of their own bench and everyone returns to their own place" (p. 315).

Wongs, 1998   *The First Days of School*

"To increase the amount of time the student works to learn: 1. have an assignment posted daily to be done upon entering the classroom 2. teach procedures and routines to minimize interruptions and maximize uninterrupted learning time 3. constantly monitor students so as to keep them on task" (p. 206).

"An axiom of handling behavior problems is that little or no instructional time should be lost. Time is wasted when you stop to find a place or move furniture around for the offender. The good students resent this waste of time just as much as you resent the troublemaker" [italics mine] (p. 95).

"9:00 bellwork, 9:05 morning message, 9:10 change helpers, 9:15 journal writing, 9:50 listening skills activity, 10:20 recess (*supervision*), 10:30 handwriting, etc." (p. 124).

"The effective teacher teaches RESPONSIBILITY. This is because effective teachers have their schedules and assignments posted. It is a joy to watch such teachers and classes in action. The students in these classes know what to expect during the day and where to look for assignments. They can now go about doing their work on their own. You cannot teach children to be responsible unless they know what you want them to do" (p. 124).

"Technique for smiling, speaking and pausing. Step 1. SMILE Smile as you approach the student, *even if your first impulse is to behave harshly toward the student* [emphasis mine]. Step 2. FEEDBACK Observe the reaction to your smile. Are you receiving a smile in return or at least a signal that the student is relaxing and receptive to your approach? Step 3. PAUSE (Timing, timing). Step 4. NAME Say "Nathan" with a slight smile. Step 5. PAUSE. Step 6. PLEASE Add please, followed by your request. Do this with a calm, firm voice, accompanied by a slight, non-threatening smile. Step 7. PAUSE. Step 8. THANK YOU. End with "thank you, Nathan" and a slight smile. ...Practice this in the mirror, over and over again" (p. 74).

Means **A Precise System of Command**

Here one is trained to automatically react to a system of signals, verbal and otherwise. Repetition and intense attention to detail leave no space for impulsive actions or any kind of action requiring individual thought.

Foucault, 1979   *Discipline & Punish: The Birth of the Prison*

"The training of schoolchildren was to be carried out [with] few words, no explanation, a total silence interrupted only by signals-bells, clapping of hands, gestures, a mere glance from that teacher...[and] a system of signals to which one had to react immediately. Even verbal orders were to function as elements of signalization: 'Enter your benches. At the word enter, the children bring their right hands down on the table with a resounding thud and the same time put one leg into the bench; at the words your benches they put the other leg in and sit down opposite their slates" (p. 167).

"To make a sign to stop to a pupil who is reading, he will strike the signal once.... To make a sign to a pupil to repeat when he has read badly or mispronounced a letter, a syllable, or a word, he will strike the signal twice in rapid succession. If, after the sign had been made two or three times, the pupil who is reading does not find and repeat the word that he had badly read or mispronounced...the teacher will strike three times in rapid succession, as a sign to him to begin to read further back; and he will continue to make the sign till the pupil finds the word he has said incorrectly" (p. 167).

Wongs, 1998   *The First Days of School*

"Shirley Lee's class is a joy to behold. She doesn't even have to open her mouth when the bell rings. She may say 'Good morning' or compliment the class on their appropriate behavior, but while the students are quickly and quietly [emphasis mine] at work, she completes her chores, which typically must be done by all teachers, like taking roll" (p. 125).

"Students, I have a procedure when I want your undivided attention. You will see me stand here with my hand up. Or I may tap a bell because some of you may not be able to see my hand when you are working in a group. When you see my hand or hear a bell, the procedure is as follows: 1. Freeze. 2. Turn and face me; pay attention and keep your eyes on me. 3. Be ready for instruction. I will have something to say. Let me repeat and demonstrate what I said...Byron, please tell me the procedures when you see my hand or hear a bell" (p. 181).

"Students readily accept the idea of having a uniform set of classroom procedures, because it simplifies their task of succeeding in school. Efficient and workable procedures allow a great variety of activities to take place...with a minimum of confusion and wasted time. If no procedures are established, much time will be wasted organizing each activity and students will have to guess what to do. As a result, undesirable work habits and behaviors could develop which would be hard to correct" (p. 168).

Means **Surveillance**

Here one gains power over others by observing them. The surveilled begin to accept docility and being regulated by the surveillor due to the knowledge gained and the threat implied by the constant (or seemingly constant) observation.

Foucault, 1979   *Discipline & Punish: The Birth of the Prison*

The Panopticon provided a model for using Discipline in prisons. Constant observation and penalties for the smallest infraction of the many rules would start the process. Every second of the day and night could be carefully structured. "He is seen but does not see; he is the object of information, never a subject in communication. The arrangement of his room...imposes on him an axial visibility, but...imply a lateral invisibility. And this invisibility is the guarantee of order...if they are school children, there is no copying, no noise, no chatter, no waste of time....Hence the major effect of the Panopticon: to induce in the inmate a state of conscious and permanent visibility that assures the automatic functioning of power" (p. 200 – 201) and so guarantees a docile student who does as ordered without question.

Wongs, 1998   *The First Days of School*

"As soon as the tardy bell rings, your first task is scan the room, not to take roll, but to look for students who are not at work" (p. 130).

"It is wise to begin the year with the desks in rows facing the teacher. This minimizes distractions, allows you to monitor behavior more readily...have a strategic location ready for students who need to be isolated from the rest of the class" (p. 95).

"Place the teacher's desk so that you can easily monitor the classroom while at your desk" (p. 98).

Means **Normalizing Judgments**

Disciplinary power not only punishes deviations from normality, it rewards "normalcy" (good behavior) with gold stars and candy. Those who transgress are defined not only as bad, but as abnormal. It is a more subtle use of power that works on the transgressor from the inside and consolidates the ranks of the "normal" against all others.

Recall: no one else got out of line to help Reuben.

Foucault, 1979   *Discipline & Punish: The Birth of the Prison*

"The school [was] subject to a whole micropenality of time (latenesses, absences, interruptions of tasks), of activity (inattention, negligence, lack of zeal), of behavior (impoliteness, disobedience), of speech (idle chatter, insolence), of the body ('incorrect' attitudes, irregular gestures, lack of cleanliness)... and that punishment would include everything that is capable of making children feel the offence...of humiliating them, confusing them...a certain coldness." (p. 178).

Wongs, 1998   *The First Days of School*

"One teacher taught her class to look down whenever a child was behaving in a way which would be reinforced by their attention. This same teacher made herself a badge with 'Not now Jason' written on it. Whenever the child in question interrupted her yet again all she had to do was tap the badge without so much as looking at him. Eventually he would learn that he would get attention at more appropriate times, not on demand" (Roffey, in Wong 1998, 130). "Heart: Have the students make a pattern with their name on it.

Place all the patterns inside a heart—your heart—on the bulletin board. If there is a violation of the rule, kindly remove the pattern and place it outside of your heart. Encourage the students to return to your heart" (p. 158).

"After a few weeks or months, if someone should ask you, 'Why are you picking on me?' all you have to do is stand and smile at the student."

Means **The Carceral**

The idea that some hold the power to punish is not only accepted, but embraced! Therefore, the judges of normality are everywhere, and the normalizing practices very difficult to resist.

Foucault, 1979   *Discipline & Punish: The Birth of the Prison*

"The 'carceral' with its many diffuse or compact forms, its institutions of supervision and constraint, of discrete surveillance and insistent coercion, assured the communication of punishments according to quality and quantity...I shall note the slightest irregularity in your conduct" (p. 299).

"Perhaps the most important effect of the carceral system is ...that it succeeds in making the power to punish [and reward] natural and legitimate, in lowering at least, the threshold of tolerance to penalty" (p. 301).

Wongs, 1998   *The First Days of School*

"Many people...believe that nothing is wrong until they are caught. Imagine this typical classroom setting. A teacher is speaking at the front of the room....Student A, without permission, goes to the pencil sharpener...student C abruptly speaks up to ask the teacher a question not relevant to the topic, student D leans over to say something to Student E. Students F through Z look on. Students are aware of a teacher's enforcement or non-enforcement of the rules...POST YOUR CONSEQUENCES" (p. 151–152).

"The consequence should be suitable and proportional to the violation; in other words, the penalty should fit the crime" (p. 156).

"Failure to work off the penalty automatically moves the student up to the next level of the consequences or doubles the penalty" (p. 157).

An important consideration of Dewey's conception of democracy is that each person is best served by a democracy created to maximize the common good. However, as Dewey noted, school cannot maximize the common good when, by virtue of the systems of control described above and by its institutional nature, it serves—at least ostensibly—to privilege those who most comply with what Goffman terms "house rules." Goffman (1961, in Macdonald 1995) described the privilege system of total institutions via three elements:

1. 'House rules' or a formal set of prescriptions and proscriptions that sets the requirements of inmate conduct
2. A small number of clearly defined rewards or privileges held out in exchange for obedience
3. Punishments designed for occurrences of rule violations. (p. 43)

Macdonald joined schools to prisons and mental institutions as one of Goffman's (1961) "total institutions" and further named them as "degree factories" and, in Thoreauian fashion, a place to prepare for the occupation of war. He cautioned that "a careful examination of this allegation suggests that it is overly simple, yet how [else might our] authoritarian relationships, and our prizing of docility, punctuality, and attendance be more readily explained?" (p. 41).

The pervasiveness of an objective to produce normalized "docile bodies"—including the common exclamation of how *easy* it can be!—is further addressed in a later section of this chapter. But first, what follows is an overview of the two schools in which the study took place.

The Schools

The two schools housing the research classrooms are similar in ways that nearly all schools are similar. The buildings are large with multiple classrooms into which children are divided (partitioned, in Foucauldian terms) according to grade level, determined by chronological age. There are particular rooms for the principal, counselor, special teachers, custodians, and for activities such as art, music, gym, therapy, tutoring, and for teachers, lounging. The segments of the school day are punctuated by ringing bells and amplified announcements. In both schools, there are signs and posters in common areas to represent to all who enter what kind of place this is and what is valued there. Both school systems have purchased a character program, and so each building has posted prominently *The Six Pillars of Character* as determined by the purchased program: trustworthiness, respect, responsibility, fairness, caring and citizenship. These traits are displayed on walls throughout the buildings as are other posters and signs admonishing all who enter to ask themselves, "Have you signed in at the office?" and to inform them that they are "about to enter a learning zone," and that the school community "strives to provide a positive learning environment to prepare caring, responsible citizens," and that "our mission is to teach students not only how to walk, but where to walk."

Each building bears signs of the institution: hard, cold linoleum floors and hard, rough, cold, pastel-colored concrete walls. Described by Somers (1976, in O'Donaghue 2006) as the "hard architecture" typical of prisons, hospitals and schools—the walls, halls, doors, floors, and furniture of the schools "resist any form of human imprint" (p. 24). These schools share physical characteristics with the school building described by O'Donaghue (2006): "Overall, surfaces are hard and flat and exposed and unsympathetic even to the smallest of creatures such as a spider. For a spider crawling on the wall, there is no hiding place…clearly, ideas of strength, resilience, resistance are echoed in the architectural surfaces in the [schools]" (p. 25).

Mrs. Krinkle's School

Mrs. Krinkle's school is one of 46 elementary schools in a large city system located in a midwestern state. The city is racially mixed, 66.7% White, 28.5% Black; however, the neighborhoods within the city are much more segregated—by race and by income. This is reflected in the racial make-up of the population of children in Andrews Elementary School which is approximately 68% Black, 27% White and 5% "Other." Most of the children—99.6%—in this school qualify for the federal free lunch program and so are named "economically disadvantaged" on the state's department of education report card for 2005-2006. This is reasonable given the median income in the city ($32, 937, according to *http://www.city-data.com/city/[city]-[state].html*, per year). According to the state report card, this school was in "Academic Watch".

When I visited the school, its appearance did not offer the sense that this was a place for or of children. It was a quiet place, and nearly all movement was subdued and uniform: children moving in lines from one place to another and gathering on command in different places in classrooms. There was evidence that the school had adopted techniques similar to those discussed in the Foucault/ Wongs comparison. Laminated and posted on school walls and individual classroom walls were the following:

Andrews Schoolwide Rules

Follow directions the first time they are given.
Raise your hand and wait for permission to speak.
Keep your hands, feet and objects to yourself.
Walk throughout building at all times.
No fighting.

Positives:

Praise
Recognition Program
Positive notes sent home
Fun Fridays

Mischievous Steps:

1st Offense- Verbal Warning
2nd Offense- Deprived of Privilege
3rd Offense- Phone call home
4th Offense- IC ½ day 5th Offense- IC (1 day)
      [IC was a form of in-school suspension]
6th Offense- IC (2 days)
7th Offense- 1 Day Suspension

Severe Clause:

1st Offense- 1 Day Suspension
2nd Offense- 2 Day Suspension
3rd Offense- 3 Day Suspension

**Mischievous and Severe Clause
starts over every nine weeks.**

In early visits to the school, I was often reminded of the institutional prison-school connection as described in chapter 2; and on reading this article from the *Talk.left.com* website, I thought immediately of Andrews Elementary School:

The bullhorn blares across the yard. Young Latinos and African Americans quickly scan their surroundings, noticing the many faces that watch them. A chain-link fence, 20 feet high, surrounds them on three sides. Dutifully, they fall into place in line. Heads up, hands clasped behind their backs, shoulders straight. Most know

better than to talk. A few test the rules and murmur among themselves. 'You're wasting my time!' barks the attendant. Rumpled
play dollars are doled out to the well behaved; order is maintained
through this token economy. Thus begins their day.

This is elementary school. First grade. Our inmates are 6
years old. They are not criminals. Small and wiry, these are children whose usual offenses are pulling braids or not sharing Hot
Cheetos. The children must walk in straight lines. Hands must remain behind their backs, as though in handcuffs. The high fences
separate them from the outside, physically and symbolically. What
does it mean when you are 6 and your school is run like a prison?

It is lunchtime. The students are herded through line, picking
up their cardboard trays of chicken nuggets and milk. Eating must
be done in silence. Misbehaving children face a 'three-strikes-you're-
out' policy. The same policy that puts many neighborhood men in
jail is also used to deny chattering children recess. (Jeralyn 2004)

Except for a few details (I saw no bullhorn; the standard token
in this school was not play money, but instead, candy; and the children at Andrews Elementary are afforded seven strikes instead of
three), the description above could easily have been made of an observation of Andrews Elementary School.

Mr. Scott's School

Mr. Scott's school is one of six elementary schools located in a me-
dium-sized suburban district in the same state as Mrs. Krinkle's
school. In fact, the town is a suburb of the city that houses Mrs.
Krinkle's school—the two schools are less than thirty minutes
apart. In distance.

By other standards—funding, socio-economic status of students, state rating, racial make-up, condition of physical plant—
the two schools are worlds apart. The children who attend Shadow
Lake Elementary School come from families in a town with a 95%
White population with a median income of $59, 800 (*http://www.
city-data.com/city/[town]-[state].html*). The school's state rating is
"Excellent." Reflecting the city's racial distribution, the population
of children who attend the school is 93% White, and those designated as economically disadvantaged according to the same state
report card include 13.5% of the school population.

While there was slightly more movement and ease in this

building—on entering, it was not uncommon to see children moving through halls on their own without reprimand, and there was a lighter feel to the place—there was evidence of tight and narrow school expectations here, too. On the walls in the hallway near the office, one can read signs of the Institution:

- School versions of corporate motivational posters: success, risk, friendship, and commitment.

- Character Counts at Shadow Lake: RESPONSIBILITY (with an elephant): Are you responsible? Do you do what you are supposed to do? Do you think about how your actions will affect others? Do you always try to do your best?

- Bulletin Board outside a classroom: "HAVE A SLICE OF OUR CHARACTER." Pizzas with pepperonis which proclaim: "I am citizenship because I don't hit" "I am trustful because I keep secrets" "I am respectful because I respect people."

- "In accordance with state laws, visitors must sign in at office."

- The school system's vision statement and core beliefs posted throughout the school and on many classroom doors:

Our Mission, Our Vision, Our Purpose Statement

Shadow Lake staff has worked cohesively to develop a framework to identify our belief systems. Our mission, vision, and purpose statement reflect this collaborative effort.

MISSION: Our purpose is to focus on the child, and as adults, create a positive learning atmosphere in which we model dignity and respect for others.

VISION: We believe that every day, every child will be actively engaged in a nurturing and successful environment and that every adult will be passionately dedicated and inspired to motivate the development of children (as individuals) who will be leaders.

PURPOSE STATEMENT:
1. Every child is provided with an opportunity to learn at his or her own level.
2. Every child should feel safe in the school environment.
3. A strong partnership between parents, children and school personnel should be developed to ensure equal responsibility.

Also posted is the school's schedule along with consequences for variations.

DAILY SCHEDULES

8:45 Students may enter the building
9:00 Students must be in classrooms
11:45 AM Kindergartners dismissed
11:45-12:30 All-Day Kindergarten,
            1st and 2nd Grade Lunch/Recess
12:00-12:45 3rd and 4th Grade Lunch/Recess
12:45 PM Kindergarten begins
3:30 Dismissal begins

Students arriving after 9:00 and before 10:30 are marked tardy

Students arriving after 10:30 are marked with a "Half Day" Absence
> [Which recalls, from Foucault (1977), "Anyone who is absent for more than five minutes without warning… will be 'marked down for a half-day'" (p. 178).]

Students that leave and return during the school day are marked with a "Partial" which is equivalent to a Tardy

Students that leave prior to 2:00 are marked with a "Half Day" Absence

Students leaving after 2:00 and prior to 3:30 are marked with an Early Dismissal which is equivalent to a Tardy

---

Mr. Scott reported that in a recent faculty meeting at this school with a mission statement and vision statement that claim an atmosphere of "dignity and respect for others" and "that every adult will be passionately dedicated and inspired to motivate the development of children (as individuals) who will be leaders," he was a bit disconcerted to learn that his principal had ripped up a petition written by the students in the third and fourth grades. The students had objected to a change in arrangements of lunch periods and decided to propose a different solution. Faculty reportedly derided the petition: "What do they think this is—a democracy?"

Michael Scott reported that at parent meetings and in staff mailboxes, the principal and others who wish to share insights

about how to handle children distribute articles written by John
Rosemond, an expert who espouses the traditional values of behaviorism. Mr. Scott reminded me that Rosemond, in his column, radio
show and website, persuades parents and educators to be decisive
authorities, rewarding compliance and punishing misbehaviors. In
one column, Rosemond (2006a) suggested that the world would be a
better place if children remained little fishes who would not dare get
"too big for their britches." Getting too big for one's britches would
be associated with high self-esteem, and as Rosemond claimed, the
best research correlates high self-esteem with anti-social behavior.
James Macdonald (1995) explains the impact of a viewpoint such
as this:

> We may in other words, 'teach' our youngsters to be 'good' and
> right' so that they learn to see themselves in these terms and
> to have feelings of shame and anxiety when 'bad' or 'wrong.'
> The 'badness' and 'wrongness' encapsulates the developing in-
> dividual in an affect-embeddedness which becomes a powerful
> drive for equilibrium, for returning to the security of what is
> 'good' and 'right'. (p. 27)

And if the shame, anxiety and resulting drive for equilibrium
do not work, Rosemond (2006b) offers another suggestion: to lie.
In confronting one of the many annoying behaviors of children—
rudely, selfishly and mindlessly talking too much—Rosemond
advises parents to trick the child by telling him that they have met
with a child specialist who has informed them that the bad habit
of motor-mouthing is caused by too little sleep, and so, the child's
bedtime will be moved to an earlier time. Rosemond further advises
that telling the child this on a day on which he planned to stay up
later (maybe on a weekend) would disappoint him even more. This
should, as MacDonald suggests, teach the youngster to be "good".

By distributing articles such as these to parents and teachers
who are caring for the children of Shadow Lake Elementary, the
school (via the principal and some teachers—who are not alone as
educators in considering this author an expert worthy of consulta-
tion) communicate that the Alfie Kohn question (see page 117) they
are responding to is "how can we get these kids to obey?" and that
the goal is to find the easiest means possible to do so. The message

here is one of the adults somehow banding together against the children who were once "our kin and our kind."

While the promotion and implied endorsement of Rosemond may not faithfully signify the heart and mind of this school, it does offer an indication that while this school may not appear quite as prison-like as Andrews Elementary, it does operate (as do most Schools) as a place where children are *calculable* and to be controlled by means that may include a well-placed lie.

Kindergarten

Based on more than twenty years of experience as a teacher in elementary school and as facilitator and supervisor of field students based in elementary school sites, and backed up by a somewhat cursory survey of early childhood texts (Althouse, Johnson, and Mitchell 2003, Bredekamp and Copple 1997, Dever and Falconer 2008, Driscoll and Nagel 2002, Gordon and Browne 2008), I offer the following as typical of what can be found in the physical environment of kindergarten and of the way kindergarten time is allotted.

Space

While to be certain a visit to any kindergarten classroom may suggest variations on these descriptions and listings, there is a tradition of what is "kindergarten" that allows for easy distinction between a kindergarten classroom and other classrooms in an elementary school. While most graded classrooms fill more than half the space with individual desks and chairs in scale to the grade-level/age of the child, in the kindergarten classroom, one will see tables seating two to six children with shared materials on them. The rest of the space is devoted to a gathering space for meetings and whole group lessons, and to areas set up as centers. In most kindergarten classrooms, one will find areas for blocks/construction; dramatic play with play props; a library including puppets, books on tape, pillows/beanbag chairs; a writing center; an art center with easels; and a play-dough or another kind of tactile center. One might also see a sand or water table; computers; science centers, sometimes with plants and/or animals; a felt board center; an invention center or a take-apart center; and a music area with instruments and song tapes.

Time

Again, according to the early childhood texts (Althouse et al. 2003, Bredekamp and Copple 1997, Dever and Falconer 2008, Driscoll and Nagel 2002, Gordon and Browne 2008), information shared on teacher and school websites, and personal experience, the kindergarten day is typically divided into particular times or events. If one were to visit a hypothetical kindergarten classroom, one might expect to the find the children and their teacher engaged in any of the following: arrival, whole group time, small groups, active times and quiet times, calendar time, learning centers, rest/nap, seat work/ work assignment, snack, language, transitions, free time, center time, project time, recess, PE, art/music, outdoor play, shared reading, class meetings, and/or closing.

Space and Time

In one popular source in the early childhood field, *Scholastic.com*, teachers and parents are presented with examples of typical kindergarten days. In these descriptions, the components of kindergarten time and space blend:

> Let us take an imaginary walk around a good kindergarten classroom. One of the first things you might notice (and be surprised by) is that not everyone is doing the same activity at the same time! Children are happily playing and working in small groups, or independently, in learning centers around the room:
>
> ° Four or five children are using math and science skills as they build a complicated structure in the block area.
>
> ° In the dramatic play area, a small group is creating a pretend restaurant complete with waiters 'writing' orders and cooks 'reading' recipes.
>
> ° The book area is filled with children enjoying library books and books written by their peers.
>
> ° Nearby, some children are writing and drawing in the writing center.
>
> ° 'Hands-on' science is happening at the water table as a group of children investigate which items will float or sink.

- In the math area, children sort, classify, weigh, and measure small rocks and stones.

- The teacher moves from group to group answering and asking questions, keeping the learning going.

- Later the students will all gather together to share what they have learned in the centers, read a story, and practice literacy skills. (Church 2007)

This is representative of many kindergarten classrooms. However, there is more going on here. Recall the tale that predicated this study—the story of Reuben's fall. Julian's difficulties in his kindergarten classroom derived from his inability to adhere to "silent playtime" and the inflexible structures that discounted his competence as a social member of his group. Mrs. Buttercup's classroom, like the one described above, had the accoutrements of kindergarten: blocks, a dramatic play area, easels, puzzles, a library with puppets, even a cage with a gerbil. In this space, filled with child-friendly materials suggesting accommodation of children's interests and social needs, were specific rules and standards to which children had to comply in order to enter and take part. On most days, Julian did not qualify.

In classrooms I have visited, while children were certainly engaged in playing and working in small groups, or independently, in learning centers around the room, there were nearly always a few who had been removed from this context: sitting in "time out" or completing a paper left over from bell work or last night's (or last week's) homework. Their participation in idyllic and typical kindergarten was contingent on compliance to the narrow expectations regarding how to properly "do" kindergarten. The following incidental observations made during various school visits include examples of children's noncompliance to—and so removal from—the order of kindergarten:

- Briona was sent from her kindergarten class's carpet time nearly daily to stand on a taped-out square in another classroom because she sat too close, or even touched, other children.

- Three boys in a kindergarten class were sent to sit in chairs placed in three different parts of the room during center time because they carried materials from the art center to use in the block center.

- Jamil, a kindergartner, had to stay on the carpet while his classmates were dismissed to free time after he started to stand up before his name was called.

- Third-grader Phillip had to turn his card yellow—which indicated a range of penalties—for stopping to look at the hamsters on his way to line up for the restroom.

- Janeen "lost 'Discovery'" when she tickled Olive while walking in line back to their first-grade classroom from a special.

- Five-year-old Bruce was forbidden to participate in recess because he forgot to put his homework in the basket before the second bell rang.

- Yana, a kindergartner, was sent to the principal from music class for shaking her hips to *The More We Get Together* ("...the happier we'll be...").

- Six-year-old Hank had his card flipped (and so missed recess *and* the chance for the weekly reward for having all "greens") because he attempted to lick his own elbow.

- In front of two other classes of children, six-year-old Stephan was sent to walk up the stairs the "right" way five times—until he got it right.

- Tevin, a first-grader who missed eight days of school due to a family tragedy, had to stay in from recess until he completed the large stack of worksheets that had collected on his desk during his absence. Tevin had not had recess for quite a while before this event—he often did not finish his work in time to join the good workers for recess.

- Forty-four of the fifty-one first-graders in one school sat in one classroom with their heads down for an entire Friday afternoon while the seven children who "stayed on green" for the whole month enjoyed a pizza party and movie in another room.

- Two children, Donald and Tremonte, whispered during a heads-down afternoon in the punishment room, and in addition to missing the pizza/movie party, were banned from recess the following Monday.

These may sound unusually harsh for young children in school—harsh for anyone in any situation. But, these punishments ("consequences" in Wong's terms) are not unusual—these incidents are representative of kindergarten and other primary grade interactions as observed during informal and formal visitations made to kindergarten classrooms in nine different schools, including Shadow Lake Elementary and Andrews Elementary, across four local districts (one urban, three suburban).

Just as the earlier descriptions of idyllic kindergarten environments are typical, so is the following posting on a teacher's classroom website titled *Mrs. White's Kindergarten Class* (White 2007) and representative of many kindergarten classroom discipline policies to be found in classrooms and on the web:

Please refer to my classroom discipline letter/policy given to you at Parent Orientation for complete comments. Below our rules, rewards and consequences are listed again for quick reference:

RULES:

1. FOLLOW DIRECTIONS (please remember that this includes daily routines)
2. KEEP HANDS, FEET AND OBJECTS TO YOURSELF
3. USE INSIDE VOICES (SILENT IN ALL HALLWAYS) AND WALK AT ALL TIMES WHILE INSIDE
4. BE KIND AND RESPECTFUL TO OTHERS
5. CLEAN UP AFTER YOURSELF

REWARDS:

1. Praise
2. Hand stamps and stickers
3. Weekly treats for good behavior
4. Good notes home, comments on weekly work folder
5. Positive phone calls home
6. Awards at the end of each nine-week grading period: CITIZENSHIP AWARD for good behavior

CONSEQUENCES:

1. First infraction: Verbal warning with explanation ("second chance warning," does not move clothespin) will still receive hand stamp at end of the day if they remain at "second chance."
2. Second infraction: Move clothespin to yellow "warning face" circle; lose 5 minutes of free time ("S" on hand instead of hand stamp).
3. Third infraction: Move clothespin to red "sad face" circle, lose 10 minutes of free time, lose hand stamp ("N" on hand instead of hand stamp).

4.   Fourth infraction: Note or phone call to parents.
5.   Fifth infraction: Send to principal.
6.   Severe clause: SEND DIRECTLY TO PRINCIPAL/POSSIBLE
      DETENTION.

Mrs. White's description of her rules and expectations are pub-lic—shared with not only the parents of the children in her class-room, but with other teachers and parents via the Internet. There are many such plans distributed and copied—with little variation in content or form. Examples of these have been included in the appendix.

Kohn (in Watson 2003), assuming the pervasiveness of such plans and their high recognizability to the reader, can then share, with little explanation, an example of one teacher's rating scale for her young students:

> The boy explained to [his father] how the system works: a '1,' the lowest possible rating is very rare; a '2' is essentially a punishment for any action frowned on by the teacher; and a '3' signifies that the child has followed the rules. 'What about a "4"?' asked the father. 'Well,' replied the boy, seemingly awed by the mere mention of this number, 'to get a "4," you'd have to be a statue!' (p. *xiii*)

Kohn used this example, as I did Mrs. White's, as representative of the programs and variations on behavior management that are out there (see appendix), "from cutesy to sadistic" (p. *xiii*)—programs, strategies and systems that are designed to control children. Even a young child "realizes that such policies are not intended to foster cu-riosity or creativity or compassion; [that] they are primarily designed to elicit mindless compliance, the ideal evidently being a student who resembles an inanimate object" (p. *xiii*).

The idea of preferring a child as a "statue" or an "inanimate ob-ject" may seem extreme—a joke made for effect. However, one of my most vivid memories of school staff meetings is about just that ideal. The teaching staff at my former school had been discussing discipline as a topic at this meeting, and the conversation drifted from general solutions to better calculate the children's behavior and how better to herd them through the day to the successes of some particular teachers' methods. One staff member told of seeing Mrs. Benn's lines when her children were standing in the hall waiting for their turn in the restroom. She praised Mrs. Benn's quiet lines as the other staff members nodded and commended Mrs. Benn, one person praising her orderly lines this way: "The children were so still and quiet—they were almost lifeless!" My heart nearly broke.

The Kindergartens

The following section details the two kindergarten classrooms which served as the sites for this study: Katie Krinkle's, a full-day kindergarten in Andrews Elementary School located in an urban district; and Michael Scott's, a half-day morning kindergarten in Shadow Lake Elementary School located in a nearby suburban district.

On entering either Mrs. Krinkle's or Mr. Scott's room, one would recognize it as a kindergarten classroom. Each has the following "places," as listed in the earlier description of Kindergarten: a gathering space for meetings and whole group lessons, dramatic play center (or housekeeping as some call it), blocks/construction, books/literacy (including puppets, books on tape, pillows/beanbag chairs), manipulatives, puzzles, computers, games, music, play props, tables seating four to six children with shared materials on them, and a teacher's desk.

However, while each had the appearance of kindergarten, the rooms are as different as are the teachers and children in them. Mrs. Krinkle and Mr. Scott bring unique backgrounds, experiences, interests, and priorities to their classrooms.

Mrs. Krinkle's Space

Mrs. Krinkle, who has been a kindergarten teacher in the same room for more than three decades, has devoted those years to collecting, building, and designing a wide range of instructional materials and spaces for her kindergarten class. The classroom is very large—more than 30 feet by 60 feet. Half of the floor space is carpet and half is linoleum. The classroom, like the building, is old. The bulletin boards, chalkboards, and doors are framed in dark, aged wood. On one wall is a vintage fireplace in which Mrs. Krinkle has placed shelves that hold boxes of educational materials. There are four tables for the children to sit at—each made of two trapezoidal tables placed together into hexagon shapes—and the chairs (six at a table) have chair pockets placed over them where the children place their supplies and where the teachers place papers.

The room has obvious functions in different parts of the room, and the areas included spaces for the following: five computers (but not all of them work); math tubs; flannel board; two separate tanks for turtles (one turtle per tank); a fish tank; several large containers with plants and grow-lights; a block center; puzzles; a range of make-believe areas; a library area with puppets, flannel kits, hundreds of books; big books with pointers and easels; an art center with painting and other art media; and book shelves loaded with manipulatives, more books, learning boxes, and labeled boxes of seasonal and thematic supplies. Mrs. Krinkle's classroom leads into a separate anteroom with storage areas for her, and also hooks and shelves for the children's coats and other belongings. Off this little area is a restroom—a very old restroom. Because of this arrangement, the children do not have to leave the classroom to use the restroom or get belongings from lockers.

Mrs. Krinkle has grown children who over the years have donated many of their toys and books to Mrs. Krinkle's classroom, and she has also contributed a great deal on her own. Mrs. Krinkle is successful at writing grants, and with the funds she receives from those, she purchases more materials for the children (her most recent was an assortment of elaborately authentic wild animal puppets) and funds field trips, such as the trips to farms during that current school year.

On her walls are soft sculptures, dozens of commercial, homemade and child-made posters—including ones of color words, senses, seasons, numbers, ABCs, Martin Luther King, animals, flowers, maps, trees and more. She keeps a word wall that, at the time of the research, had the children's names and words related to the farm.

Mrs. Krinkle maintains a chart of behavior using weather as a theme. If the children's stars remain under "sunny," it means they had a good day. However, some children are asked to move their stars, and so progress from cloudy to rainy to stormy with consequences of similarly progressing seriousness. Mrs. Krinkle does not ask the children to move their stars very often, but the possibility is always there.

Mr. Scott's Space

Even given the similarities they share as kindergarten classrooms, Mr. Scott's room is quite different from Mrs. Krinkle's. First, his classroom is housed in a newer, more modern building (Shadow Lake Elementary was about 40 years old, while Andrews Elementary was constructed in 1920). The room itself is much smaller, yet it looks larger because Mr. Scott does not have nearly the amount of materials that Mrs. Krinkle has collected. Many of Mr. Scott's materials have come from the school system as part of kindergarten, and from the PTA—which has been generous in providing him with materials he has asked for. Generalizing by gender can be dangerous, however I venture to say that on looking in at Mr. Scott's room, I would have guessed it was a "man teacher's" room. While certainly functional, and containing (as will be detailed in a moment) what might be expected in kindergartens, it is somewhat sparse with obscure attempts at "décor."

Areas in Mr. Scott's room include housekeeping/make believe (wooden stove, sink, etc), blocks (in tubs, plastic, cardboard and wooden blocks), library (books in fronted-shelf, tubs, and beanbag chairs), gathering area (calendar, big book easel and box of big books, games, chair), computer center (four computers with children's programs installed), and shelves with art and math materials. Hanging from the ceiling are an inflatable fish, a disco ball and a sun mobile. Mr. Scott has labeled items in the room with cards reading: door, closet, light, sharpener, chair, computer, teacher's desk, flag, wall, pencil, and clock.

Like Mrs. Krinkle's room, Mr. Scott's room has a fish tank: prompting children to ask "Where's the fish?" as it is empty. On his walls at the time of the study were a number line, posters with color words, an ABC chart across a whole wall, Character Counts posters: Respect, Trustworthiness, Honesty; and on a word wall, Aug/Sept words: pencil, scissors, backpack, computer, books, crayons, paper, lunch box.

Mr. Scott no longer uses a formal discipline system. He once did, but was influenced by conversations with his student teachers and by his own study to abandon the "box" system he once used. At the time of the research, he was studying his new, more relational means of constructing a workable kindergarten classroom with his students, and was including that studying in his in-progress master's thesis.

Teachers

Much of what I have learned about teachers I have learned by listening to their conversations about children. In the past, I could overhear such insights into teachers' views of their students and of their responsibilities as teachers in the teachers' lounge or in the hallways. In my travels to schools as a university supervisor and facilitator, I am still privy to some such discussions, but as a relative outsider. However, one particularly pertinent and available source of the teacher-to-teacher conversations is the Internet, on bulletin boards and chat rooms. These are sites where teachers can take part in conversations on particular topics, grade levels, issues, etc. related to school. These are of particular interest to me for several reasons. First, I am interested in the opportunity to "overhear" teacher talk in places other than the schools and systems where I have taught, facilitated or observed, so that I can learn if the topics and views that I have overheard and witnessed in the schools I worked in and visited are particular to my geographic area.

I am also eager to observe the exchanges where there is, in many ways, no observer. Virtual observations can be made by visiting teacher websites such as *teacher.net*, and reading the chat-boards under the categories of "classroom management" and "classroom discipline." I find the conversations to be very similar to those one overhears in the teachers' lounge: candid, venting, commiserating, and often somewhat shocking. What follows are outtakes from sequences of postings—postings that are highly representative of the hundreds of posting sequences of teacher conversations on teacher.net. I have also included some examples of these pages in the appendix.

Classroom Management and *Classroom Discipline* are common topics to be found on teacher websites. Teachers post discussions that request and describe punishment and reward systems (see appendix). The following is a list of phrases and titles found on various pages of *teachernet.com* describing a wide range of such systems:

Fish Bowl
Gumball machine
Three strikes, you're out!
Friday Fling
Checkbook reward

Token/box of prizes

The Ladder Plan

Caught being Good Stickers

Banana Bucks

Bonus Bucks

Bulldog Bucks

Barnyard Bucks

Behavior Bucks

Mrs. Angelo's Angels

Dragon Dollars

Space Race

Mystery Envelope

Mystery Walker/ Mystery Person: "every time we walk in the hallway, I pull a name out of a jar and that is the "mystery walker." I look for the "mystery person" walking there and back. If they were successful, they color in one gumball and when they are all colored in, we have a bubblegum party. Nothing is better than gum in school!"

100 minute club

Class compliments

Goody drawings

Green, yellow, red (or green, yellow, yellow, red; or green, blue, yellow, red; and other variations of this—green always meaning good and red being the worst)

Clothespins

Bonus Days

Ice cream contest

Hole punches

JABBERJAWS – "write JABBERJAWS on the chalkboard. Each time children talk when they are not supposed to be, erase a letter. At the end of the day, if there are letters left, the children get that many minutes of free time."

PAWS

Class store

Apples on apple trees

Class piggy bank

Behavior puzzle

Surprise!

A silent cheer

Pasta discipline

Who's watching

Proper Pennies: pennies (copied from math book) to be spent in prize box

Class stoplight

Round'em up

I spy

Reward jar

Colored cards

Frogs on lily pads

Puppy love

Rockets to the moon (to space, to Saturn, to the universe)

And on, and on, and on...

One particular online exchange, titled "ocean themed discipline plan"—which will follow this discussion—is representative of the nature of these systems and the effect of a misdirected focus on the techne' mode of inquiry as cautioned in Henderson and Kesson's (2004) *Curriculum Wisdom*:

> Educators are often so caught up in the refinement of craft knowledge, the day-to-day business of teaching, and the pressures of the profession that we...fail to continuously ask the more meaningful 'why' questions. Concern with techne'—with the details of method, process, and technique—can cause us to fail to see the forest for the trees. (p. 49-50)

The trees in this case may be what is presented as "moral education"—a picture of moral growth and education that conforms to the general notion that children should get morally better as they develop, and that moral education entails a process of gradual building up of virtue through socialization into one's "cultural norms" (Bennett 1993, Lickona 1991, Wynne and Ryan 1993). If this is true— *if* moral development is built on preset "cultural norms" which children must be molded to fit, then systems of coercion may make sense, at least when admiring the trees and, so, losing the forest.

Recall Noddings's (2002) question: "Can coercion be a sign of caring?" She notes that many teachers would insist "that the coercion they exercise...is indeed a manifestation of caring. It is 'for their own good.'" Alice Miller (1983/1990) describes this as "poisonous pedagogy," a rigid and coercive pedagogy that "seeks to substitute the will of the teacher for that of the student...insisting that what they are demanding is right and that coercion and cruelty, if they are used, are necessary 'for the child's own good'" (in Noddings 2002, 29).

Indeed, in reading over the content in the following chat room excerpts, the concept of coercion for the children's own good is clearly evident. This chat board posting from *http://teachers.net/ chatboard* requesting help with a craft-oriented discipline plan elicited a number of responses. It concerned a teacher's question about a system of management to "go with" her current academic theme: the ocean.

Post: Any ideas about an ocean themed discipline plan?
Posted by Ann on 5/31/07

For next year I am having an ocean theme. However, I cannot think of any cute ideas for a behavior plan. I read somewhere (can't remember where though) the behavior board said, "Behavior Bay." I am not really sure what I would do for a board like this but I like the title. If anyone has any good ideas please share.

Ann

Posted by HDGuy on 5/31/07
    Hmmm...

SUPPORT: As the ocean supports the ship, we Support each other. We want each other to not only float, but swim really well. And so, in our shipboard classroom (on our island), we want each other to succeed at everything!

SAFETY FIRST: In order for us to have fun without endangering anyone else, we must create Safety. That might mean "No Running" aboard ship, but it means "Be Kind" in our shipboard classroom (on our island).

Good luck!
Tom

Posted by Carolyn on 6/01/07
You can also have a board that has clown fish and sharks. The clown fish represent good, respectable fish. The sharks represent bad behavior.

As the main theme, the clown fish (students) are trying to get across
the ocean safely without being disturbed by the sharks (disrespect,
bad behavior). Put the clown fish across the board as you feel they
deserve it. If that student misbehaves, start moving a shark down from
above (or up from below), indicating the clown fish is getting closer
to the "danger zone." Corrected behavior, and the shark is sent back
down (or above). This way, you're not punishing the child (clown fish),
but pointing out the inappropriate behavior that is being done (the
shark).

You can even incorporate different kinds of sharks to represent
different kinds of misbehavior (great white = rude to teacher, nurse
shark = talking out, etc.) You can even add dolphins in to indicate
overall good classroom behavior or really smart choices (because
dolphins are so smart!) If there are five dolphins by the end of the
week, the kids are given some sort of reward/recognition. Make the
board interactive and allow students with exceptional behavior to add
their own "ocean" contribution: coral reef, another type of fish, etc.
Watch how the board comes to life!

I can hear it now: "The teacher told me I was a dolphin today!" "I got
eaten by two nurse sharks AND a great white in class today"...That
would make for interesting dinner conversation!
Posted by Tom(HDGuy) on 6/01/07

___

Carolyn,
WOW!! I love this! What a great idea, and what a terrific way to have
fun while enabling a whole new understanding of the support process!
This makes me want to go to whatever classroom uses this notion and
live there for awhile!!
All my best,
Tom

___

Posted by Carolyn on 6/01/07

Why thanks, Tom!

I literally thought it up while sitting here at the computer. I've never
seen this done in the classroom by any other teacher, it was just
a burst of creativity from my brain. One thing that should probably
be said about this idea: There needs to be some form of back up
or notetaking the teacher needs to write down at the end of every
day—should kids decide to manipulate the fish themselves. That way,
the teacher has some way to pick up where they've left off from the
day before, should there be any type of "creative interference."

The great thing about this board idea (sorry to brag) is that it offers
an immediate assessment of how the class is behaving overall. By

> knowing what the fish represent, the teacher can turn to the students at any time of the day and say, "Wow, there are way too many sharks on this board right now—let's try to get them to swim away, ok?" or "Look at all the dolphins in the water! Wow! What a wonderful view of the ocean we have all created together!"
>
> Carolyn
>
> (posted on 5/31/07 and 6/1/07 on teachernet.com)

The above represents a "how to" notion of teaching, schooling and especially *managing* children—a focus on techne'—the *craft* knowledge that sometimes blurs the view of the forest. Further troubling is the issue of variously deficient children whose presence serves to complicate the smooth application of these methods and techniques. The children in this teacher's room were to be eaten by a shark for disobedience such as talking out (a nurse shark), or being rude to teacher (a great white); only the children with exceptional behavior would be permitted to add their own ocean contribution; and finally, the children were *expected* to cheat and so force the teacher to make contingency plans via note-taking in order to circumvent any creative interference by the children (maybe a tiger shark would eat those children). The obscuring trees in this forest were assumptions these teachers held about the children as deficient and therefore in need of coercion and manipulation—for their own good—by those who are less deficient.

This view of children as in need of socialization and better preparation for the world of school was brought to the front page of the local section of a city newspaper in a report on pupils' readiness, or lack thereof. Leading with a headline asserting that urban districts cite insufficient preparation, the article claimed that research correlated poor kindergarten readiness as the most important reason for the gap in achievement between rich children and poor children. The featured kindergarten teacher expressed shock upon returning to teaching in the city schools, comparing those children to the students she had been teaching in the suburban top performing school that her own children attended. She was exasperated and claimed to be killing herself while trying to catch them up on what *they didn't have*. Like the teachers who communicated on the next chat board entry, these deficient children had become in her eyes (and heart), not kin or kind, but were killing her.

While most of the discussions on the chat boards are related
to techne'/craft, a good number are related to teachers' similar
viewpoints about children—that they are killing us with their deficiencies, immaturity, disobediences, inadequacies, and negative
character traits, such as being ungrateful. Here is one chat-board
discussion, also from *http://teachers.net/chatboard,* titled "How to
handle ungrateful students":

Post: How to handle ungrateful student????
On 11/24/06, kat wrote:

Hi, everyone! I've been teaching 3rd grade for a few years now and I
do really enjoy this grade level. I have set rules and procedures in my
classroom and the kids understand them. As a bonus, I have a bulletin
board (For November it was titled 'Turkey-rific Behavior'), where the
kids have to ALL be following the rules to earn a reward to staple to
the board. They must earn 25 and then we can vote on a class-wide
reward. On the back of a few of the rewards, there are short (5 min)
games that we play or I spontaneously read a fun poem aloud, etc.
This system has been fun for the class (and me) in the past, but this
year, it seems that after we do the fun small reward, I'll have kids that
seem ungrateful. For example, I heard someone groan after the small
reward was revealed! After the class-wide reward, I actually had a kid
tell me that he didn't have a good time! The kids do know that this is
just a fun 'extra' thing I do....I've decided that if I leave school at the
end of the day unhappy or bothered, it's not worth it to me anymore. If
I tell the kids that the games have to stop, am I punishing the kids who
are grateful and deserving? Your thoughts are appreciated.

On 11/26/05, ha ha wrote:

Over the years I have noticed that kids have more of a sense of
entitlement and no ability to express gratitude whatsoever. Last
Christmas, I gave each kid a ruler with his or her name painted on it.
All of the kids looked very miffed. One actually said, 'This is it?' So, I
took all the rulers back, broke each one in half, and threw them in the
trash. It was worth every dime to see the look of shock on their faces.
Extreme, but it got the point across.

On 11/26/06. ellen wrote:

Wow. That must have felt good. But really, doesn't this sort of thing just
make you want to not spend a dime of your own money on them?

The content of these postings is extraordinarily telling. My experience in schools, as a teacher and as a university facilitator/ researcher, has provided a long-term window into the zeitgeist of teacher/child relationships—one that frightens me. For teachers adhering to relationships with children based on systems of rewards and punishments and the advice of child-rearing experts such as John Rosemond, their regard for children is conditional on how well the children meet their adult needs ("I've decided that if I leave school at the end of the day unhappy or bothered, it's not worth it to me anymore"). Indeed, "children who fulfill their parents' [and teachers'] conscious or unconscious wishes are 'good' but if they ever refuse to do so or express wishes of their own that go against those of their parents, they are called egoistic and inconsiderate" (Miller 1979/1990, 12).

As in many of the exchanges on this chat-board, the initiator asked for help with a problem or concern. And, again, as in many of the exchanges asking for input, the concern had to do with: (a) fill in the adjective (some deficiency—e.g., ungrateful, noisy, tantrum-throwing, interrupting, talkative, lazy, defiant, disrespectful) students; (b) efficient and easy ways to manage said (some deficiency) students and/or; (c) techniques that no longer seem to work like they did before. If one spends time reading through any random sampling of these unsolicited and candid discussions, one might get the impression that these teachers don't much like the children in their classrooms.

The Teachers

The following are brief introductions to Katie Krinkle and Michael Scott, the teachers who volunteered their classrooms for this study.

Katie Krinkle

I have known Mrs. Krinkle for over twenty years. I previously had taught in the same school district, although never in the same school building. We became acquainted as we participated in kindergarten curriculum development for the school system and as we facilitated system-wide workshops for kindergarten teachers. In these inter-building associations, it was often Mrs. Krinkle and I who were aligned together against the majority of the teachers and administrators in selection of system-wide texts, curriculum decisions in math, science and language arts, and especially in advocating for children in those contexts. We shared a similar concern that many educators involved in large-scale decision-making grossly underestimate the intellectual, moral and social capabilities of young children. Even though we also share some fundamental differences in our beliefs about ways to enact our regard for children, I have considered Mrs. Krinkle an ally in the schools for a very long time.

While Mrs. Krinkle and I do not always agree about everything related to Kindergarten, I trust Mrs. Krinkle's deep regard for children. I have observed her with children, and have listened to her talk about her students—always with respect and enjoyment.

I am not the only one who sees Mrs. Krinkle as different—her colleagues do, too. She is highly respected and is/had been a leader in her building. I qualify the leadership part because of what Mrs. Krinkle told me when I expressed concern to her about what seemed to be happening with math in a first grade classroom upstairs. She said, "Yes, I thought I had them convinced—it was much better a couple of years ago, but with the tests and all the pressure for the kids to get those scores up, they're [the teachers] too scared to think for themselves anymore."

More significantly, teachers in Mrs. Krinkle's school demonstrate their view of her by sending her their problems. Every year, Mrs. Krinkle receives two to four "new" students. These are generally not children who had recently moved into the neighborhood, but are children from other classrooms. When a teacher can't handle a child anymore, the student is sometimes sent to Mrs. Krinkle's room as a time-out, but just as often, the child is moved to Mrs. Krinkle's classroom permanently.

A note to include here in a discussion of Mrs. Krinkle is her smile. It is not the practiced, scripted smile described by Wong and Wong, nor is it the measured smile of David Jardine's (1998) puzzled student teacher. Rather, Mrs. Krinkle's smile is an artifact of her connection to the children. She looks deeply and smiles, for "the source of a true smile is an awakened mind…[and] smiling helps you approach the day with gentleness and understanding" (Hanh 1990b, 3).

Michael Scott

On my first visit to Mr. Scott's school, I noticed outside every class-room a bank of lockers. Every single classroom had labeled these lockers with children's names. Moreover, *nearly* every single class-room had placed on those lockers die-cut, store-bought shapes with the children's names written on them by teachers. And *nearly* every classroom had a theme: dogs, frogs, smiley faces, apples, triceratops, stars, balloons, bulldogs (the local high school's mascot), compo-sition books (various colors), bees, bones, "school"(bells, apples, books, crayon boxes, pencils, rulers). However, Mr. Scott's lockers had wrinkled up, somewhat scribbly nametags. He had given each child a half sheet of white paper on which the children wrote their own names and decorations. Without even benefit of lamination, the children proudly hung their nametags on the lockers they shared with one another and with the afternoon kindergarten (one locker had **five** nametags on it!), and I noted that individual children some-times made adjustments to their nametags when passing them.

Michael Scott was, during the time of the study, an eight-year veteran of teaching. His experience, like Mrs. Krinkle's, was all in kindergarten and in the same classroom where he started. He teaches next door to another male kindergarten teacher—his men-tor teacher during student teaching. At the time of the study, I had known of Mr. Scott for about two years. While I did not meet him until he was a student in a graduate class I taught in the summer of 2006, I knew of him from his role as a mentor teacher to a student I had had in class the previous fall. This class was a *Guidance of Young Children* class—and I had learned through the field student in Mr. Scott's class that her mentor teacher was interested in the ideas we talked about in class regarding ways to teach with care and regard for children as a paramount consideration. By coincidence, he came to join my course that summer—a course that was relat-ed to building thoughtful, caring "sociomoral environments" for early childhood classrooms. Mr. Scott devoured the readings and engaged in discussion with an intensity derived from a deep inter-est in the intellectual, moral and emotional aspects of the teaching relationship.

Mr. Scott, like Mrs. Krinkle, reported that the colleagues in his building view him as "different." His method of trusting children to travel to the bathroom individually as needed, his rule of not talking *too much* (as opposed to not at all) in the hallways, and of course, his less-than-stellar locker design mark him as perhaps (as colleagues warned him about three of his incoming kindergartners after seeing them on the first day of school) "out of control." He also told me that after one trip to the restroom too many for some, he realized that "my children have defiled the sanctity of the hallway," and playfully called the reactions of the other teachers the "sanctimonious and the profane."

Summary

This chapter presents an overview of Schools, Kindergarten, and Teachers, as well as of the particular schools, kindergartens and teachers involved in this study. These descriptions represent, as qualitative inquiry requires, "experience or create[d] qualities worth experiencing...[requiring] an ability to notice and to appreciate the symbolic import of social objects and activity....We can ask: What are our classrooms made of? What is the character of the tasks we ask students to engage in?" (Eisner 1998, 126).

The purpose of this chapter is twofold. The first function is to provide a picture of, and an educational criticism of, school, and especially its structured order, including the procedures and rules that the children must negotiate. In order to discuss children's disobedience in kindergarten classrooms, one must have an understanding of what is expected of obedient children. This chapter serves to remind that, for the most part, teachers in schools expect obedient children to be quiet, to be in the right place at the right time, to keep oneself to oneself, and to cooperate with the adult in charge.

The second function of this chapter is to introduce the particular teachers, schools and kindergartens involved in this study in order to place them in the larger context of school, but also to provide a context for the moments of disobedience that are described next in chapter 5.

Chapter 5

Moments in Kindergarten: Findings and Analysis

Small things—the morning, perspective—can be lost in
    the bowels of the earth,
in tunnels where trains convey bodies, human beings with
    purposes,
human beings surviving.

~ Wenner (2004, 3)

Introduction

I worry about small things being lost. This chapter serves to hold small moments up to the light in order not only to see them, but to value them just as much as big things. This book seeks to see through experienced and concurrently fresh eyes qualities (which can be very small things) worth experiencing in a kindergarten classroom, and to express and complicate these qualities via rhizomatic logic to the readings of the children's moments of disobedience in order to "build complex and diverse pictures of " the texts of children's interactions (MacNaughton 2005, 144–145).

In considering these readings of children's texts uncovered in classroom contexts, MacNaughton (2005) has cautioned:

> The everyday language, ethics, routines, rituals, practices, ex-pectations, ideas, documents and invocations of quality in early childhood services are formed through and motivated by very particular understandings of children and how best to educate them. Over time, some of this knowledge has settled so firmly into the fabric of early childhood studies that its familiarity makes it just 'right', 'best' and 'ethical'. (p. 112)

In the previous chapter were descriptions of the structured expectations of schools, classrooms and teachers in general—including the rules, routines and regulations constituting the implicit lessons that Phillip Jackson (1968) has termed the "hidden curriculum." In descriptions of the two schools, two classrooms and two teachers involved in this particular study, the hidden curriculum is in play, "socializing students to the norms, values, purposes of schooling" (Pace and Hemmings 2007, 13)

It is important to note here that the goal in spending time in these classrooms with these teachers is not to comment on these discourses or to say the teachers are "wrong." As Pillow (1997) discusses, the teachers in her work and the teachers I watched and engaged with in the process of this research are dedicated, caring professionals for whom I have the highest respect. However, in the process of "situat[ing] and attempt[ing] to understand what impact the regulatory function of [teacher control] may have on [the moments of disobedience] spoken and embodied in these classrooms" (p. 361), it is necessary (and desired) to confront the choices and actions made by these teachers in the course of their actions within the context of the selected moments.

This chapter details particular events that occurred within the walls of Mrs. Krinkle's and Mr. Scott's classrooms and schools— events that I have named "moments of disobedience." Disobedience, in this study, describes an action or interaction that appears to disregard or defy structured expectations. These expectations might be explicitly stated (verbally or textually), or they might be implicitly expressed via the physical arrangement of school, normalizing procedures and rituals, and/or something as simple as a glance from another child.

For each of the three moments of disobedience that comprise this chapter—*Right Here, Right Now*; *Behind Her Back*; and *Shoulder to Cry On*—I offer the following: (a) a context, (b) a description of the moment via transcriptions and narrative, (c) a recap of the moment, (d) a rhizomatic analysis of the moment by laying another text or texts over the text of the moment, and (e) a brief description of what those texts do to the original text (the moment of disobedience).

Recall that rhizoanalysis is a means to explore the politics of a text in order to create new texts as it serves to both deconstruct and reconstruct a text. It deconstructs a text (e.g., a research moment or child observation) by "exploring how it means; how it connects with things 'outside' of it, such as its author, its reader and its literary and non-literary contexts; and by exploring how it organizes meanings and power through offshoots, overlaps, conquests and expansions" (Alvermann 2001, 120).

Moment of Disobedience: "Right Here, Right Now"

The following moment of disobedience is representative of children's responses to the time and space constraints of the kindergarten classroom. A kindergarten teacher is expected to marshal each year's crop of kindergartners into the very specific structure of school. As described by Wong and Wong (1998), "the effective teacher establishes good control of the class in the very first week of school" (p. 4). And the job of the kindergarten child is to synthesize the stated, the implicit, and the structural cues in order to seamlessly take on the role of the good kindergartner. These school/kindergarten expectations are guided by normative rules of events. Complicating matters is that these tacit rules vary according to situation. Children and teachers must learn the rules and expectations for each situation, recognize the differences, and produce behavior appropriate to each situation (Mehan 1979).

As in Mehan's work, studying the lessons learned by taking part in the organizations of school, children are actively involved in making sense of the everyday events of the kindergarten classroom, and are, in fact, working with their teacher in contributing to its organization. Often this organization is taken for granted and not remarked upon. Attending to the organization can sometimes require an outside or sideways viewpoint.

One of my earliest recollections of looking askance at what I see involves a long-ago visit from my brother to my kindergarten classroom. He had come to chaperone a field trip that day and was early. I remember feeling embarrassed by what I assumed he would view as disorder and chaos and a lack of control on my part as the teacher in this kindergarten classroom. But instead, here is what he said: "It's amazing. (And I waited for the hammer to fall.) You ask them to come to the carpet and they come. You turn the page in the book, and they get quiet so they can hear the next page. You say 'clean up' and they do. It's amazing." And I realized—it was!

An important aspect of any effort to study moments of disobedience is that an understanding or at least an awareness of the fundamental order of the context situation is required if one is to be able to spot disorder. And most certainly, the fundamental order is generally taken for granted as it was above when all I could see in that particular instance were the parts that stuck out: the disobediences. My brother saw the order and rule of kindergarten—and probably saw the minor disobediences that so concerned me as part and parcel of that larger order. In all discussions of moments of disobedience in this chapter, the larger compliant order is included as a necessary prerequisite for said disobedience.

Setting Boundaries

The arrangement of Mr. Scott's classroom (and any kindergarten classroom) reflects the expectations of each space. Table arrangements—the placement of the tables as well as the distributions among them—determine whether and with whom children can interact during the times the children are directed to sit at those tables. Spaces for gathering—the carpet and the lesson areas—are open with a designated teacher chair to cue the children where they should direct their attention. Some center areas—the block area, the library, make-believe and the math tubs area—are somewhat hidden. Placed in corners or against walls with furniture dividing the spaces from clear lines of vision in the classroom, these places offer the children opportunities to act without consistent surveillance. Field notes documenting the children's interactions while working in these areas of the classroom often included a range of bawdy or bathroom talk (whispered, snickering comments about butts and heinies, giggling and pointing out pictures of partially naked characters in books like *In the Night Kitchen* and *I'm Going to Run Away*, and one gasp-filled, mouth-covering conversation about whether or not Mr. Scott poops), as well as physical interactions that included sword play (with snapped-together math cubes), paddling one another with the long wooden blocks, and, on a more gentle note (but just as frowned upon in school) lying on top of one another and stroking hair.

However, while children recognize these spaces as places of relative freedom from surveillance, it is the teacher who generally arranges the spaces and determines who may go to these spaces and when. While kindergarten is unusual among school classrooms in the relatively generous allotments of free space, classroom arrangements are still "designed to maximize the teacher's ability to keep an eye on students" (Nespor 1997, 133). This is true in Mr. Scott's room, too.

Mr. Scott's Articulations of Order

The following are descriptions of a selection of the many and varied attempts by Mr. Scott to help the children in the morning kindergarten at Shadow Lake Elementary School adapt to the time and space constraints inherent to kindergarten. The moments were gathered via videotape during the first few weeks of school as Mr. Scott carefully articulated the boundaries that define the time and space of kindergarten. The following transcripts and descriptions offer some examples of the means Mr. Scott used to engage the children in kindergarten expectations regarding where they should be and when. This particular snapshot of Mr. Scott's classroom was taped as the children arrived on that September morning.

The children on entry moved independently to seats at three rectangular tables and two trapezoidal tables pushed together to make one hexagonal table—with about six chairs at each table. Most children placed their backpacks on their seatbacks—hanging them by their straps—even though they had lockers in the hallway.

The children were talking and some moved from table to table before choosing one at which to sit. The conversations remained generally confined to those sitting nearby—either at the same table or at chairs that were adjacent to one another at the closest tables. The talking rose and fell in volume. Some children were absently playing with the crayons that fill the plastic tubs. While there was some movement once seated—turning in seat to speak to another child, arm reaching into crayon tub—it was as if their bottoms were glued to chairs; not one child left his or her chair once seated (although Fred and Jamie dawdled choosing a chair, walking from table to table with their book bags held in front of them as if ready to place them on their chairs).

Line

103.   T: ((walks between and around the tables carrying a laptop, which he is absently looking at and typing as he walks))

104.   T: ((looks at the clock periodically and as the time draws near to 9:00, moves toward the chair that is placed against the chalkboard very near one of the tables, and sits, slowly typing))

105.   T: OK friends, that bell's going to ring any minute

106.   (unknown child): Yes sir

107.   ((Buzzer from loudspeaker))

108.   ((Children continue to talk loudly and engage in hand play—at one table four children have their hands in the crayon tub, two of them pulling at one crayon)).

109.   T: Boys and girls, there's the bell

110.   T: There's the bell and it tells us be ready to listen. Because the uh ((1.0)) the morning announcements are coming on

Mr. Scott's actions and statements indicated an awareness of the time elements inherent in the kindergarten day. Even during a relatively relaxed portion of the day— arrival—a time in which the children were engaged in casual conversation with one another and there is some ease in the structure of time and space. Recall: "The children are talking and some move from table to table before choosing one at which to sit"; Mr. Scott checked the clock (Line 104) and as he anticipated the impending announcements, cued the children via a gentle warning (Line 105, "Okay friends, that bell's going to ring any minute"). Finally, he directly explained the function of the bell (Line 110: "There's the bell and it tells us be ready to listen").

The children's actions for the most part demonstrate that the lessons of kindergarten are clear. With very little direction, the children know where to be and when. They have entered the classroom on their own—and have selected places to sit where they will stay until directed to move elsewhere. The children who resist these elements of the day are, for the purpose of this work, disobedient. Mr. Scott, for whom time was of paramount importance, and for whom the children's adherence to the "school" expectations was facilitative to his role as their teacher, expended a great deal of effort explaining to the children the time and space constraints of kindergarten. The following are brief non-sequential excerpts representing these efforts:

Line

111.   T: And the song is over. That means that it's time to walk on over to the calendar

112.   T: You're expected to be quiet and listening in three, two, one, zero, Mason, you need to scoot up I am worried that you'll bump your head

113.   T: Once again there are people who are not ready… it's not time to talk to a friend

114.   T: This is a turn-taking time.

115.   T: That'll have to wait ((to a kid who has offered a non se-quitor during sharing time, implying that it's not time for that))

116.   T: Wait till I say go ((spoken when one child gets get up too soon to go to centers—before all the groups were named))

117.   T: Noowww, I would like you to be able to move around the room and talk to anyone you want ((0.2)) however we're still sharing things from home. That's what we're talking about. That's what should be in our hands

118.   T: ((turns out the lights))—would everyone please put ev-erything away... carpet time is coming up

119.   T: Boys and girls, here's what we need and we need it right now

120.   T: Terocko, right here, right now. ((1.0)) Right here, right now

121.   T: Right away, I'm seeing a problem with our circle. The first problem we had was it took too long to make our circle

122.   T: ((after sending children back to their chairs)) Look at me right now. Our meeting is a waste of time ((0.5)) when people don't come to the carpet ready to listen when we get to the carpet

123.   T: That circle was a problem too, I saw people coming over and they were spinning around friends, like this ((demon-strates this while talking)).... And...(0.5). It was probably about two minutes before we could sit down.

124.   T: If you wanted to try out Billy Bob Joe's machine, Now's the time to do that. We're going to stay at the carpet. You can talk to anyone you would like now. You don't have to raise your hand for a turn. You can get up and move. You don't need to stay in a circle. You can talk to anyone now

125.   T: Boys and girls, here's what we need and we need it right now. Right here, right now. Right here, right now. And sit!

Mr. Scott used language along with nonverbal behavior and cues in order to continuously orient the children to expectations of the kindergarten classroom. He used the word "time" over and over, actually naming parts of the day: "time to walk on over to the calendar" (Line 111); "not time to talk to a friend" (Line 113); "turn-taking time" (Line 114); "carpet time" (Line 118); and "the time to do that" (Line 124).

In addition, he demonstrated to the children that he was actively keeping time and noting the passage of time. For instance: "You're expected to be quiet and listening in three, two, one, zero" (Line 112); "carpet time is coming up" (Line 118); "the first problem we had was it took too long to make our circle (Line 121); "Our meeting is a waste of time" (Line 122); and "It was probably about two minutes before we could sit down" (Line 123).

Finally, Mr. Scott delineated the places children should be at particular times and the importance of coordination of those elements. More often than not, he noted time as the children were to transition from one place to another: to come to the carpet, line up, go to the tables, get in a circle, go to centers, clean up, even to stand or sit (so, in the chair or not in the chair). In these non-sequential examples, Mr. Scott implied or specified place as follows: "That means that it's time to walk on over to the calendar" (Line 111); "Mason, you need to scoot up I am worried that you'll bump your head" (Line 112); "Noowww, I would like you to be able to move around the room" (Line 117); "((after sending children back to their chairs)) Look at me right now. Our meeting is a waste of time ((0.5)) when people don't come to the carpet ready to listen when we get to the carpet" (Line 122).

Mr. Scott named times via their function and implied function of space in his directions. Sitting in chairs implied a stasis—the children tended to stay there until called out, and a return to chairs was often used as means to interrupt what was occurring and/or as a means of control—because as the children sat in chairs, they were less likely to be in contact with one another, and their freedom of movement was impeded. A call to the carpet did not only name the place to come, but also the time to come (right now), and what to do/be on arrival (ready to listen). When expectations are different from this default structure, Mr. Scott must articulate as much: "We're going to stay at the carpet. You can talk to anyone you would like now. You don't have to raise your hand for a turn. You can get up and move. You don't need to stay in a circle. You can talk to anyone now" (Line 124).

Pushing Boundaries

As Mr. Scott and the children collaborated on their use of the time and space of the kindergarten, the boundaries were drawn and redrawn. Contrary to the inflexibility of the disciplined classroom as described by Wong and Wong and other experts in the field of classroom management, the teacher and the children in this classroom were responsive to one another as they interacted within it. Most of the children consistently remained within the boundaries with very little variation—and, in fact, did not move from one place in the classroom to another until cued to do so. When the cue did come—a verbal direction, a hand wave, a nod, a ringing bell—these children responded immediately and as prescribed. A few, though, often operated on the edges of these boundaries, sometimes pushing them out of shape a bit. When these boundaries of time and space *were* pushed, the teacher responded by either making new space for the broader boundary or pushing it back in. The following details a particular event involving snack time in which the time and space kindergarten boundaries were pushed by many of the children. Following this example, I will focus on one particular child, Mason, whose engagement with the time and space restrictions of kindergarten was particularly flexible.

Line

126.   T: We've got about two minutes to enjoy our snack (.01) before we go out to play.

The children continue to enjoy their snack and to talk with one another. Snatches of conversation can be heard related to what color the food is, how much one can put in a mouth, and lots of laughter, children generally stay in chairs while talking and laughing and eating, but periodically a child will get up to throw something away, to talk to someone at a different table, to walk out into the hall to get a drink, to put a lunchbox away, and to walk into the hall to use the restroom. The teacher is walking between tables and casually talking to the children and responding to their questions.

127.   Sally((to Mr. Scott)): Can we tell jokes?

128.   T: Yes, you can tell jokes, it's an excellent time for jokes

129.   Fred: knock knock....

130.   ((More of the enjoyment of snack (180.0).

131.   ((Mr. Scott has been checking the clock and is gauging the time left before the kindergarten recess is scheduled to begin.))

The three kindergarten classes in the school had arrangements to meet outside for recess, and the three kindergarten teachers took turns in supervision. In addition, Mr. Scott's class had lessons and specials scheduled for the time remaining for morning kindergarten after the scheduled recess. Mr. Scott was acutely aware of the constraints of time here, and to gently initiate the transition between snacks and clean up, he began reminding the children about some solutions they had suggested during a class meeting they had had before regarding concerns about snack.

Line

132.   T: There were a few helpful hints from you guys. ((.05)) One person said we need to get started right away. Another person said it's, ahh ((.02)) probably a good idea to talk quiiiietly while we do this; another person said as soon as you're done, see if you have a friend that needs your help. As soon as you are cleaned up, please sit down quiiietly at your table so we'll be getting ready for the playground

133.   ((As he is talking, the majority of the children are busily cleaning up: putting left over snack in lunch boxes, throwing away trash, leaving the room to go in the hall with lunchboxes or book bags, and then sitting down. Some are not.))

134.   T: Mason, are you all cleaned up, friend?

135.   Mason: ((off camera)) yeah...

136.   T: One helpful hint was to do it right away ((checks two more tables))

137.   T: Now, Mason, it's time to clean up so close the lunchbox

138.   Mason: ((enters camera range with lunch box))

139.   T: And put it away.

140.   Mason: ((with lunchbox, trots over to another table, swinging the box, and after weaving in and out of every chair and table with arms outstretched, reaches the counter by the sink and carefully sets his lunchbox on it and then crawls beneath Cupcake's and Fred's table and disappears from view))

141.   T: Mason, you're done cleaning up? Have a seat in your chair

142.   T: ((continues to walk from table to table making suggestions for cleaning up)) Hey, guys, have a seat in your chair when you are finished cleaning up ((2.0))

143.   ((Most of the children have already cleaned up and are sitting quietly and patiently waiting for the next direction from Mr. Scott—the direction that will transition them outside. However, some children are still eating, some are talking to a friend while their snack wrappers lie in front of them on the table, and some children have not yet returned to their seats.))

144.   T: Hey guys, recess is starting without us. We're having the same problem that we did before ((walks out to the doorway and checks down the hall for children to return from restroom ((3.0))

145.   ((Na'ton and Billy come back in the room—either from the restroom or from their lockers))

146.   ((Mason and Lemmie are seated at their tables but are engaging in hand play—each taking turns laying a hand flat on the table, palm up so that the other can smack it, if they can time it before the hand-on-table person snatches it away.))

147.   T: C'mon over and have a seat at the carpet

148.   T: Now. Come to the carpet and come ready to listen...

149.   Sally: Can I throw this away?

150.   T: Please do—it should have been thrown away about 10 minutes ago

151.   T: Mason, I want you right here and I want you to listen

152.   ((Mr. Scott has walked to the carpet— and the children have followed him, many pushing in chairs as they rise and are, for the most part, silent as they make this transition. When they are all seated, Mason included, Mr. Scott reasons with them.))

153.   T: Does it matter if we get outside?

154.   ((children indicated their answer with raised hands, and)) "yeah, yeah"

155.   T: Now what you guys are telling me is that you want to go outside on time, and you are also telling me that snack time is important to you. But you need to be trustworthy in order for it to work. Right now do you think I am thinking we're going to have a good clean up time tomorrow?

156.   (children): noooooooo

157.   T: I am worried about it

158.   Sally: ((fingers in mouth, kind of cute-girl-ish)) no you're noooootttt

159.   T: Yes. ((1.0)) I am

160.   T: We have only about 4 minutes. Very quick play time. We wasted a lot of time cleaning up

161.   T: Now let's line up behind Allie

162.   ((The children, en masse, get up from the carpet and hurry into what approximates a line. Terocko has hurried enough that he is the first in line, not Allie.))

163.   Sally: ((loudly)) There's a boy in front ((2.0)) There's a boy in front!!!

164.   ((The children are in a rough line, many are talking, hands are snatched, pulling one another, hands around necks, hands touching hair....))

165.   (unidentified child/ren): OWWWW

166.   Sally: There's a boy in fr....

167.   (unidentified child) OoHHHH

168.   T: We have about three minutes left guys

169.   (unidentified child): Ohhhwww!

170.   (unidentified child): OOOOWWW!

171.   (unidentified child, loudly): STOP!!

172.   T: Sit down in your chairs. We're out of time. Sit down in your chairs. We're out of time

173.   T: Sit down, we're out of time. Sit down, we're out of time.

In this excerpt, a small number of children were engaged in various kinds of disobedience: taking too much time (Lines 134-139; 142-153); disregarding function of space, in this case the quiet and physically separate space of The Line (Lines 162-173); and disdaining the expectations of transitional times as ones in which one is to be relatively quiet and so ready to listen, and still, and so ready to move on command (Lines 148; 150; 161-172). What I did not clearly describe, however, is that of the 23 children, most of them—18 or so— were totally compliant with the stated and unstated expectations. These children assisted in drawing and maintaining the kindergarten boundaries and quietly pulled back as individual members pushed them out. It was not Mr. Scott alone who set these boundaries, but it was with the children's tacit agreement. They were complicit in the process of setting these boundaries, and their compliance pointed to the non-compliance of the dissidents.

In later conversations, Mr. Scott worked to reason with them about the bargains to be made with time and about the basic idea of time as a commodity—IF it takes too long to clean up from snack, we're late for recess. IF it takes too long to clean up for snack, we might not have snack anymore. IF we cannot line up quietly in the allotted amount of time, we miss recess. He must also communicate that having snack is not necessarily a done deal by saying, "Every day, in school, you guys have been able to count on me to say, 'Time for snack.'" This while problemitizing whether or not to have snack or not. Ever again.

Mason Stretches Boundaries:
Right Here, but Not Now; Right Now, but Not Here

After the children were out of time and sent back to their seats, Mr. Scott reluctantly went to the board to where he had posted the schedule for that day.

Line

174.   T: So let's take a look at our schedule here. Also outside recess is finished

175.   Mason: But we always go outside

176.   T: Not today

This little exchange is important because in this next series of moments of disobedience, I will be focusing on Mason and his particular brand of negotiating the time and space boundaries of kindergarten. Watching Mason push and pull boundaries of time and space in kindergarten led me to sometimes wonder if he had any idea of what is happening in the kindergarten, and at other times, to wonder if he is anticipating and aware of more than even the teacher. He bridged from moment to moment a vagueness about, and an acute awareness of, the workings of the kindergarten. His statement above, "but we always go outside" was a reminder to Mr. Scott that he (Mason) knows the way it (Kindergarten) works. And the absence of going outside became a palpable presence to Mason, as he questioned Mr. Scott three times later that morning about going outside: "Don't forget: outside, Scott," "When are we going outside?" and "Have we gone outside yet?" In making sense of the events of kindergarten, Mason had built some structures that were indelible: the components of the day remain constant even though the timing of them and their actual enactment may vary.

This holds true in the following descriptions of Mason's flexible participation in the kindergarten. Each vignette offers some context and then Mason's response to that context. These moments of Mason's disobedience are ones in which he engages with the boundaries set by kindergarten, Mr. Scott and the other children as if those boundaries were elastic—stretching but not breaking.

"I Said It, Too": Mason Fakes the Pledge

Mr. Scott and the children were preparing to participate in saying the Pledge of Allegiance at the close of the morning announcements.

Line

177. PA: I would like ...

178. ((Fred stands))

179. PA: you to stand as

180. ((Mr. Scott lifts both hands in a rising motion and the children begin standing and pushing in chairs. Some turn to face the place in the room where the flag is placed))

181. PA: we slowly and proudly recite the pledge of allegiance

182. T ((with some approximations by most students)): I pledge allegiance to the flag

183. ((Bravo puts knees on chair))

184. T and children: of the united states of America

185. ((Bravo sits))

186. T and children: and to the republic

187. ((Fred sits, Mason scratches knee while facing the chalkboard (not the flag)))

188. PA: I pledge allegiance to the flag

189. T: Oh! They just started ((laughs)) to...To the flag of the united states of

190. ((Eric picks a wedgie))

191. T, PA and children: America and to

192. ((Bravo taps Fred))

193. ((Frank, with both hands on his stomach escalates his twisting motion))

194. T, PA and children: the republic

195. ((Eric begins shifting weight from foot to foot))

196. T, PA and children: for which it

197.   ((Mason scratches his head and is facing the back of the room))

While the disembodied voice of the principal gave direction, the children took their cues from Mr. Scott. Their compliance was generally complete—all the children stood when signaled to by Mr. Scott; many took part in a choral recitation of words approximating the pledge of allegiance—although the tape only picked up Mr. Scott's words as decipherable; the children's recitation was a low mumble with a random cadence. Within that space of compliance— that structure which presumes uniform participation—the children offered a wide range of variations within the small geographic area of "the seat" (not one child moved more than six inches away from his or her seat) and within the expectation of individual participation with the whole-group action. During the recitation of the pledge, I had trained the camera on a table of seven boys—including Mason. In fact, these children did comply—with variations—during the pledge. Some variations:

- Billy sat down before Mr. Scott even said "America"

- Frank turned his shoulders from side to side—the movements becoming progressively larger as the pledge continued

- Corn-on-the-Cob faced the wall that is 90 degrees to the left of the flag wall, but his right hand did approximate heart position

- Fred sat and stood at will throughout the pledge

- Mason looked around the room and rubbed his neck, scratched his head and faced every direction except toward the flag. He appeared totally oblivious to the event of the pledge—saying nothing, not even mumbling

- And yet, when the principal thanked them for joining her in say the pledge, Mason called out: "I said it, too!"

Mason did not stand out in this instance. His variations on compliance were not so different from many of the others at his table. What is telling about this particular event is that Mason moved quickly from an apparent disinterest and obliviousness to what was happening to making an overt attempt to reclaim his membership as a compliant member of the kindergarten, claiming for all to hear: "I said it, too!" This, on very small scale, was what defined Mason as a disobedient child in Mr. Scott's kindergarten class. As will be seen in the snapshots of Mason to follow, Mason worked the boundaries with a particular elasticity that stretched the time and place kindergarten boundaries in unexpected and inconsistent directions. In considering Mason's association with the kindergarten boundaries of time and space, he was a Mummenschanz performer, and the boundaries were the colorful spandex that covered him. As Mason contorted and pushed out against the rubbery fabric, he reshaped it—even while staying within the flexible confines of the fabric.

Where's Mason?

The following excerpts of the kindergarten day are contextualized, non-sequential snapshots of Mason as he interacted with the time and space constraints of kindergarten. Throughout the observation periods of this research, Mason stood out as he resisted these constraints, and as the majority of the other kindergartners did not.

It should be noted that Mason stood out in other ways. In this midwestern suburban kindergarten class, he was the only child of color. Mason is biracial: his mother is White; his deceased father was Black. He was also the youngest, entering school at four, and turning five during the first month of kindergarten. Mr. Scott also shared with me his understanding of Mason's sensitivity—acutely aware of any disapproval from Mr. Scott and transparently vocal when his feelings were compromised by that sense of disapproval. Later, Mr. Scott reported to me that Mason's father passed away several months after my visits and discussed with me how the respectful and caring relationship between the Mason and Mr. Scott (and the caring classmates) may have somewhat ameliorated the difficulties inherent in such a tragic and emotionally devastating circumstance.

Snapshot #1

Mr. Scott and the children were on the carpet discussing my presence with the camera. The children were sitting in a circle, and recall, sitting on the carpet implies not only a place to sit, but also a way of being: a call to the carpet not only names the place to come, but also the time to come (right now), and what to do/be on arrival (ready to listen). And as gleaned from hours of observation in this kindergarten, "ready to listen" means being quiet, looking in a prescribed direction (at the speaker, in front), and sitting down (whether on the carpet or on a chair). Therefore, Mason's moments of disobedience were related not only to his presence in the right place at the right time, but to his way of being in that particular place.

Line

198 . T: No one can really have a turn because if everyone's talking then no one's listening. We won't hear what we have to say unless you're gonna ask for a turn

199. T: Billy, did you have a question or something to say about this camera?

200. Billy: I think she's ((some talk about taping so that my kids can see what kindergarten is like))

201. Mason: ((sings)) dah dah dah dah

202. ((Mr. Scott touches his head gently and then his back))

203. Billy: ((quietly)) I think she's going to make a video to show her kids

204. T: You think she's going to make a video....

205. Mason ((begins singing again)) doo doo doo doo

206. T: Oh—right now, what are we talking about?

207. Mason: ((looks behind himself and very slowly begins to scoot backward away from the circle and toward Mr. Scott's chair. Eventually he has removed himself from the circle and then slowly and surreptitiously shifts toward Mr. Scott's empty teacher chair placed immediately outside the circle and next to the book easel. With little fanfare, Mason backs up to the chair—still scooting—and slides up into it. While in the chair Mason kicks feet together, slides down and pushes back on the chair.))

208. T: Right now we are talking about Ms. Leafgren and her camera....

Once Mason had left the circle, he was free of the constraints inherent in the rule of kindergarten circles. First, he continued to slide up and down in Mr. Scott's chair—the chair that was out of Mr. Scott's line of sight. No other child remarked on Mason's desertion of the circle. He quietly slid up and sat in the chair, turning first and touching and seeming to count the magnetic letters on the board behind him, and finally getting up and walking to the easel, which was behind where Mr. Scott had squatted in the circle. He took a book from the easel, sat back down in the chair, and opened the book. Mr. Scott, who had not remarked on Mason's exit from the circle, now looked at him. He gently removed the book from his hands and placed it back on the easel. He shook his head. Mason frowned and slid down the chair onto the floor and remained seated on the floor but outside of the circle.

Snapshot #2

There was a period of time on the carpet where the children who have brought something to share show it to the others while still seated on the carpet. Mason had brought something, so had re-joined the circle. He was the second to share and told about the little notebook his mother gave him to "write in and draw in." After his turn, and while the other children spoke, he absently turned the pages in his notebook. Bravo had taken his turn last and was walking from child to child in the circle to let them touch his keychain. Mr. Scott began a transition:

Line

209.   T: While Brrrravvvo is showing everyone ((0.30)) his key-chain, ((0.5)) please put your eyes on me. I'm going to tell you what you're going to do next. ((1.5)) Next we're going to take, give everyone a chance to talk

210.   T: ((to Billy, touches his head)) did you hear that?

211.   T: You can talk to any person that you want. If you wanted to see something that someone brought or maybe try out Billy Bob Joe's ((1.0)) what did you call it? Machine?

212.   Billy Bob Joe: yeah

213.   T: If you wanted to try out Billy Bob Joe's machine, now's the time to do that. We're going to stay at the carpet. You can talk to anyone you would like now. You don't have to raise your hand for a turn. You can get up and move. You don't need to stay in a circle. You can talk to anyone now

The children moved in, closing the circle. Mr. Scott moved to the library area where he teaches language lessons. He was prepar-ing a tape and a book for the next lesson. Mason sat with the other children for 44 seconds. He looked toward Mr. Scott and rose on

one knee announcing: "I'm gonna read a book." He waited two seconds and repeated, "I'm gonna read a book," and he rose and walked
quickly and stiffly over to the area where Mr. Scott was working.
Mason slowed down as he approached him and tugged at the fabric
of his own shorts as he stood by Mr. Scott and repeated more quietly, "I'm gonna read a book. Scott. I am reading a book." Mr. Scott
listened and then pointed to the children still sitting and sharing
on the carpet: "We're doing this now." Ariel had picked up Mason's
notebook that he left on the carpet, and as he turned away from
Mr. Scott, she followed him and handed him his notebook. Mason,
still grasping the cloth of his shorts and the notebook, fake-limped
back to the group of children, but upon reaching them, took a slight
detour, placing the notebook on the chair he had sat in earlier, and
then arriving at the book easel, he once again took the book off its
shelf. Ariel stood beside him. Mason placed the book back on the
shelf and turned toward the board just as Mr. Scott arrived back at
the circle area. Mr. Scott gently touched Ariel, cueing her to return
to the group of children four to five feet away, and Mason turned
further toward the board and quietly walked to farthest corner of
the carpet and sat, watching the groups of children as they shared
their items from home.

Snapshot # 3

During a class meeting about whether or not to keep backpacks on
the chair backs or out in lockers, Mason, while remaining on the
carpet and basically in the circle, was:

• On his knees, with finger in mouth

• Balanced on combination of knees, forearm, head and hand, until
  lifting the hand to tap Na'ton, then leaned forward on hand and
  knees, shifting weight so that feet go upward, then shifted back to
  sitting on heels—raised hand in response to wanting to use locker
  and then swung back down to knees and forearms

• Sitting on his bottom but reached out and rubbed the curve of
  Na'ton's head, ending with a slight push. Na'ton looked briefly
  at Mason and Mason made a "yeah, so…" face…and put his arm
  akimbo against his side

• In crab walk position, on hands and feet, stomach up, bottom
  tucked under, head back

- Lying down on his back, knees bent and feet sliding back and forth across the carpet
- Sitting up and with legs straight in front of him, began to tap feet together
- Tapping Billy Bob Joe's head
- Pushing Billy Bob Joe's head back like it was a Pez dispenser

Thirty minutes later, when Mr. Scott had called them to the library area to listen to a book, Mason did the following while Mr. Scott read:

- Turned his body away from Mr. Scott, facing me
- Lay on his back with his feet in the air
- Bicycled his feet
- Turned to watch Corn-on-the-Cob rub the fabric of his pants
- Faced "wrong" directions
- Rolled as if putting out flames
- Walked his fingers up Corn-on-the-Cob's pant leg
- Stroked Flower's hair (but only for a moment—she yanked her head from his reach)

Snapshot #4

The children were sent to assigned centers. There were four or five children assigned to five centers, and Mr. Scott "rotated" the children though each center by timing them and announcing when and where to move. At first Mason remained with his group of five, but soon left the others and, anxious to get a book, joined Cupcake's group at the library. During his transition, he again made his stiff-legged (and I think tentative) walk—the walk that seemed to signal an awareness of being in/going to the "wrong" place. Mason lifted a book from the bookshelf. Terocko said "Hey!" and Mason took the book away from the library to the carpet part of the room.

Where's Mason? He Knows.

Mason's understanding of the kindergarten structures of time and place is clearly demonstrated in these snapshots. While his movements were not normalized to the class's movements, his flexible interpretations of their shared boundaries were apparently accepted and even expected. Even though Mason directly disobeyed several of Mr. Scott's directions and expectations (not "ready to listen" while on carpet, leaving assigned centers, otherwise being at the wrong place and the wrong time and with the wrong things in hand), he never totally pushed through the kindergarten boundaries. He was out of place, but still within the boundaries of place. He was "out of step and still part of the parade" (Leafgren, in Henderson 2004, 136).

The final example of Mason's elastic sense of time and space boundaries demonstrated his skill in negotiating the time and space constraints in kindergarten and the collaborative nature of the drawing of those time and space boundaries. Mason, once again, disobeyed the structured expectations, and so *influenced* those expectations.

Mason Sits in Mr. Scott's Chair Again

After the announcements that day, Mr. Scott noticed that some of the tables were "very very crowded" and some tables had empty spaces. So, he spent several minutes making adjustments to the distribution of children among the four classroom tables. As he named children to come join Sally at her table—first Emily and then Ariel—Mason called out: "me!!" Mr. Scott continued to name children, including Fred and Flash. "Bring your backpacks with you; come have a seat at this table." Without notice, Mason, who had not been named (and so not directed or expected to leave his seat) tiptoed by the camera on his way to sit on the chair on the carpet. Mr. Scott continued to direct the movement of the children, "Walk on over Emily. Flash will you come over, too? Keep Fred company. C'mon over here, bud. There's a chair for you right there." By this time, Mason had not only left his table but was sitting in the teacher's chair and sliding it up and down on the carpet.

Line

214.   Mason: Scott. ((Note: Mason often calls Mr. Scott by his last name sans the prefix of "Mr."))

215.   T: ((noting that Mason is seated at the gathering carpet, albeit in Mr. Scott's chair)) You're ready to go

216.   T: ((Walks over to Mason (on the carpet) and Mason mimes dribbling a basketball))

217.   T and Mason: ((Private exchange)).

218.   T: Oh it's not time to play basketball right now. I know what you're talking about, but we won't be using that

219.   Mason: ((stands with arms akimbo)).

220.   T: BOYS AND GIRLS. ((2.0)) Please stand up, push in your chairs ((1.5)) And join Mason and I on the carpet

221.   (Unknown child): Hey! He already knew we're going to be on the carpet

In this moment of disobedience, Mason was at the right place, but at not at the right time. Mr. Scott—he of the elastic boundaries—did not reprimand Mason, and in fact, used Mason's anticipatory position on the carpet in his transitional instruction to the other children (Line 220: "And join Mason and I on the carpet"). Mason (one of the children described as "out of control" by colleagues of Mr. Scott in chapter 4) demonstrated here his profound understanding of how his classroom works. He was making sense of the social situation of kindergarten and was able to apply his overt and tacit understandings of the boundaries co-drawn by Mr. Scott and the children in order to resist and so push those boundaries. In this way, Mason was an anomaly, as described by Mehan (1979), and acting purposefully even while acting anomalously. It was precisely his skill at learning the kindergarten boundaries that allowed him to effect change on them. Even the child who remarked on Mason's precipitate presence on the carpet did not point out that he was there at the "wrong" time, or that he wasn't in his seat where he was supposed to be—but instead, remarked: "Hey! He already knew we're going to be on the carpet" (Line 221). Mason "worked ahead," anticipating what was to come, and entering that place.

Mason played with these boundaries with great awareness and aplomb. Even with Mr. Scott's generous latitude with boundaries of time and space, Mason stretched them— he was often two steps ahead, behind, or sideways. His behavior sometimes seemed to indicate that he was oblivious to the expectations and the moment-to-moment occurrences. When Mr. Scott had spent so much time working through the causal relationship between snack clean up and recess, Mason was not actively attending, and so was, I believe, unaware that a fundamental shift in the structure of the kindergarten day had been made.

In fact, it was this rift that seemed to trouble Mason more than any stretching and misshaping had done for anyone else. Clean-up time may take too long, the circle may be left, but not the room—but the hole left by a missing element such as recess was not acceptable to Mason: "But we always go outside."

The children and teacher in this classroom, influenced by the moments of disobedience committed by Mason and others in the classroom, were relatively aware of, and receptive to, the elasticity of their time and space kindergarten boundaries. Moreover, as a consequence, more aware of the boundaries themselves.

Laying a Skateboarding Text

Unyielding and uncaring, we slide back and forth behind your vision

In search of the forgotten and useless.

~Nelson (2004)

In considering Mason's moments of disobedience in the above descriptions, the expected connections in analysis might be to developmental stages or methods of ameliorating his lack of fit to the time and space constraints of kindergarten. However, as befits a rhizomatic analysis, in seeking surprises in order to "disrupt the familiar and obvious" (MacNaughton 2004), other texts may be found on which to lay this particular text of a child's moments of disobedience. In this case, I seek to engage the reader in considering the inventiveness in Mason's resistance—and so the following is an analysis of this quality mapping a "new entry point" (Deleuze and Guattari 1987, 134-135).

Mason's sometimes oblivious, sometimes self-pleasing, and sometimes brilliant negotiation of the social terrain of the kindergarten was fluid, transpiercing, transforming, resistant, marginal, and often "outlaw." Outlaw in a way that resonates with the skateboarding subculture celebrated in the literature of the *Outlaw Collective* in which socio-spatial resistance is a way of life. As Nelson (2004) wrote, "I felt as though skateboarding not only allowed me to feel something in the world that others didn't seem to notice, but that skateboarding also pushed me into an odd marginal space in society where I wasn't a criminal (at least not always), but I wasn't a 'normal,' respectable youth either" (p. 1).

Mason often operated on the margins—even creating new margins as he pushed on the boundaries of the kindergarten space. In describing his negotiation as brilliant, self-serving and oblivious, I note that Mason seemed to feel something in the classroom that others didn't seem to notice—and seemed to *not* feel things others did notice; thus, the simultaneously occurring states of obliviousness and awareness. In the same spaces (the tables, the easel, the centers, and especially carpet) and times (lessons, centers, snack, recess, and especially gathering times) he shared with Mr. Scott and the other children, Mason saw, felt, and valued qualities and opportunities that allowed him to pick the boundaries up and slide beneath. As if he were a member of the *Outlaw Collective*, not really a criminal, but not normal/normalized either.

Flexible Space and Time

At an African-centered school where I taught several years ago, the children adopted their African day names—names bestowed based on the day of the week they were born, and by gender. Boys born on Thursday were called *Kwa*, and their overarching trait (their contribution and responsibility to the culture) was that of "transcendental pathfinder." One *Kwa* in my classroom was like Mason—seeing, feeling and valuing the kindergarten space in ways most of us did not. Like Mr. Scott's work with Mason, it was my job to bring *Kwa* somewhat into the fold, to help him see the boundaries and remain within them, even while remaining on the margins or pushing the boundaries out of shape a little. *Kwa* and I talked about this one day. Together we devised a signal that I would give him when I noticed him drifting to the edges or ripping and tearing down the fences marking the boundaries—which in some ways we needed. With my index finger, I traced on his chest a circle and told him that the circle was our kindergarten. And that while most of the people in there liked to travel in that circle in lines like this (drawing with my finger smooth, gently curving lines within the circle), that I could see he liked to go like this (traced wild squiggly lines in the circle). I told him that I noticed that, at times, his route was so wiggly and wild, that he left the circle—transpierced the boundaries in ways that left us behind. This communication between Kwa and me was often recalled with a signal. The signal—me tracing a circle on my own chest—was enough most days to call him back to an awareness of the boundaries of kindergarten. And watching him figure out ways to interact and move in and on the edges of kindergarten space and time allowed me to see the circle as much larger than I had thought it to be.

As the children in classrooms interact and co-create the space of kindergarten, they re-imagine the conditions of both their childness and of the school, often through a "youthful reinvention of the form and function of [school] spaces" (Nelson 2004, 4). In abandoning the vertical tree logic which separates the concept good from the lived good, children can find goodness in their own encounters with the world.

Like *Kwa* and like the skateboarders, Mason's reinvention of his school space was not only physical/functional, but generative and, in micro-ways, revolutionary. Borden's (2001) discussion of "micro-spaces" furthers the concepts of reinventing and revolutionizing spaces:

> When skateboarders ride along a wall, over a fire hydrant or up a building, they are entirely indifferent to its function or ideological content. They are therefore no longer even concerned with its presence as a building, as a composition of spaces and materials logically disposed to create a coherent urban entity. By focusing only on certain elements (ledges, walls, banks, rails) of the building, skateboarders deny architecture's existence as a discrete three-dimensional indivisible thing, knowable only as a totality, and treat it instead as a set of floating, detached, physical elements isolated from each other…skater's performative body has 'the ability to deal with a given set of pre-determined circumstances and to extract what you want and to discard the rest', and so reproduces architecture in its own measure, re-editing it as a series of surfaces, textures and micro-objects. (p. 214)

In the case of Mason, he was often clearly aware of the totality of the intersection of the time and space boundaries articulated by Mr. Scott and the other children: boundaries that included expected behaviors in certain places at certain times, and that also included each child as a member of the Kindergarten. Mason, however, more often experienced this totality in "micro-spaces," indifferent to its structured expectations. The elements of the classroom were acted on by Mason as floating, detached and isolated from each other. Coming to the carpet did not automatically mean the total package of "coming to the carpet" for Mason. While most of the other children knew what coming to the carpet meant (right now and ready to listen, which in turn meant sitting down, being quiet and looking at the speaker and/or up front) as a package deal, Mason did not behave as if he knew this. Mason came to the carpet often before or after the rest of the class. He did not just sit down: he sat, rolled, somersaulted, bicycled, touched, pezzed, wiggled, kicked, slid, scooted, and lay down. He re-edited the carpet space as a place to explore—a flat surface on which to lay the shapes and designs his body made, and a flexibly purposed space where, at least for a moment, one can come ready to listen or not.

Mason's interaction with the space in the classroom reflects the role of skateboarders in the city. Skateboarding transforms and mutates the objects and spaces of urbanity and "suggests that cities can be thought of as series of micro-spaces, rather than comprehensive urban plans, monuments or grand projects architecture is seen to lie beyond the province of the architect and is thrown instead into the turbulent nexus of reproduction" (Borden 2001, 217). Just so, The carpet and the classroom are not sacred, and while the teacher lays the design, it is disobedience that, like skateboarding, throws the structured expectations into a turbulent nexus of reproduction.

However, in these ultimately adult-owned spaces, freedom such as Mason's is hard won. As is detailed in chapter 4, in the name of their own good and in order to earn and keep the regard of their caregivers, children are admonished and driven to be good, to keep their hands to themselves, to mind their own business, to stay on task, to be still—ultimately to disengage from the world that envelops them. For most children—ones who are less likely to risk a normalizing adjustment—school does not offer skateboarder-like generativity. Rather, "their education destroys the special bent and leaves a dull uniformity" (J. Dewey 1916, 116).

When Lynch (1979) summarized his work on children's conceptions of the material environment, he was surprised by "how rarely we heard discussion of a playing field or of a school" (p. 104). Children, according to Lynch, believe that playing fields and school impose an order that limits bodily movement that might organize childhood space and so chart the shapes of pleasures and pains. Because of these limits, the children in Lynch's 1979 study focused on spaces that could be reworked for their own uses. Lynch suggested this was partly because children's spaces are too often "controlled by adults and their time controlled by adults" (p.107). Kids value settings for the possibilities they allow for bodily play and performance.

It is often suggested in studies of youth and skateboarding that there is a specific attraction to spaces of potentiality and possibility, to open spaces in which to play (Bradley 2001, Woolley and Johns 2001). This, however, causes problems for youth as "open space is highly regulated or closed and is where young people are expected to show deference to adults and to adults' definitions of appropriate behaviour" (Woolley and Johns 2001, 3). It is deceptive in its permission; there seems always to be a "but": "You can.... but..." And so, children learn quickly and thoroughly to gauge adult expectations—and learn about themselves in the process: "Kids are taught to control and regulate their bodies in ways acceptable to adults. But more important, as kids grow up the body ceases to be acknowledged as a primary tool for mediating relations with the world" (Nespor 1997, 122). As language literacy and other representations of communication replace the body for connecting to the world, those who resist sometimes feel a difference in their world experience—as this skateboarder describes:

> I started to realize that due to skating I was always looking down or my eyes were always scanning the surface for ledges, gaps or bumps.... I knew which lights I could make, which hills were smooth and where all the good curb cuts were. I even knew some neighborhoods right down to the last crack. That's when I realized that, as skaters, we live in an entirely different world. Our minds are no longer processing things in normal terms. (Scott Bourne, in Woolley and Johns 2001, 8)

Processing in normal terms may be considered the linear, arbolic model of thought, while the skater mirrors what Deleuze and Guattari (1987) might exhort us all to do: "Make rhizomes, not roots, never plant! Don't sow, grow offshoots! Don't be one or multiple, be multiplicities! Run lines, never plot a point! Speed turns the point into a line! Be quick, even when standing still! Line of chance, line of hips, line of flight!" (p. 24–25).

In the fashion of the rhizome, skateboarders and those others— such as a kindergarten child—disobey/ resist enclosure and stasis. However, when skateboarders are relegated to the reservation—the skatepark—it is recognized as a means of control. Lundry (2003) warned the skater:

> Skateparks should be ridden only as a matter of convenience or out of laziness, as an alternative to streets, backyard ramps, pools, pipes, ditches, banks, plazas, handrails, etc.... Once they have us isolated and classified, we are much *easier to control* [italics mine]. And if we continue to rely on them for our spots at the exclusion of finding or creating our own, we are allowing them to dictate to us how, what, where, and when we ride. And if the day ever comes when they decide to take them away, we'll be left with nothing. Progress can be good, but we must always ask: 'At what price?' (p. 149)

In like form, in his relatively elastic classroom with Mr. Scott, with its appealing play centers, colorful posters and compliantly content classmates, Mason would very likely soon have become more acclimated to kindergarten constraints. He might one day have existed within the boundaries of time and space without pushing against or warping those boundaries and might have enjoyed the inherent rewards of compliance. This might have been considered progress—as Mason "matured" and "developed" an appropriate school(ed) self. But at what price?

Moment of Disobedience: "Behind Her Back"

Miss Juste's police whistle rent the air with two awful blasts. The two hundred little girls in green rompers stopped dead in their tracks. Two blasts meant line up. Line up like at the beginning of the period.

Obediently, the green rompers milled about and found their appointed places in regular lines the length and breadth of the gymnasium. With grim pleasure, Miss Juste watched the girls respond to her command. She had called them back, after once dismissing them, as a master might jerk her dog back on a leash...Standing at attention, her shapeless white sneakers side by side, her knees like two cauliflowers below the voluminous serge bloomers, Miss Juste waited till every movement in the lines should cease. As usual, it was Edith Polizetti who could not find her place. Edith Polizetti who, under the terrible eye of

Miss Juste, tried to squeeze her way anywhere into a line and was mercilessly shoved out by the other little girls.

~Highsmith (1941/2002, 53)

"Under the terrible eye..." Just as in Ms. Highsmith's rendition of Miss Juste's gymnasium, there are places in school—for instance, The Line, The Carpet, The Tables—where children are "under the terrible eye," the inescapable eye. These places share their own kind of time and space: surveilled, constrained and highly restricted. The restrictions usually include some reference to noise, but much more often than not, a prohibition related to touch. The following descriptions of moments of disobedience span the classrooms in both schools, Andrews Elementary and Shadow Lake Elementary, but culminate in one moment at Andrews Elementary involving Moby touching and being touched on the carpet. Within these moments are examples of the means employed in both schools to keep children apart from one another. A normalizing and controlling technique described in chapter 4—surveillance (the terrible eye)—serves to actively limit interaction between and among children, especially physical interaction.

In kindergarten classrooms, children are kept apart from one another. Structures, procedures, rules and early childhood norms serve to explicitly and implicitly place children in the right place at the right time, and, especially, apart from one another. Walking in lines with hands at sides or clasped behind backs, standard school-wide rules—"keep hands, feet and other objects to yourself," assigned places on gathering carpets, admonishments to stay "in your bubble," all are in place to prohibit touch. As Tobin (1997) noted, "children's spontaneous, enthusiastic bodily expression and pleasure are contained and traded for the adult's sense of order, propriety and control" (p. 63). Yet children find ways to surreptitiously connect, using said hands, feet and other objects to do so. As school places children in close proximity—in clear view of one another—the children see, and so desire. Desiring in revolutionary, productive ways (Deleuze and Guattari 1972/1983), children join and so create new connections in the classroom space.

This particular series of moments of disobedience details the ways that the children in Mrs. Krinkle's and Mr. Scott's classrooms learned to recognize unsurveilled places and unsupervised (sometimes for merely a moment) times in their kindergarten classrooms, and how they found in this temporary freedom, a space to connect flesh to flesh. In these secret touches, children found spiritual pleasure and erotic pleasure: an "Eros born of Chaos, personified [by] creative power and harmony. [The erotic is] a life-force manifested in a capacity for joy, intense feeling, and a deep sharing with others" (Lorde 1984, in Phelan 1997, 87).

Slipping Surveillance

Long ago, when I was in elementary school, the teacher would sometimes leave the room, and without discussion, one child would immediately go to the classroom door to serve as the look-out. While remaining for the most part in the room, the lookout would keep close watch on the hallway for the approach of any adult and still manage to take part in the goings-on of the classroom. The worst of these goings-on were usually merely conversations taking place out of our seats, and a periodic peek at what was on the teacher's desk, but I can still recall the feeling of release—until—"SHHH!! She's coming!!!" There were always a few of the children who remained sitting quietly in their seats, and looked on disapprovingly, and a few who looked on longingly—but none of them ever "told." In my mind, these moments had extraordinary potential. I was greatly influenced by televised episodes of *The Little Rascals* and by *Peanuts* specials where the adults were invisible and the children accomplished wonderful things.

Earlier in this chapter, at the time of snack clean-up in Mr. Scott's room, Lemmie and Mason were engaged in hand-play (recall Line 146: Mason and Lemmie are seated at their tables but are engaging in hand play—each taking turns laying a hand flat on the table, palm up so that the other can smack it, if they can time it before the hand-on-table person snatches it away). Before the hand-play began, Lemmie committed three checks—turning her head to gauge Mr. Scott's attention. Each time, Mr. Scott was looking in her general direction. She remained still. After her third check, Mr. Scott turned to the door to look for stragglers coming from the bathroom—and instantly, without committing another check, Lemmie reached across the table with both hands and gently smacked them on top of Mason's. He snatched his hands back, and she laid hers out on the table. Mason, without checking, smacked hers carefully, too. They reversed roles, and as Mr. Scott was coming back in, he saw them. Mr. Scott said nothing, but soon after called the entire class to the carpet to talk about the problems involved in getting ready for recess.

This exchange is typical of those where children seek out time and spaces that will permit them to physically connect. In this instance, Lemmie and Mason were in one of the most public places in the kindergarten—at their tables. Yet, because it was a transitional time and because Mr. Scott was partially occupied with other children who are at various states of preparation in the clean-up process, Lemmie and Mason sensed a space for illicit physical play.

What is not typical, given the information we have about kindergarten in chapter 4, is Mr. Scott's response. He may have been frustrated about the distractions that were keeping the children from moving on in a timely fashion from snack to recess, but he did not impose consequences on children for the various transgressions committed—as recommended by Wong and Wong (1998) and as detailed by the myriad discipline and behavior plans described in the previous chapter and in the appendix.

However, both Mr. Scott and Mrs. Krinkle are participants in school. Components of their roles as teachers in kindergarten classrooms in their public schools are surveillance and partitioning. One of Gatto's (1992) seven rules of *The Seven-Lesson Schoolteacher* is "One can't hide." He related:

> I teach students that they are always watched, that each is under constant surveillance by myself and my colleagues. There are no private spaces for children, there is no private time...the meaning of constant surveillance and denial of privacy is that no one can be trusted, that privacy is not legitimate. Surveillance is an ancient imperative, espoused by certain influential thinkers, a central prescription set down in *The Republic*, in *The City of God*, in the Institutes of the Christian Religion, in New Atlantis, in Leviathan, and in the host of other places. All these childless men who wrote these books discovered the same thing: children must be closely watched if you want to keep a society under tight central control. Children will follow a private drummer if you can't get them into a uniformed marching band. (p. 12)

Surveillance by Lining 'Em Up

In school, children are herded, in preemptive, panoptic fashion, by their teachers from one teacher-dominated space to another (from classroom to library, from art-room to classroom) and are expected to "walk in single file, facing forward, in silence" (Nespor 1997, 126).

While visiting Mr. Scott's classroom, I could often see or hear lines of children from other classes in the hallway. Lines are places where children can be carefully surveilled—no place to hide, highly constrained space, expectation of very limited variation in movements; and yet lines are a place to hide in plain sight—behind the rest of the line—and a place where one is able to see easily if the teacher is looking. In the line, this is often not the case. If the line is moving, the teacher usually leads the way, and if it is stopped, the teacher may be committed to watching restroom doors and water fountains. This odd juxtaposition of high surveillance and high freedom was apparent in the incidental observations of a variety of lines over the course of two months in the two different schools.

As I sometimes watched the lines moving though hallways, I saw children doing the following (in addition to standing and walking):

Touching
Spinning
Squeezing faces
Touching butts
Stomping
Doing the bump to people
Jostling for first (or other places) in line
Holding arms behind heads (own and others')
Drifting
Walking backwards
Engaging in conversation
Flipping papers hanging in hallways
Arm flapping
Yelling
Riding other kids (then falling)
Falling (in general)
Tossing balls (on way to recess)
Wiggling
Shaking butts
Pulling/twirling/stroking/braiding/and/or brushing hair

Crawling
Walking on/jumping over furniture
Wall-rubbing
Taking giant steps
Taking steps so small they might be absent of forward motion
Skipping
Hopping on one foot
Hopping on the other foot
Laughing

On one day, I made the following observation of a teacher's line moving through the hallway at Shadow Lake Elementary. There were 20+ kindergarten children walking in a line past the door with **no** talking at all. The line stopped, and from Mr. Scott's classroom door I could see a portion of the line—the last seven children. There were two girls at the end of the line—the second-to-last girl (The Toucher) turned and ran her hands down the last girl's arms, starting at her shoulders and rubbing up and down. She did this several times. The Toucher then lifted the arms of The Last Girl so that they were perpendicular to her body. She was shaped like a "T." The Toucher now ran her hands from The Last Girl's fingertips, down the inside of her arms to the armpits and then down her body again. She did this twice. Then she hugged her hard four times. While still turned around toward the back of the line, she bent down to do several toe touches, checking to see if The Last Girl was watching (learning?). The Last Girl did one toe touch. All of this was accomplished with no talking or noise whatsoever. When the children began walking again to go back to their room, the only one who talked was The Toucher—she was correcting (and holding back!) her silent friend from passing her by saying, "Don't run in the hallway." Thus, immediately following a prolonged period of unnoticed, silent touching, the girl who touched risked a reprimand to help the one who needed to be cared for. She went unnoticed.

Even so, on further incidental and purposeful observations of lines of children at both schools, I made note of teachers' attempts to maintain an active surveillance, and so to inhibit the children's freedom to deviate from the standard line rules and expectations: silent, lines straight, arms at side, facing front, walking, staying in your place. Here is what I overheard as teachers walked with their children in the hallways of Shadow Lake and Andrews schools:

- No skipping. You can skip in gym class.
- Kevin, you're going to trip. Don't put that on your head.
- _____'s table, you may put your books away quietly and line up for art. [This four times in a row.]
- Walk quietly down to the art room.
- Someone else is talking.
- Okay, some girls came out but you wouldn't know it since you aren't facing front!
- Arms at your sides—now!
- Are you in line?
- I'm waiting for everyone to face the front.
- Not now, not now we don't ask any questions.
- I can hear your feet—stop it!
- Brian, you're behind Bobby.
- Do you think this is a playground?
- You're the first person so the line should be behind you.
- Don't do that in here. It's distracting!

Intriguing here is that the adults, in defining the line as a place to be still and quiet, name places designated as settings where bodily play may be permitted—the gym, and a playground. Yet, even in these spaces—the ones not like the line—play is considered permitted, so still in the control of the adults who can name where and when to play, where and when to touch. The function of these adult admonitions for order in line is to promote the expectation that a reprimand or reminder to one child will in the process keep the other children acutely aware that they are being watched and that chances are, variations of the lines rules will be seen and corrected through normalizing, civilizing controls. In true swaddling fashion, as teachers join the children in the corridor, they may "be demonstrating caring and responsive styles of management while they are simultaneously engaged in acts of policing or surveillance" (Clarke 2004). Rogovin (2004) advocates consistent enforcement of hallway (and other) rules:

Our 'no talking in the stairway' rule is always in force, not just when I feel like enforcing it. If you are not consistent, you end up wasting a lot of time dealing with misbehavior. If you enforce a rule consistently, after a while, it is internalized and stays in place. In time, the children will become silent in the stairway when they see me hold up two fingers or if I simply turn to look at them with a serious (not mean) look. In time, I don't have to do any of that, they just walk in silence. (p. 7)

In *Discipline and Punish*, Foucault (1979, in Clarke 2004) described the way in which docile bodies are induced to discipline themselves through practices of rituality "in which they take on the monitoring, scrutiny and appraisal of their own practices as if they are constantly subject to the gaze of unseen others. While corridors might thus be construed as part of the disciplinary architecture of educational institutions" (p. 9).

Thus, the hallway joins the ordered structure of school toward the children's progression from what Bakhtin (1968/1984) described as the "grotesque body," one with "shoots and branches [and] all that prolongs the body and links it to other bodies or to the world outside" (p. 315-317), to the "civilized body...an entirely finished, completed, strictly limited body" (p. 320)—so the kindergartner's body becomes a civilized body. Nespor (1997) named the civilized body as a "schooled body, one that stays silent, walks in line, keeps its hands to itself, and doesn't get out of its chair and walk around the room" (p. 131).

A vivid example of the civilized kindergarten body involved Fireman, a child in Mrs. Krinkle's class. One day, as the children in the class were cleaning up and then preparing to line up for dismissal, Fireman, who had cleaned up very quickly, helped other children and then gathered his belongings, and stood "in line" to await the other children. Because the other children were taking so much time—talking, dawdling, playing—he stood for several minutes. Alone. And because his "place" in line was toward the end of the line-to-be, he was standing in an odd place: toward the end of the carpet and right in the path of the children as they moved from clean-up to the cloakroom and back out to their tables to gather more items. As minutes ticked by, Fireman looked at me and shrugged. Finally, he said, as if to himself, "I'm standing in line for nothing." But still he stood.

Touch

An article in the *Washington Post* (Glod 2007) related the story of one middle school setting in place a rule against all touching. Claiming benefits of safety and convenience against the cost of a lack of physical human contact, the school's decision included even handshakes and high-fives in its ban on touch. The rule conveyed to students as NO PHYSICAL CONTACT was designed not only to prohibit inappropriate touching or fighting, but forbade *all* contact. Some officials compared this ban to similar rules in other schools of "keeping hands to yourself." Those schools, however, tended to enforce disruptive behavior and touches, but did not enforce a rule against all touching as did this middle school. The school's principal cited an overcrowded school and the desire to keep lunchrooms and hallways orderly and safe. She also expressed doubt in the students' ability to make decisions about what might make another student uncomfortable, suggesting that they were too immature to understand what kinds of touches would be acceptable. In protecting the students' personal space, the adults in this school decided that *for their own good,* they should not be allowed to touch.

Earlier in this chapter, Lundry wondered at what price progress? Here we must wonder at what price safety and order. As structures are put in place to separate children from one another in ordered isolation, the effect becomes dehumanizing. The structured order of kindergarten serves to prohibit fully "vivid and highly charged" (from Mead 1951) interactions with other children and their environment, and so interferes with children's potential to act on spiritual-moral opportunities. This recalls the earlier discussion of Buber in chapter 2 regarding the relational nature of the human spirit and cautions that nurturing the spirit-self is not passive or restrained, but that "the human child... gains his world by seeing, listening, feeling, forming. It is in encounter that the creation reveals its formhood; it does not pour itself into senses that are waiting but deigns to meet those that are reaching out" (Buber 1958/1970, 76). Reaching out implies the freedom to do so.

As implied in the *Washington Post* article above, those involved in setting these norms do not seem to realize—or possibly care—that the consequences of the imposition of these norms are the loss of humanity and joy. It is for the good of the child that adults swaddle (constrain, protect, prevent, remove from one another and from the environment, the world). This brings to mind the words of Tommy Trantino as he recalled his own time in school in chapter 2:

> I liked to be around the other kids and I used to look at the sky out the windows of my classes and smile at the women across the street looking out of their prison tenements and sometimes we'd catch each others eyes but they hardly ever smiled back and sometimes I would wave to them but the teachers would always say VERBOTEN. People were being kept apart and we were keeping ourselves apart and we were all hurting like a motherfucker but no one was telling. (1972, 23)

Recall also, Upton Sinclair's 1922 account related in chapter 1 of the little boy who marched in line and talked in chorus, "saying the same thing as nearly at the same instant as could be contrived," and how he " found that a delightful arrangement, for he liked other boys, and the more of them there were, the better." This little boy and the little boy who was Tommy Trantino claim a need and a liking to be around the other children. And both end their tales apart from the others: being laughed at and having "a sense of triumph over other little boys" that one could laugh at such as "being kept apart" and "keeping ourselves apart"—all functions of the schoolroom.

Moby Gets Caught

Mrs. Krinkle's children "come to the carpet" for lessons. As in Mr. Scott's classroom, the children here have expected carpet behaviors—coming ready to listen, sitting down, facing the speaker and/or front—and in this class, the children have assigned places to sit on the carpet in three rows of six or seven children. Another expectation on the carpet here is that the children stay in their assigned places—and so, apart.

Of course, though, the children do touch. Often it is with Mrs. Krinkle's tacit approval, but usually it is not approved. On this particular day, the children were seated on the carpet in their rows facing Mrs. Krinkle's chair while she cut one of the sweet potatoes the class had been growing in their garden.

Line

222.   T: Are you guys allowed to bring knives to school?

223.   (students): Noooooooooooo

224. T: Knives are not toys; but they are a tool...

225. ((The children are passing around a potato and touching it and smelling it and squeezing it to see what it's like.))

226. T: Bumblebee—did you get to feel the potato?

227. T: I am going to peel off the skin

228. T: Is it hard like a brick?

229. ((While Mrs. Krinkle is cutting the potato—Jacob and Peter are on their knees; both swing their arms in wide circles—this escalates. Jacob shifts into using his fingers and right hand to make a "gun" and begins to pretend to shoot. Francesca (Mrs. Krinkle's daughter who is helping out that day) says—"Stop Jacob"))

230. T: Please sit... look how nicely Clark is sitting. Thank you Clark

231. ((Most of the children shift on the carpet, sitting straighter, placing hands on lap to await their chance to touch the potato making its rounds to touch; and then to receive their cut piece of potato to taste.))

232. T: Look how nicely Scrappy is sitting, too

233. Moby: I want some potato

234. ((Moby is at his proper space on the carpet but is on his knees. Mrs. Krinkle continues to slice off pieces of potato and hand to children, but not yet Moby.))

235. T: Sit down and you'll get some. Take a seat. Take a seat and you'll get one

236. T: Oh I love the people I heard saying thank you

237. Moby: Thank you!

238. ((There is a general murmur as children exclaim over their taste of potato and/or worry over when theirs is coming. Mrs. Krinkle gives a slice to Bruce Wayne and then runs out.))

239. T: hold on ((to Dora who was next)). Hold on ((to class, in general))

Mrs. Krinkle walked away from the carpet toward the front part of the room near the door to get another potato. The classroom is large, and so Mrs. Krinkle's walk to corner of the room was slightly

out of earshot and—as long as she was walking away from the carpet and looking for the potatoes—out of eyeshot.

What occurred there and then was a striking example of the
children's awareness of their teacher's presence and the impact of
her surveillance (and lack of). Mrs. Krinkle had not taken more than
six steps away from the carpet when the spaces between children
disintegrated and the rows collapsed into piles and bundles of children. Dre, Scrappy, Jacob and Peter wrestled each other; Cinderella,
Princess, and of course, Briona—she of the too many touches—tickled each other and twitched and flinched as the others tickled them;
and Gabriella, Tommy, Mr. Policeman and Bumblebee, still in their
places with hands on laps, quietly watched them, Bumblebee with
pursed lips of disapproval. New York, Leela, Dora, Bruce and Moby
wrestled and rolled on one another on the corner of the carpet closest to Mrs. Krinkle's corner.

The shift from the children sitting, straight and silent. to the
state of crumpled, quiet, and intersecting was instantaneous. Nearly
as one (except for those who watched and frowned), the structure
of the carpet imploded. Mrs. Krinkle had her back to the children
for less than 60 seconds, and she continued to talk to them as she
walked and bent over the bag. Those sixty seconds were full of action and interaction.

Then, as Mrs. Krinkle started to turn back to the carpet, at that
very moment—as if the children were one entity perfectly attuned
to their teacher's anticipated movements—the structure of the carpet reasserted itself.

Except for Moby. Moby, who was geographically the closest to
Mrs. Krinkle from his assigned place on the front-door-side corner of the carpet, somehow missed the message of Mrs. Krinkle's
impending turn back toward the carpet. He continued to bury his
head into Bruce's stomach, joyfully kneading it. The other children
merely sat straighter, some looking forward at the teacher's empty
chair—the others looking toward Mrs. Krinkle as she began walking to the carpet. Bumblebee shook her head even while looking
straight ahead at Mrs. Krinkle's chair.

Moby lifted his head from Bruce's tummy and smiled at him,
puzzled. It was then that he must have noticed that all of the children had returned to their carpet state—and just as he began to
form an approximation of a listening position, Mrs. Krinkle, three

steps into her return—sang out, "OH, Moby...," and the rest of the children gave no indication of their participation in the break-down of the carpet.

Observing this moment was surreal. It seemed in slow motion—the tightly stretched, straight-lined carpet of children and then its collapse upon the moment of Mrs. Krinkle turning her back. Then the elastic seemed to snap back as she returned her attention to the carpet. Within this moment lay children's collective awareness of the teacher and her gaze; the willingness of children to risk that gaze in order to physically, sensually, and playfully connect with one another; the role of surveillance in children's opportunities to physically inter-act; the role of the compliants in the group interaction on the carpet; and the willingness of the class to sacrifice one on the outer perim-eter (like a zebra herd to the lion) to the teacher's gaze.

Laying a Picture Book Text

Rhizoanalysis reconstructs a text by creating new and different un-derstandings of it; and it does so by linking it with texts other than those we would normally use. For example, we can use rhizoanaly-sis to replot the links between an observation of a child and a child development text, a sociology text or a popular culture text. As did Kylie Smith (in MacNaughton 2005) in her analysis of gender roles using Munsch's *The Paper Bag Princess*, here I "read" an observation of Moby and his classmates by linking it with popular children's texts to reconstruct my understanding of disobedience and compliance in that observation. As I construct a rhizome of disobedience and com-pliance meanings in the observation, I rethink what it means to do disobedience at six years of age and how this might influence me to rethink the possibilities for responses (p.120).

Nicholas Burbules (1986, in Merriam 2002) discussed building understandings of ideologies on models of literary texts, claim-ing that "the process of ideology analysis and ideology critique is akin to literary criticism; it includes an attempt to hold a portray-al accountable to social reality while recognizing that ideologies capture the popular imagination" (p. 330–331). He demonstrated this approach by laying texts of school beside texts of the classic 1945 children's text, *Tootle*. In his analysis he sought to consider how the assumptions and values of a particular social worldview "underlie a seemingly simple and innocent text [and so are] better able to recognize them at work in other educational contexts" (p. 343) and argued that *Tootle* "presents an account of schooling that cheerfully endorses some of the most repressive aspects of the process by which schools restrict the impulses and aspirations of children" (p. 331). Like the character Tootle, Moby's "sensitive, emotional and relational qualities are not 'relevant' to their work as kindergartners and actually impede it, therefore, it is 'clear which must give way'" (p. 340). Burbules (in Merriam and Associates 2002) asks, "What can we learn about ourselves and our culture by examining the kinds of books we produce for our children [and ourselves] to read?" (p. 331).

Engaging with this question via a more current popular children's text, *David Goes to School* (Shannon 1999), one finds the character David as the joyful, spirited dissident, an autobiographically cartooned version of the author/illustrator, David Shannon. The cover depicts David standing in front of a classroom chalkboard, mouth open in gapped-tooth laughter, preparing to toss a paper airplane. However, the back cover represents, in the Bart Simpson mold of school-coerced compliance, first-grade writing paper covered with the child-printed words, *I will not disrupt class* over and over again. The single I will not *dirsupt* class in a field of correctly copied sentences is circled in red.

David Shannon continues to represent the spare text in the same child-like print on depictions of first-grade lined handwriting paper, and begins: "David's teacher always said... NO, DAVID! No yelling. No pushing. No running in the halls." Even so, David the disobedient child is represented in the pages of the book in variations of:

• Tardiness ("David! You're tardy!")

• Out-of-seat behavior ("Sit down, David!")

• Gum-chewing ("Don't chew gum in class!")

• Talking out ("David, raise your hand!")

• Touching the red-haired girl sitting in front of him ("Keep your hands to yourself!")

• Daydreaming, off-task behaviour ("PAY ATTENTION!")

• Cutting in line ("Wait your turn, David!")

- Food fights ("I don't care who started it!")
- Mason-like delays in joining the class ("David! Recess is over!")
- Noisiness ("Shhhhh!")
- Having to go to the bathroom ("Again?!")
- And vandalism via drawing on the school desk ("That's it, Mister! You're staying after school!")

One might recognize the teacher in this book—although in *Peanuts*-fashion we never see her face. In fact, except for her voice, she is absent until the very end of the book, as we shall see. Her voice, however, may be almost any teacher's voice. Her invisibility serves a purpose. The faceless power of the teacher contributes to the panoptic quality of her control. She may always be watching. As well, the reader may be enjoying David's transgressions, especially as depicted by Shannon's wildly joyful and scribbly drawings—and, if the teacher were to be shown, with the disapproving face and posture which surely must be the case given David's perseveration in willful disobedience, we may resent her and so resent the voice of reason that must present the inviolate rule of order. Since we cannot see who is behind them, these unquestionable rules are "abstracted from any social context or set of conventions—they just are" (Burbules 1986, 342).

The character of David's naughtiness—his fully-present and active engagement with what he sees, feels, and desires in the space of his school and classroom—is a problem to be addressed via verbal admonishments; reminders of likely rules (I recognize "keep your hands to yourself" as one of the most common rules relayed earlier: "Keep hands, feet and other objects to yourself."); and peer pressure toward Foucauldian normalization as on several pages, Shannon depicts the children in the class viewing David's antics with disapproval. Examples of these normalizing behaviors include:

- The red-haired girl is depicted with stunned despair as she raises her hand while David calls out;
- Children in the lunch line who were passed by as David takes his turn before theirs are drawn with anger, shock and confusion on their faces;

- Children trying to read through David's pencil-tapping noise-making look at him with down-pointing, furrowed eyebrows and frowning mouths;
- And finally, a punishment and reward.

After his act of vandalism, David stays after school, and works to please his teacher by washing all of the desks in the classroom. Shannon illustrates David's face and demeanor in this drawing as one seeking approval: eyebrows slanting upward, very slight smile, arms open and palms out as he holds the sponge and quietly begs the teacher's attention to the shining desks. At last, the teacher is shown—actually only her blue-dressed torso—as she awards David a sticker representing her gold-starred approval ("GOOD JOB, DAVID!") and he is released.

Finally happy, David skips home and passes on the sidewalk the red-haired girl who now deigns to smile and wave at him. His compliance has earned her approval, too. As Burbules (1986, in Merriam 2002) concluded in *Tootle*, "It appears that the child's desire for a happy ending can be satisfied only when [he] learns to follow the rules" (p. 335).

The characters of Tootle and David permit us a peek into the complexity and norms within children's picture books. In order to further disrupt Moby's moment and consider the themes of surveillance and compliance that were among the limitless possible rhizomes to follow, we can lay the observational text next to another classic children's text, Dr. Seuss's (Theodore Geisel's) 1957 *Cat in the Hat*.

Throughout this story, the author shared a theme of unseen surveillance and so a kind of self-regulation. The children in the tale, a boy and a girl, were left home alone on a gray rainy day—the mother went shopping and left them to their own devices. Unlike my child-character heroes, who do their best work in the absence of adults, these children sat quietly looking out the window with the approval of their watchful goldfish.

Then, The Cat appeared—the cat who is like an adult and not like an adult—and disrupted the household ("You shook up our house," said the fish) with his antics. The children never joined him, but did not stop him either... and soon the Things came in, too.

Then those Things ran about
With big bumps, jumps and kicks

And with hops and big thumps
And all kinds of bad tricks.
And I said,
'I do NOT like the way that they play
If Mother could see this,
Oh, what would she say!'

Then our fish said, 'Look! Look!'
And our fish shook with fear.
'Your mother is on her way home!
Do you hear?
Oh, what will she do to us?
What will she say?
Oh, she will not like it
To find us this way!'

'So, DO something! Fast!' said the fish.
'Do you hear!
I saw her. Your mother!
Your mother is near!
So, as fast as you can,
Think of something to do!'

(Geisel 1957)

The mother has gone out. From the earliest page in the book, the adult in the situation has absented herself, and so—like *The Little Rascals* and *Peanuts* characters again—the children are unobserved by the constraining and calculating (terrible) eye of the adult. However, as is the case in the panoptic nature of carpets and school lines, the adult's actual presence is not required in order to compel some compliance. In the story, the fish (like Bumblebee on the carpet, and the red-haired girl in the David book) worry about what "She" might see ("if Mother could see this; Oh, what would she say!"); Thing One and Thing Two (like the bad kids who do transgress against the rules of the carpet once the calculating eye of the adult is not actually present) do not concern themselves with this possibility; and the two children in the story (like the ones who watch with smiles and a sense of possibility for joining in) are paralyzed by the conflicting goods of Mother's approval and the tricks of the Cat, Thing One and Thing Two.

Surveillance

Enacting their understanding of surveillance, many children, especially disobedient ones, do not act (or fail to act) on the assumption
that they are being watched when they are not. In this way, children
are perhaps more savvy about surveillance than are adults. I think
this may be related to their intense engagement with the geography of the classroom. Nespor (1997) wrote that while a teacher's
perspective is a problem of organizing, managing and controlling
children's bodies in classroom and school spaces, the children view
the classroom and school as "negotiable terrain" (p. 131). As noted
in the earlier discussion of highly-surveilled school spaces of lines
and carpet, "there is surveillance, but it is hardly suffocating" (p.
131). Teachers and other adults cannot monitor most of what children do, and children are acutely aware of this.

The disobedient ones operate under the latitude provided by
this fact—that while much effort is made by the adults to carefully
order the time and space of school to provide tight and standard-
ized control, and also to relax those rigid boundaries at expected
times and places, the free spaces are there. Not much is required in
time or space to take advantage. As demonstrated in Moby's carpet
incident, the public, teacher-controlled space of the carpet became
a free space when Mrs. Krinkle turned her back for only a moment
("your mother is out") and the children acted out their resistance
to "constraints placed on their spontaneous natures" (Pace and
Hemmings 2007, 4).

As Fifield (2008) commented of Moby, he was "not so much an
innocent victim coercively domesticated by school, but was a creative, flexible and accommodating participant in the construction
of school life" (p. 3). Rather than resistance as open disobedience,
Fifield noted a system of reciprocal surveillance, in which teachers
are every bit as much under the eye of children as children are under
the eye of teachers. Although teachers and students are partners in
surveillance, "they are up to different things." While teachers' surveillance of students seeks to homogenize space and time in school,
placing children under rules of conduct that apply across space/time,
the children seem to experience a much more fine-grained space/
time. They are in the moment, sensitive to fleeting opportunities
that open and close possibilities. Fifield further clarifies:

Phenomena like the instantaneous reassembly of crystalline social order from chaotic bodily collisions on Mrs. Krinkle's classroom carpet reflect this reciprocal surveillance. This was not so much a broad strategic resistance to institutional control, as a lack of sustained presence in any single regime, a facility for being present in multiple regimes, purposes and identities nearly simultaneously. Even as these Foucauldian children are induced to discipline themselves through practices of rituality, they use the rituals for purposes and pleasures of their own. I wonder if the children's touch would have been so pleasurable, without the opportunities that surveillance of bodies paradoxically affords? (p. 4)

Laying a Pleasure/Sensing/Spirit Text

The body, source of self, lived for self and others;
Encapsulating and encapsulated by social order and chaos.

~Virginia Oleson (in Leavitt and Power 1997, 39)

I met a man in Nigeria one time, an Ibo who had six hundred relatives he knew quite well. His wife had just had a baby, the best possible news in any extended family. They were going to take it to meet all its relatives, Ibos of all ages and sizes and shapes. It would even meet other babies, cousins not much older than it was. Everybody who was big enough and steady enough was going to get to hold it, cuddle it, gurgle to it, and say how pretty it was, or handsome.

Wouldn't you have loved to be that baby?

~ Vonnegut (1999, 16)

As they enter the school building, children are to leave their bodies at home. School personnel lament the inconvenience of feeding, watering and elimination as the most difficult portions of the school day to manage. And the functions and desires of the body—to move, to touch, to be touched—are an anathema to the adults who are there to ensure that "nothing goes on."

Poor Tootle, the train in Burbules's (1986, in Merriam 2002) analysis of the children's book, *Tootle*—he of the loud toots, meadow frolics, and races with horses off the rails—leads children to share the lessons he learns from Bill and "The Mayor Himself":

Attempts at independent judgment, sensual investigation, and peer-group formation are at best naïve; at worst, they interfere with the important task of becoming responsible and productive adults. Becoming an adult...means learning self-control and self-denial; it means foregoing childish pleasure; it means accepting tasks and constraints that one may hate; it means suppressing certain emotions and desires; it means abandoning play and learning to work in a compulsive manner; and it means accepting without question the discipline of externally imposed rules. (p. 345)

The surveillance described above plays an important part in ensuring that self-control and self-denial are learned. The erotic, "the lure of human beauty that releases pleasure" (Browning 1998, 96), in early childhood classrooms is public. In other words, touch is monitored explicitly with the implicit understanding that "sexuality exists in the classroom and is antithetical to compliance, obedience, and conformity" (Broadway, Leafgren, and Gilbert 2007).

Decades spent in primary classrooms and elementary school hallways inform me of the pervasiveness of this theme. The ubiquitous rule, "Keep hands, feet and other objects (or body parts, in some classrooms) to yourself" is an almost universal classroom rule. Beyond the direct admonishments and reprimands, teachers carefully prepare the time and space elements of the classroom toward separating and controlling the children and their bodies. Note that Mrs. Krinkle has assigned places in three straight rows on her carpet with sufficient space between children so that touching takes an effort. "From birth, children construct themselves subject to the 'civilizing' controls of adults" (Elias 1978).

There are notions of uncontrollability applied to young children, "thus we find young children and women locked in a daily battle to civilize children's volatile bodies. By the time they reach kindergarten, children are to be moved from sensory-motor engagement with the world to abstract thinking, from unbridled expressions of bodily desire to socially sanctioned forms of play, from excessive pleasure to good clean fun" (Tobin 2003, 19). Control means controlled by others' demands and expectations. Recall that three of Mr. Scott's students, including Mason, were named out of control on first glance by other teachers in the building. On probing, Mr. Scott learned that the three had been skipping or hopping in the hall and smiling. One was singing. Physical demonstrations of joy, evidence of energy and enthusiasm became signs of being out of control.

In the case of Moby, head buried into the soft belly of Bruce, he had gone too far. He not only missed the returning surveillance, but he crossed the invisible fences between children. Missed them by a mile. Like Mason, Moby was often off the beaten path of kindergarten, marching to his own drummer; but unlike Mason, Moby seemed not to be sure where the fences were. So rather than stretching and pushing them, he tripped over them or overshot them. For this, Moby sometimes sacrificed other freedoms; as his body transgressed the boundaries of time and space carefully laid out by Mrs. Krinkle, he sat in the time-out chair or in places separate from other children. If Moby could not control his body, Mrs. Krinkle's decision to partition him away from other children who might touch or be touched would control it for him.

Moby's need to be physically close and engage in body play with other children is, as Buber (1958/1970) noted, the "reaching out" that permits one to relate and connect to the other. "Part of the aim of tactile stimulation and close, warm, gentle, caring affirmation and intimate communication in infancy and childhood is to eroticize the child, to arouse, to awaken, to turn the child on to life" (Martinson 1994, 11).

Elizabeth Grosz (1994) delineated what she terms "two kinds of approaches to theorizing the body—one, 'inscriptive,' a Nietzchian, Foucauldian notion of the social body upon which 'social law, morality, and values are inscribed'" (p. 33). In this case, the children's teachers determine where each body should be and what it should be allowed to touch and do. Even lining up in girls' and boys' lines are practical and nominal only—the boys are named boys and the girls, girls, not to delineate their sexuality, gender or interests, but to make two relatively even lines matched to restrooms also named "boys" and "girls".

Grosz's second theorizing is the "lived body," which references the "lived experience of the body, the body's internal or psychic inscription" (p. 33). Grosz suggests that, while we are becoming adept at naming the inscriptive details of the body, we tend to shy away from the messiness of the corporal body—the lived experiences... especially sex. An assertion that "practically all children indulge or are prone to indulge in sexual activity; and that, being...at the same time, 'natural' and 'contrary to nature,'...posed physical and moral, individual and collective dangers; children were defined as 'preliminary' sexual beings, on this side of sex, yet within it, astride a dangerous dividing line" (Foucault 1980b, 104).

Indeed, two of the most uncomfortable and confrontational times of my own teaching career were related to children's sexuality. In each case—the incident involving two kindergarten boys in the bathroom, and the incident involving three girls in the classroom library where pillows and knitted blankets could be used to hide—parents, counselors, and agencies were activated to stem the possibility of crossing that dangerous dividing line. As Deleuze and Guattari (1987) described the body as "not simply a sign to be read, a symptom to be deciphered, but also a force to be reckoned with," so did the children's bodies and the connections made manage to "align themselves to other things [and] produce what [is] called a machine ...in itself, the body is not a machine; but in its active relations to other social practices, entities and events, it forms not simply a sign to be read, a symptom to be deciphered, but also a force to be reckoned with machine connections." In this case, the alignments the children's bodies made served to engage other entities (counselors, agencies, frightened/angry parents— "Does this mean he's gay???") as surveillance machines imposed in the classroom to join the machine of the sexualized events in the school. "The body is thus not an organic totality which is capable of the wholesale expression of subjectivity, a welling up of the subject's emotions, attitudes, beliefs, or experiences, but is itself an assemblage of organs, processes, pleasures, passions, activities, behaviors linked by fine lines and unpredictable networks to other elements, segments and assemblages" (Deleuze and Guattari 1987, 120).

If we take one more backwards look at Mrs. Krinkle's walk away from the carpet, her body's distance and position was the catalyst linked by "fine lines and unpredictable networks" to the carpet, and like a Rube Goldberg machine, put into motion the series of motions and interactions that included every child in the room— watcher or wrestler.

Moment of Disobedience: "Shoulder to Cry On"

breathing in, I am so happy to hug my child
breathing out, I know she is real and alive in my arms

~ Hanh (1990b, 36)

The final moment of disobedience revisits the conflicted notions of good and goodness as introduced in chapter 1 in the discussion of the moment of Reuben's fall. In the space of the kindergarten classroom, a space where interactions with time and space are, to different degrees, highly restricted, and a space where children are surveilled closely and kept apart from one another, there is also space for children (and their teachers) to act with generosity and kindness.

Clark and Jacob Go to Time-Out

On a day in this same classroom, during a time when the children were in various parts of the room working and playing, Jacob had committed an act of disobedience (which I did not witness) and was sent to sit at a table for a time-out. He had been there for about four minutes, head down but eyes up, calmly surveying the room and waiting for a signal from Mrs. Krinkle that he could rejoin the others. I watched him. And so missed whatever occurred that sent Clark to a time-out table, too.

Clark was a new boy. At the time of this incident, he had been a member of Mrs. Krinkle's class for about two weeks and was adjusting slowly to kindergarten. He had been living with his mother until the courts took him away from her to live with his father immediately before joining Mrs. Krinkle's class. Before moving in with his father, he reportedly had had almost no interaction with anyone besides his mother. He suffered language delays, according to Mrs. Krinkle; and in the classroom, everything was new to him. In my view, having everything seem new can be a very exciting prospect, and Clark sometimes evidenced this enthusiasm in surprising circumstances. For instance, once while sitting in the front row on the carpet while Mrs. Krinkle read a big book aloud, Clark spotted a picture of a cat on the page. "A CAT!!" he cried... and rose to his knees to point to it. "LOOK!! A CAT!!" he said and rubbed its picture on the page. Mrs. Krinkle turned the page to read what followed, but Clark reached up to turn the page back to again touch the cat and murmur, "It's a cat."

Jacob in many ways had the opposite relationship with the class as did Clark. Jacob seemed to know everything about his kindergarten class, his teacher, the university students who spent time in his classroom, and details about each child in the class. In the month that I spent there, he had transitioned from the boy who had soaked his paint shirt in blue and yellow (and so green) paint and seemed oblivious to the impact on the adults who witnessed it, to a perceptive child who moved with confidence through the classroom and to whom Mrs. Krinkle often turned for assistance. The children viewed him as a leader, and Mrs. Krinkle understood that he could and did serve as an ally to her purposes. I noted this in my visits and asked Jacob to help me out more than once.

For instance, during one of my early visits, I asked the children to choose their pseudonyms that I would use in this document. I had planned to explain it to them, let them think about it, and then get the names on my next visit. However, the children were excited at the prospect of having an alias and began calling out their new names instantly. I rushed to write down their choices and then checked against the class list for who was missing. One child, who later became "New York," was absent. On my next visit, I caught up with he-who-would-become-New York and attempted to explain the process and ask him to name himself. He ignored me. I tried again. And he ignored me again.

I turned to Jacob. I asked him to help me out with he-who-would-become-New York, and Jacob said, "Sure," and joined the boy at the library. At first, he just said, "Hey, you have to name yourself!" and the boy ignored Jacob, too. Without giving me a glance, Jacob persisted. "It's easy," he coaxed, "we all got new names. I'm going to be Jacob in the book." And he proceeded to walk he-who-would-become-New York from child to child and told him their names. Jacob remembered the names from the previous visit, and was able to name the children as they had named themselves. Finally, Jacob held the boy's hand, walked to me, and said, "That's a good one. Tell her!" and New York said, "I'd like to be New York." Jacob smiled and returned to his work at the table.

On this day, however, both Jacob and Clark had committed some misbehavior that sent them from the group. While Jacob dutifully did his time, Clark balked. He walked slowly from where he had been in the block area toward the chairs and tables—but then stopped, frozen, and began to cry. Loudly and wetly. Mrs. Krinkle calmly said from across the room, "Clark, you need to go sit down at the table," and continued working with the small group she had joined in the library.

Jacob Leaves Time-Out

Clark continued to stand exactly where he was and cry. Louder. Jacob, from his time-out seat, had been watching, too. He rose from his time-out chair—no checks for surveillance, no request for permission—and walked to Clark and placed his arm around Clark's shoulder pulling him tightly to his body. Jacob was tall and Clark was small. Jacob was Black and Clark was White. Jacob was highly experienced and knowledgeable about Kindergarten and Clark was inexperienced and knew little about kindergarten.

Jacob rubbed his hand up and down Clark's shoulder and upper arm and said, "Hey, you don't have to cry. It's just time out. You sit down. You sit down for five minutes.... five months.... five somethings, and then you get back up. Come on. It's not that bad."

Jacob, a highly knowledgeable student of kindergarten understood time-out as part and parcel of the kindergarten experience. He explained that time—as it seems to in all aspects of school—played a role in this particular event. While he was not certain exactly the length of time (minutes, months, "somethings"), he did know that it was relatively predictable, that it *would* end, and that once again, the bad would re-join the good. Jacob was offering Clark hope and a sense of the future.

Clark, however—to whom everything was new—experienced this time-out without faith in what would happen next, remained frozen, and did not move from the spot where he had stopped. Although his crying was a bit less loud.

Jacob finally checked—looking toward Mrs. Krinkle, who, while she must have heard and probably seen this exchange and Jacob's abandonment of time-out, did not offer any indication that she noticed, thus providing her tacit approval. Jacob then shifted—he faced Clark and placed both hands on Clark's shoulders. "Hey, buddy," Jacob said, bending his knees a little to look Clark in the eye, "I'll stay in until you get out. Okay?" He checked Mrs. Krinkle again. "Okay?"

Jacob shifted from teacher and informer, explaining to Clark the logistics of time-out, to comforter, more directly offering his emotional support toward alleviating Clark's sadness and confusion. Jacob demonstrated a quality of care and regard early on—rubbing Clark's shoulder and arm as he comforted him with words; and then he extended his comfort to Clark by promising to remain with him for as long as he was required to stay in time-out.

Finally, Jacob let go, and as he turned to return to his time-out seat, he repeated, "Okay?" and while Clark still stood on that spot, Jacob returned to his chair and laid his head down. His eyes remained trained on Clark.

Clark sniffled and finally, still in the same spot, sank to the floor. He had stopped crying.

Laying a Spiritual-Moral Text

Is a leaf smart?
Does it keep secrets
Or
Is there a secret I don't already know?
No
I know every secret
That roams this earth,
But one...
The secret that breaks my heart.
To not know what I did wrong.
                ~ Eva, age 8 (in Kohl 1998)

Moral: Goods and Bads

Watching Jacob, who had been bad and so sent to the time-out table, disobey Mrs. Krinkle by leaving his designated spot in order to comfort his crying classmate Clark recalled for me the moment of Julian's care of Reuben many years ago. As I had then, I troubled the notions of good and bad and what meaning the children may have made of those terms, those qualities, for themselves.

Vivian Paley has troubled the same notions in her long-term work with kindergarten children. In *Wally's Stories* (1981), she shared excerpts of conversations she has had with children about how they understand their value as good or bad on the basis of the adult response to their actions. Here are a few of those excerpts:

Eddie: Sometimes I hate myself.

Teacher: When?

Eddie: When I am naughty.

Teacher: What do you do that's naughty?

Eddie: You know naughty words. Like 'shit'. That one.

Teacher: That makes you hate yourself?

Eddie: Yeah. When my dad washes my mouth out with soap.

Teacher: What if he doesn't hear you?

Eddie: Then I get away with it. Then I don't hate myself.

Wally: If I'm bad, like take the food when it's not time to eat yet and my mom makes me leave the kitchen. Then I hate myself because I want to stay with her in the kitchen.

Eddie: And here's another reason I don't like myself. This is a good reason. Sometimes I try to get the cookies on top of the refrigerator.

Teacher: What's the reason you don't like yourself?

Eddie: Because my mom counts to ten fast and I get a spanking and my grandma gets mad at her.

Deanna: Here's when I like myself: when I'm coloring and my mommy says, 'Stop coloring. We have to go out.' And I tell her I'm coloring and she says 'okay. I'll give you ten more minutes.'

Teacher: What if you have to stop what you are doing?

Deanna: When she's in a big hurry. That's when she yells at me. Then I don't like myself. (p. 54-55)

And in a later conversation:

Wally: In my old school, if you tore someone's picture you sat in the hallway all alone by yourself until you were good.

Teacher: Did it make you good?

Wally: Yes. Hey, you know what we did in the hallway? We tore off the pictures on the wall.

Teacher: Then being in the hallway didn't seem to make you good, did it?

Wally: They didn't know it was us. (p. 55)

As Paley (1981) wrote, "Bad and good depended on the adult response. If the schoolteacher used a hickory stick, it meant the children were bad; the stick made them good. An angry parent denoted a naughty child. To the adult, the cause of the punishment was obvious, but the child saw only the stick and judged himself accordingly" (p. 55).

In Mrs. Krinkle's classroom, the children often discussed who was good and who was bad—and the basis for naming the subject of the conversation was the adult response to the child's action, almost never the action itself. When Jacob had been sent to his seat from the carpet a few weeks earlier, Leela had clicked her tongue, shaken her head, and said under her breath, "He's so bad," as Tommy nodded his head in agreement. I had leant over and asked Leela what he'd done, and she had shrugged and said, "I don't know, but he's always bad." Adults are just as susceptible to this juxtaposition of cause and effect. One afternoon I witnessed the following:

Line

241.   T: Time to clean up! All join in but in their own way!

242.   Clark: ((claps and jumps up and down))

243.   ((the children busily move through the room, putting things away))

244.   Dora: ((as she passes by the behavior chart, she notices that the only star under the cloud is the one with Moby's name on it)) What did Moby do? ((loudly))

245.   T: Nothing. ((to Moby)) Why did you move your star there?

246.   (University student): ((moves the star back so that it lines up under the sunshine cut-out)) ((to Moby): If your name is there, it means you're bad.

This exchange was striking in the truth of this arbolic logic: if you are punished, it means you are bad.

Clark and Jacob had been sent to time-out chairs for disobedient behavior. When Clark refused to go, and instead sobbed his sorrow and frustration, Jacob responded to his sadness and committed another disobedience when he left the time-out table. Jacob's comfort was two-fold: he reassured Clark about the punishment itself ("It's not that bad."), and he demonstrated his regard for Clark even though he was bad. If being punished means one is bad, Clark's tears may have been just as much a product of his sudden badness as it was due to the time-out punishment. Mrs. Krinkle, the adult in Clark's school-life, reprimanded Clark and so—in good/bad logic—named him, in his eyes, as bad.

Groening (1988) explored the notion of being good (or bad) in Chapter 19, Crime 'N' Punishment, of his cartoon book, *Childhood is Hell*. Bongo engaged in conversation with himself:

B: Ok—what is crime?

B: Crime is when you break the rules.

B: What are rules?

B: Rules are the general guidelines to follow so nobody has to think. Parents dig rules 'cause they get to enforce them on you.

B: That's the one rule parents obey: Makin' the kids obey all the other rules.

B: And you know something? Most kids actually like to follow the rules.

B: That's 'cause, for better or worser, it's easier to obey a rule than to think for yourself.

B: Plus the rules give you this safe target for when you get mad. You get mad at the rule instead of the parents who made up the rule.

B: But eventually, you wise up and begin to notice that some rules are stupid, pointless and crazy.

B: So then you gotta ask yourself: Why am I following this rule?

B: Does obeying this rule make sense or I am just being a little wimp? What happens if I break this rule? Will anyone get hurt?

B: If I break this rule, will I be happier?

B: Or I am just being a little wiseguy, trying to get even for some past injustice?

B: How much punishment will result from this crime? Can I handle it? Yes!! I can! I can!! I am free!!! Free, I tell you!!!

Mom: I thought I told you to go to bed.

Mom: ((turns Bongo over her knee and spanks him)) You're so bad.

B: Now where was I? I know it was important.

B: Dang. I lost it.

B: I'm so bad.

And once more, the dominant (adult) naming of bad is convincing and final. As defense lawyers know, their clients begin with at least one strike against them: that many people (jurors) believe that if a person has been arrested, he or she must have done something to deserve it. Therefore the conversation shifts from what Dewey (in Gouinlock 1994) referred to as the reflective morality of "goodness" to the customary morality of "good," as had been carefully negotiated in Makarushka's (1998) analysis of Bess, the protagonist of von Trier's film, *Breaking the Waves* (in chapter 1). In this discussion, good means "not to make waves, not to destabilize the 'natural' order of things, not to express deeply felt emotions, not to experience pleasure...[else to be] interpreted as a flaw, an emotional deficit" (np). Makarushka further notes that the good assumes an "external reference against which all choices and behaviors can be measured and assessed .... If the 'good' is a static moral category that assumes compliance, goodness is 'dynamic, transgressing, and, therefore, dangerous'" (np).

Jacob's generous act was also dangerous. Reading between the lines of the hundreds of discipline books, the words of thousands of experts on how to handle children, and the dozens of teacher websites, we realize that many teachers are fearful of losing control and of the chaos that will result.

Spiritual: "Seeing" the Need to Act

Living is easy with eyes closed, misunderstanding all we see.

~ John Lennon (1967)

At a recent conference, William Ayers (in Pinar, Ayers and Schubert 2007) shared the premise of the 1998 Brazilian/French film, *Central Station* (*Central do Brasil*), in which Dora—a former school teacher who writes letters for illiterate people at Rio de Janeiro's central station, Central do Brasil—transports a young boy, whose mother has just died in a car accident, to Brazil's remote Northeast, in search of the father he never knew. However, later in the film, Dora finds out that she was duped, and that she has placed the boy in danger.

Initially, Dora did not have a moral choice to make because she did not know about what happens to the children so transported. She was not aware.

Ayers used this plot line from the film to discuss social ethics. The film was striking in its portrayal of this incident due to the sequence of its progress. Dora—who sometimes throws away the letters she writes, and who speaks denigratingly of some of the people she writes for—is not aware that she is doing any evil by taking a large amount of money to transport the boy across the city. Once she recognizes the boy's need, she does all she can to help him.

Ayers's point is that moral choice requires one to be aware. In the moment of Jacob's disobedience above, his ability to see Clark's pain required him to act. Jacob's presence and intense engagement with his own senses created for him a kind of conscious awareness—making explicit the moral commitment.

Noddings (2002), in her description of the state of the "carer" in a caring situation, names this special form of attentiveness as "engrossment." Engrossment is a kind of attention that is "acutely receptive and is directed at the cared-for" (p. 28). Hay and Nye (1998) further discuss "seeing the need to act w/ kindness" as a spiritual awareness, a special kind of "attention" within a reflexive process, "being attentive to one's attention or "being aware of one's awareness" (p. 65)—what I might call a meta-awareness.

In many instances of non-compliance or disobedience, the child may not be responding to the teacher's demands or to the order of the structure of the room, but rather, he or she is responding to his or her attention/awareness to something or someone else. In Jacob's case, he did not attend to his teacher's expectation to stay seated in his time-out place, but instead evidenced an intense, irresistible attention to another child's needs.

As introduced in chapter 2, there is a deep connection between "attention" or "sensing" and morality, indicating that moral action "is not so much a matter of choice or values, but a matter of seeing the moral context clearly... moral sensitivities develop from continuous attention to the moral aspects of experience" (Murdoch 1970/1985, in Sherblom 1997). Murdoch's sensing/attention is similar to Eisner's (1998) discussion of the experience of "quality", noting that while the sensory system is the instrument through which we experience the qualities that constitute our environment, the ability to truly experience these qualities requires more than merely their presence—it requires action.

Jacob, like Julian who saw and therefore acted, allowed himself to be fully engaged with the space that surrounded him. As discussed in earlier chapters, this intense awareness and wide-awakeness is associated with their spirituality. Within the ordered structures of school—structures that are very effective at separating children from one another, from nature, and from real interactions with space and time—it is often the children, in more consistently and actively resisting those structures, who are able to maintain their spiritual relationships. There are many instances of children and their teachers caring for one another in their settings. The students in Michael Scott's class demonstrated a "spirituality of caring" for Flash's hurt neck (this will be described in chapter 6); Jacob did so for Clark, and Julian did so for Reuben. Even Moby's playful wrestling with Bruce seemed to come from a regard for Bruce and a desire to connect his body to another's. To feel alive and human:

> *Spirit* is that property of being fully and wholly human that fuels our predisposition to transcend each and every condition in our experience. 'Spirituality' is a construction of meaning meant to inform the human way we engage in that process of transcendence. Margaret Chatterjee (1989) appropriately suggests that there 'can be no spirituality shorn of community' (p. 6). A spirituality of caring is a way of naming what it is we do as a community to nurture and educate spirited young children for the invitations to transcendence presented by life; that is a human activity performed by and for whole people in a whole community. (Kimes-Myers 1997, 62)

Kindergarten classrooms are rife with moments of disobedience—moments in which children (and their teachers) push and transpierce boundaries of time and place; seek out the free spaces that allow the pleasure and comfort of a touch; and trouble to see one another in ways that allow deeper, fuller, spiritual and human connections. It is in these moments of disobedience that we may find our way into kinship and love.

> *The thought manifests as the word*
> *The word manifests as the deed*
> *The deed develops into habit*
> *And the habit hardens into character.*
> *So watch the thought*
> *And its ways with care*
> *And let it spring from love*
> *Born out of respect for all being*
>
> ~ Buddhist tradition (in Das 1998, 132)

Chapter 6

Discussion and Implications: The Moral of Julian

We are what we think. All that we are arises with our thoughts. With our thoughts we make the world.

~ Buddhist tradition (in Kornfield 2007, 4)

Introduction

In 1893, Emma Goldman was arrested for inciting a riot while advocating for unemployed workers. And in 1995, Julian, age five, lost his recess for getting out of line to help Reuben, also five, when he fell hard in the hallway of his school. When Reuben fell, Julian joined the ranks of those morally and spiritually unswaddled who practice disobedience even in the face of known consequences. I witnessed Julian's moment of disobedience many years ago and am still haunted by it. Haunted by seeing two lines of children not moving, not helping; by a child in pain disregarded by his teacher; by my own inaction; and by Julian.

While I didn't share a classroom with him, I quickly got to know Julian. He was unfailingly cheerful, polite and respectful. He was also unfailingly moving, talking, and asking questions. I began to expect him to take his place "on the wall" every kindergarten recess, and day after day, there he was. Most of our conversations took place there. Risking Mrs. Buttercup's admonitions that I was rewarding him, I would stand by him on the wall and talk. We talked about the reasons he was being punished and made plans on how he might comply with the rules in his room. He always planned to try, but was also almost always eerily realistic about his chances of meeting his teacher's rigorous standards for order. His sentences on the wall went unabated.

I don't know what became of Julian. I left the school the following year, and when I asked about him of teachers who stayed, they said he had left, too. I have always hoped his spirit sustained and that he remains cheerful, polite and respectful as well as full of energy, curiosity, and joy.

I do know what became of me as a result of Julian's lessons to me. I hold the moment of Reuben's fall, Julian's commiseration and Mrs. Buttercup's reprimand and punishment in vivid memory. I think back to my observations of his kindergarten experience and regret my choice to be considerate of a colleague over being responsive to the needs of a child. While Julian seemed capable of overcoming the event, I am not sure about me, and even more profound is my concern for the children who witnessed the event. I wonder about the effect of seeing a child's pain disregarded and another child's kindness devalued, even punished. One of my greatest regrets is that although Julian and I exchanged glances and slight shrugs of resignation at that moment, I did not communicate to the *other* children—the ones who stood in line—that there was goodness to Julian's action.

Over time, as I have reflected on my relationship with Julian, my feelings of guilt are ameliorated by my realization of how my relationship with him likely served as a "helping witness" or "enlightened witness" (Miller 1990). I know Julian knew that I *saw* him, that I noticed when things happened that weren't fair, and that I cared about his feelings and actions. He knew because we related. He knew by the exchanged glances, the smiles, the shrugs, the conversations, and the time spent together. He knew that I *chose* to be with him *because* of the very qualities that were the catalyst for the punishments doled out in his kindergarten classroom. I hold hope that this relationship assisted him in keeping his indomitable spirit—that it contributed to his spirited resiliency.

The moral of this event for me is related to the complexity of each moment of interaction—and especially those moments of what we would categorize as moments of disobedience. While such events are typically named as bad—and reacted to accordingly, these acts of disobedience are much more complex than those reactions imply.

And yet, it seems that nearly every strategy offered to teachers is aimed at making those interactions easier and *less* complicated. This troubles me. On beginning the inquiry that led to this book I wondered if there were goodnesses to see in other moments of disobedience. I wondered in what ways it might be possible to engage teachers in the spirited surprises to be found in the small acts of disobedience that are so much a part of a child's school life. So, in order to find ways to complicate teachers' understanding and interpretations of children's disobediences, I studied moments of disobedience in kindergarten classrooms to see what else I could find in them. Rather than looking at the disobedient acts toward determining cause or solution, my purpose in casting a light on these moments was to disrupt the typical early childhood/classroom management understanding of children's school disobediences.

Research Questions

Research intended to disrupt and destabilize the familiar and obvious in what is known and to form new logic and understanding about what is happening in the moment requires a method that supports that intention. In preparing to embark on the study of kindergartners' moments of disobedience, I tried on one qualitative method after another and abandoned each one: too linear, too prescribed, too critical, not critical enough, too predictive, too definitive, too *expected*.

Then, after two years of searching, I was fortunate enough to hear a panel presentation on rhizomatic methodology at a Reconceptualizing Early Childhood Education conference in Madison, Wisconsin. A group of Australian researchers led by Glenda MacNaughton presented for twelve minutes and I was up and running out the door with notes and names, revisiting Deleuze with a new purpose and ready to frame and pursue the research questions that eventually became the substance of this book.

In considering the first two research questions —"In what ways do kindergarten children disobey in the context of the kindergarten classroom?" and "In what ways are kindergartners' moments of disobedience representations and enactments of something more than merely disobedience?"—my research findings focused on a few small categories of disobedience, ones related to time and space, to surveillance and touch, and to observation and altruism. It became apparent in the contextual literature review in chapter 2 and in the contextual review of schools in chapter 4 that the ways in which children used the time and space of the classroom, the ways in which they kept themselves available for viewing, and how separate they kept their bodies were high priorities for classroom teachers. The rules, consequences and rewards were based on how tightly children toed the figurative line of classroom and kindergarten expectations of time, space, contact and surveillance.

I found that as the kindergarten children disobeyed, they often did so in ways that allowed them access to one another and to the environment that spoke to the next question: "In what ways are kindergartners' moments of disobedience opportunities for responding to others in caring, ethical ways and acting out the possibilities that a spiritual childhood provides?" While only Jacob openly exhibited a kind of disobedience that could be considered "responding to others in caring, ethical ways"—as will be discussed in the following sections of this chapter—I believe that all of the moments of disobedience presented in chapter 5 were acting out the possibilities that a spiritual childhood provides. Indeed, throughout my days at the kindergarten sites, I was witness to spiritual acts of reverence, awe, wonder, reflection, vision, commitment, and purpose as children daily engaged with one another and the environment in what Hay and Nye (1998) would term "awareness sensing, mystery sensing, and value sensing."

Mason, for instance, as he stretched the boundaries of his kindergarten space, was profoundly aware of the nuances of the classroom space and of the relationship he and his teacher had with time in that space. Because of this awareness, he was able to experience what one might consider the mundane, predictable, and everyday kindergarten day with freshness, surprise and a unique vision. Here then lies the mystery. Mason could look at the same carpeted area that all the children sat in every day and wonder what new possibility it would hold for him if he tried a slide, a quicker exit or bringing a ball to it. Even while engaged with an exciting prospect like the new (to him) carpet, Mason demonstrated that he could hold a dual (at least) sensitivity for value-sensing. While the ever-shifting newness of the carpet and room lent a rich value to the everyday in Mason's eyes, he also valued his relationship with Mr. Scott and the class. His actions throughout—"I said it, too"; checking with "Scott" for approval, for notice, and because he wanted to share with Mr. Scott what he was finding—indicated that he valued deeply his place in Mr. Scott's kindergarten classroom, even while pushing at the boundaries of that place.

In pursuing the questions about the ways children disobey and the possibilities and complexities of those disobedient moments, I chose to use rhizomatic analysis to simultaneously sharpen and blur the view on children's moments of disobedience in order to fold them into potential moments of humor, engagement, empathy, imagination and abandon. It was rhizomatic logic that allowed me to see Mason's spirited awareness-, value- and mystery-sensing in his non-compliance to the structured order of kindergarten. And it was rhizoanalysis that allowed me to trouble the power of techne' and seek to alleviate the pain of the morally and spiritually swaddled kindergarten children in their tightly partitioned (although not as tightly partitioned as some might think) classrooms.

Limitations, But Not So Limiting

St. Pierre (1997) wrote about her work considering the concept of data: "I took very seriously a very ordinary concept of qualitative inquiry, data, a concept that we certainly cannot do without, and opened it up to different possibilities. As a result, I will never again be able to think of data in the same way. Indeed, I am no longer sure I know what data 'means' or whether what it 'means' can assume the importance it once did" (p. 418).

In this book, I also took very seriously the concept of "data" as I, too, struggled with the considerable number and variations of moments of disobedience, and infinite variations of possible interpretations of the data generated during my time in those two kindergartens. I struggled with my own strong feelings about the data—the moments I selected to analyze, the texts I chose to include when discussing schools and teachers, the texts I selected to carefully lay over the texts of moments plucked from the kindergarten, and where I chose to lay those texts. From this experience with data, I, too, understood its meaning as fleeting and, concurrently, rife with possibilities and limitations.

In making my data-related choices, I was aware of my intentions and purpose concerning this book and of the strong biases I have related to those intentions, and so was concerned about the fairness and value of my choices. However, I found that aspects of Lather's (1991) discussion of postmodern, emancipatory research allowed some ways to think about ameliorating this concern. For instance, Lather recognizes that "ways of knowing are inherently culture-bound and perspectival [and that] ideology is the stories a culture tells about itself...[and] something that people inhabit in very daily, material ways" (p. 2). Therefore it was important to the book that I consider how my own values, my own ideologies, served to permeate my inquiry and what function they may have served as I engaged with the teachers and children. Helpful in working through the role of my values in this project was taking into account the distinction between "'coercive values'— racism, classism, sexism—that deteriorate objectivity and 'participatory values'—antiracism, anticlassism, antisexism" (from Harding 1986, in Lather 1991, 3). In rhizomatically challenging coercive values such as what I have named "compliancism" and the rational-technical teaching practices that often go unexamined, I would claim that this work operates under participatory values—taking a "change-enhancing, advocacy approach to inquiry based on ... 'enabling'" (p. 3). In this case, enabling a participant bias that advocates for children as spiritual, deeply moral people who deserve to spend their child-lives in places of comfort, joy and love.

Just as St. Pierre took very seriously the ordinary concept of data, so did I take seriously the ordinary concept of disobedience in kindergarten—now opened up in a way that I will (and I hope the reader will) never be able to think of it again in the same way.

Roads Untaken

Within those moments and within the walls of those school sites, there are many potential lines of flight in coming to understand the complexities of these moments of disobedience. Certainly obvious and not-so-obvious connections might have been followed, including those related to race, economics and culture—especially given the contrast between the two sites. However, this book is not about a comparative study of urban/suburban, Black/White, or economically advantaged/disadvantaged, but about a study of children's disobediences that a teacher of any child might see in any kindergarten classroom.

Ways in which gender connects to disobedience might have been pursued on an alternate line of flight. It was not a deliberate choice to focus the rhizomatic analyses only on moments of boys' disobedience; the acts themselves were selected for their mundaneness, and therefore the likelihood they would be familiar to kindergarten teachers; and selected for their potential in laying texts. Boys' acts of disobedience were more common than were the girls', more obvious, and, often, more prolonged—so there were more instances of disobedience involving boys from which to select. In pursuing this inquiry into disobedience, the gender of the child is not the issue, only that the child acts.

Even while focusing on the disobedient actions of children, I have selected among a wide variety of lenses with which to see those actions—lenses of possibility. But the limitations of language, pages, and one's capacities caused most of those lenses to be cast aside. Therefore, the limitations of this work derive in large part from the fact that there are few limitations to the ways in which the research question might have been answered. No matter which lines of flight I travel, there are others I have missed, and depending on which middle or fold of the line of flight I grab, other connections I might have made.

Implications: What Will this Research Do?

As different questions about educational research emerge, perhaps desires will shift from an insistence on defining concepts and predicting results to, as Linda Alcoff (1994, in St. Pierre 2000) suggests,

> an investigation of where our research goes and what it does there. This kind of inquiry, then, is always political, ethical, and material since it does not stray far from the lived experiences of those influenced by educational research. To this end, I believe our responsibility is to keep educational research in play, increasingly unintelligible to itself, in order to produce different knowledge and produce knowledge differently as we work for social justice in the human sciences. (p. 27)

I agree. I wanted to do research with young children that is about *them* and their school lives. And I wanted it to be unintelligible—not defining or predicting—but about a different kind of knowledge close to the children's and teachers' lived experiences. Taking into account Alcoff's suggestion of wondering where our research goes, a final question arises—one that is fundamentally connected to the stated research questions. "What are the possibilities in coming to understand and respond to the complexities and potential value of kindergartners' acts of disobedience?" This question informs the implications of the study in the final sections of this chapter, one each related to (a) compliancism and swaddling, (b) teacher choice, and (c) democracy.

Swaddling/Compliancism

> *The education of young children (like religion) 'becomes demonically destructive when it goes by the book and tries to make the dancing order of nature conform to the marching order of law, and force this essentially wiggly universe to toe the straight and narrow line.'*
>
> ~Alan Watts (2007, 192)

Perhaps the most succinct and cogent representation of a morally and spiritually swaddled character is that of Matt Groening's cartooned depiction of Bongo bound, gagged, and surveilled from the book *The Huge Book of Hell* (see *Figure 1,* on page 70), astutely depicting the complexity of reward and constraint as the compliant character is ostensibly privileged over the non-compliant. In considering an ism such as "compliancism" as represented in Groening's work, but also throughout the context of the study, one can clearly see that, as with every privileged ism, privilege only goes so far. Even the privileged compliant are not free.

Recall from the first chapter, Mead's (1951) description of the swaddled Russian child: "Hands that were tightly bound inside the swaddling bands could not explore... experiencing but never touching the teeming, vivid, highly charged world around it, being in it, but not of it." Rousseau (1979) also discussed swaddling in his famous text, *Emile*: "A child unswaddled would need constant watching [and children...]left free would assume faulty positions and make movements which might injure the proper development of their limbs." While the practice and act of swaddling may come about as an act of care and concern, and as a practice of security and control, the unintended consequences of the act include a muted, disengaged experience with one's world. This aligns with school swaddling, which is both a means of control and, ostensibly, for the child's own good.

In studying the child in interaction with school, it is important to be aware of the impact of the normalizing, constraining, and structural orders inherent in child/teacher relationships and even in the architecture of the school and classroom. Wrapped in the swaddling clothes of school procedures, rules and norms, the kindergarten child is similarly deprived of real association with the world, and so, also deprived of the opportunity to enact the freedom, joy, wisdom, silliness, hope, abandon, faith, beginnings, playfulness, verve, whole-hearted faith and intense awareness of what childhood might offer, given the space to do so.

We read in the previous chapters of children like Mason, Moby and The Toucher in the Other Teacher's line—children who, in spite of (in response to?) the constraints and normed order of school, threw off the swaddling clothes of normalization and coercion. We also read of children like Tommy and Bumblebee who perhaps enjoyed the safety and security of those swaddling bands. For some, these predictable and presumed constraints may feel right and proper and may serve to

> provide canopies under which identifications grow protected from the wild winds and harsh temperatures.... [These canopies may] constitute 'regimes of truth' that protect the fragile human ego providing canals or routes of thinking, or rather, logos, to which we become emotionally invested in maintaining as it constitutes in part our being and [which] define 'the situation' (regimes of truth), justify the status quo, and thingify (that is identify) what is and what is not that 'we'are: the state of things. (den Heyer, email communication, 2007)

As den Heyer's message implies, within the discussion of the consequences of swaddling and the deceptive benefits of engaging in compliancism, one might find value and a range of meaning connected to compliance and the security of the rules, structures, beliefs, traditions, and sacred texts that swaddle us and keep us, in some ways, safe. Palmer's (1998) work mirrors den Heyer's statement:

> We collaborate with the structures of separation because they promise to protect us against one of the deepest fears at the heart of being human—the fear of having a live encounter with alien 'otherness'.... We fear encounters in which the other is free to be itself, to speak its own truth, to tell us what we may not wish to

hear. We want those encounters on our own terms, so that we can control their outcomes, so that they will not threaten our view of world and self. (p. 37)

While Palmer and den Heyer lead us to understand, in gentle terms, the humanness of huddling beneath canopies of identity, I cannot help wondering what we miss while fearfully wrapped apart from the teeming possibilities from which we become separated. I presume that the same canopy that protects us from winds and temperatures also prevents us from seeing the stars and feeling the sun on our faces, and I worry about the means by which these safe places are maintained. Bunyard (2005) tells of the child protected from the messiness of childhood and so protected from his own perfection:

> Probably every reader of this essay has had to deal with a small child and its mess. Of course the child was soon cleaned up, the floor swept, and the table wiped. The clothes they wore eventually got dumped in the washing machine and some semblance of order was restored. Day after day, this pattern was repeated and eventually a level of tidiness and cleanliness acceptable to adult eyes predominated for longer and longer stretches of time. Each correction or encouragement added to the apparent solidity of the practices of everyday life surrounding the child—adults and other children creating an increasingly well-defined reciprocal to the child's own agency; and so the child grew up. This process is unremarkable, yet it presents society with two forms of danger. Adults, in wanting the best for their children, perhaps try too hard to shape them according to some image of perfection; children, in wanting love, are perhaps too willing to submit. (p. 292)

Alice Miller warned of the 'as-if personality' that emerges from children's susceptibility to adult needs and expectations. Just as education is a process of "improving" or making better children (Baker 1998), the as-if person "develops in such a way that he reveals only what is expected of him, and fuses so completely with what he reveals that ... one could scarcely have guessed how much more there is to him, behind his masked view of himself. He cannot develop and differentiate his 'true self' because he is unable to live it" (Miller 1983/1990, 27).

It thus is not only rules and structures that serve to swaddle— but also the normalizing pressures of customary moralities of good and bad and the desire to please. Under the judging gaze, the "terrible eye" of the adult, the child learns her goodness and so her value. There is no need to actually wrap the child in swaddling clothes. She will wrap herself. In drawing this picture, the intent is to blur the lens, but also to focus it on the child within the moment of the gaze—not the child who is the object of our authoritarian gaze, not the child who is the subject of a rewarding or punishing action, but the child who is "our kin and our kind" (Jardine 1998).

The children's text introduced in chapter 5, *Tootle* (in Burbules 1986), neatly portrays a world in which children and the adults responsible for them have very definitive roles and obligations toward one another. "Typically children fail by acting upon immature desires and habits; they must try to stop being 'babies' who do 'silly' or 'dreadful' things... responsibilities and expectations can be formulated as *simple* and *inviolate* rules that are absolute, not accidental—facts, not mere conventions [emphases mine]. Follow the rules and your life will work out well. The paradigm of all rules is to "Stay on the Rails No Matter What":

> School is where lessons are learned, where inadequate [innocent] children (babies) become responsible and accomplished adults. These lessons are...immutable—learning to obey rules is essential to success....Teachers are kindly and benign; what they do is always for the child's welfare...[even though some of their] techniques may be misleading, deceptive, or manipulative, such as assigning tasks without explanation or justification; using rewards and punishments to elicit desired student behaviors; relying on personal allegiances in order to motivate students to perform certain tasks; presenting incomplete, inconsistent, or inaccurate accounts of the world in order to make it uncontroversial and palatable; or avoiding conflict by presuming that consensus exists....These approaches are appealing because they *simplify* [emphasis mine] the school day for the teacher and for the student.... An educational approach that calls into question the above goals and methods would vastly complicate the tasks of teachers and students in the classroom, making their activities and relations to one another much more problematic, controversial, and provisional.... This is a picture that can convince teachers that their intentions are invariably good and that their basic endeavor can be unambiguously defined. Moreover, it can reassure students

that the path to adulthood and success is simple and linear. Neither side has much stake in examining very closely why the Great Curve of the rails leads inexorably away from many of the warmest and most vibrant impulses of childhood, or what is lost to those who do Stay on the Rails, No Matter What. (p. 344–346)

The following section, "Choice: Making It Complicated," is intended to call into question the simplifying goals and methods described here and in chapter 4, and seeks to greatly complicate the tasks of teachers and students in the classroom toward maximizing the common good.

Choice: Making it Complicated

I have always done what they wanted me to do. Teach reading, writing, and arithmetic. Nothing else—nothing about dignity, nothing about identity, nothing about loving and caring.

~ Earnest Gaines, *A Lesson before Dying* (1993)

How will you live your life so that it doesn't make a mockery of your values?

~Bill Ayers, *Fugitive Days* (2001)

In the moment of Reuben's fall, Julian saw a child's need, listened to the call of the situation, and responded with an exhibition of care. I have grown to believe that if we look carefully, we may see these qualities within the day to day actions and interactions of young children, and that many of these qualities may be present in the context of acts of disobedience.

In chapter 2, Hay and Nye (1998) discussed "spiritual awareness" as a special kind of attention within a reflexive process—"being attentive to one's attention or 'being aware of one's awareness'" (p. 65)—as a meta-awareness. Julian, Mason, Moby, and Jacob, through their actions of resistance and disobedience in their respective kindergarten classrooms, demonstrated a special kind of attention and awareness to the "other." Noddings (2002) suggested that a question we must put to ourselves as educators is whether this form of attention, which she calls engrossment, should be invisible in our classrooms or, as it is even more commonly, subject to correction. "Why do we so often fail to develop it [engrossment] and substitute instead an almost self-righteous belief in our own authority and the goodness of our coercive methods?" (p. 29–30).

Children who become engrossed in what they perceive around them are, ironically, often scolded for a lack of attention. Yet, as Macdonald relates, the school offers only a "shoddy" experience to shutter the children away from their engrossment. For example, Macdonald (1995) told of an observation made in a classroom in which some children sat in a circle and took turns reading aloud to their teacher, more often than not, having to be told where they were supposed to be reading when it was their turn; some sat copying a handwriting lesson from the chalkboard; and others were given worksheets so that they might "make new words out of double vowels such as 'oo' and work on endings such as 'er,' 'ing,' and 's.'" Of this observation, Macdonald finds nothing out of the ordinary in terms of the everyday life in schools, noting that "the hour was characterized by routine, boredom, and busywork" (p. 110).

What Macdonald wrote next recalls some of my own conversations with fellow teachers. He wrote: "I have often asked teachers why they waste their own and children's lives dealing with trivia and meaningless tasks. I have even accused them of being immoral for doing so!" (p. 111).

Macdonald then claimed he was wrong, and should have been asking, "Who really makes the decisions, and in whose interests are these boring, routine, and busywork decisions made?" (p. 111). I don't agree that Macdonald was wrong in asking teachers why they wasted a child's life, or in accusing them of immorality in doing so, for while, certainly, teachers are likewise swaddled and coerced into compliance, they do have choices in how actively and enthusiastically they unquestioningly comply. As did the children in this study, they could disobey.

A few months ago, I was struggling with what this book might do for teachers. How might my rhizomatic (meandering, reversible, detachable) connections to moments of children's disobedience mean anything to someone else? What would it mean to a teacher if she read it? And I almost quit. Then I caught a morning rerun of the medical drama series "ER" (Thorpe 1996). It was an episode in which a little girl had been shot as a bystander by a pair of pre-teen gang-bangers. The mother of the little girl and the doctor who saved her life exchanged the following:

Dr. Pratt: "They have the guys who did it. They'll pay for this."

Little Girl's Mother: "I don't want them to pay. I want it to stop. We abandon these kids, we don't educate them and then wonder when it goes wrong."

Dr. Pratt: "People make choices."

Little Girl's Mother: "Some people don't know they have choices."

And *that's* what made it clear. *Some people don't know they have choices.*

Recall what Hostetler (2005) wrote (as first related in chapter 1): "The presumption is not that people err with regard to well-being because they are evil. We err because we overlook something, misperceive something. All of us have blind spots. But we can improve our vision" (p. 20). We *can* improve our vision, if we are willing to hone our eyesight and move beyond the limited readings on each kindergarten moment that we are used to making, and if we are willing then *to disobey.*

Thoreau (1848/1966) asked us to consider those laws and rules of convention that are at times unjust, "Shall we be content to obey them, or shall we endeavor to amend them, and obey them until we have succeeded, or shall we transgress them at once?" (p. 231). Thoreau was talking about making what we perceive as unassailable, unquestionable convention into opportunities of choice. He asked that we consider that some conventions, rules, and laws are unjust and so to look more fully and carefully at what, who and how we obey and, I would suggest, what we require of children.

I think that many teachers do not know—or do not really *believe*—that they have choices. Therefore, an important aspect of this research was the careful analysis of children's moments of disobedience in ways that make it obvious that the choices are infinite! Infinite, and therefore, concurrently, even more difficult to negotiate in the constraints that the children and teachers are a part of.

MacNaughton (2004) warned that these more complete readings are not easy. They are without the "simple roadmaps showing routes to certain destinations" like those built into the path that others (see chapters 2 and 4) have so blindingly lit up for us. Taking on more complete and complicated readings leads us to a path replete with "complex ethical choices, unpredictable twists and turns and never-ending possibilities."

This path is not an easy one... and in avoiding it, teachers have a sometimes-ally in Macdonald. When he asked who is really making the decisions in school, he, in essence, absolved teachers of their moral and ethical responsibility to nurture the spirits of the children in their care. He implicitly placed the blame on those who make the decisions in a way similar to the way that the 1974 Milgram obedience experiments worked. By deferring to the Authority—whether the authority of the doctor in the lab coat, the state senator, or a suit-and-tie principal—teachers avoid the moral responsibility for their actions and interactions with the children in their care. Closing their eyes to their moral choice leaves them unaware and so free not to act on what is best and right for our children. I like Macdonald better when he takes teachers to task:

> The schools are full of a 'they won't let me' syndrome on the part of teachers...it is difficult to see how teachers who acquiesce to the authoritarian and self-serving milieu of the system could provide conditions other than those same ones in their own classrooms.... Teachers often teach from textbooks, manuals and, if possible, commercial lesson plans. Teachers teach groups of children because it is *easier* to do so, and have often acquiesced to 'homogeneous' groupings in schools primarily because they feel it is *easier* to teach this way [emphases mine]. Teachers often avoid controversial issues, deny the erotic aspects of the nature of human beings, and avoid the discussion of anything that is not planned ahead of time. Many teachers are consumed by the fear that they will lose control, that some situation will present itself in which they must operate as a responsive human being rather than as a status symbol of authority. Under these sorts of circumstances, it pays to get things 'organized' and develop managerial techniques whose primary goal is the maintenance of control. (Macdonald 1995, 44)

The children in Mrs. Buttercup's line did not seem to believe they had a choice—and, thus, compliance absolved them of their responsibility. Perhaps the same children who obediently stayed in line, who did not question authority, who did not see that there was a moral opportunity are the ones who will (or already have!) become teachers. If school "fits" the child, he or she may be more likely to wish to continue there. However, once one becomes a teacher and commits to the care and well-being of children, it becomes imperative to recognize and then confront that "part of the privilege of being a member of the dominant culture [the compliant] is a blind presumption that yours is the natural, preferred entitlement" (Whitelock 2006, 172).

In order to engage in the possibility of making choices outside of the structured order of school, the teacher must not only be brave but skilled, for "the enactment of democratic living in education requires the practice of professional deliberative judgments" (Henderson and Slattery 2006, 3). As a young teacher, I found myself almost accidentally resisting the dominant order through what was perhaps a combination of deliberative judgment and serendipity.

Here is what happened in one instance of a teaching choice that I, at first, did not realize I had—because at first I did not "see" the moral choice, and so could not practice informed deliberative judgment. Andre' Hotten was a third-grader in my class who said, "I'm am!" nearly every time I asked him to do anything, but he never was! For several months we argued. We would attempt the three-step (or, as in this instance, a five-step variation) response ala Mehan (in Mullooly and Varenne 2006):

1. I would tell him to do something or to stop doing something.
2. He would *not* do it or stop doing it [a break in the exchange].
3. I would then repeat 1. or a variation, like "NOW!"
4. Andre' would say, "I'm am!!"
5. My response would be a variation of: "No, you're not."

One day, I watched him. After I had told him to clean up the toothpicks and clay he was using to make a model of the rabbit cage we were preparing to build, he continued to move the toothpicks into a variety of positions. But this time when I looked, I didn't just check, I *watched*. And so, this time, I *really saw* him. He *had* heard me tell him to clean up. And while he continued to manipulate the toothpicks, I saw/felt a shift: he was *preparing* (fixin') to clean up.

As expressed in chapter 4, it is expected in the disciplined relationship between teachers and students that the student respond immediately to what the teacher says. What is not said aloud is that the response must be visible or otherwise apparent to the teacher!

Andre' had been listening to me; he *had* been responding. The problem between us came about as it appeared to me that he was not responding. As I became interested in this particular realization, I attended much more carefully to Andre on the occasions of our "tell, do, evaluation" exchanges. I became much more attuned to the subtle shifts as Andre transitioned between activities. He had been aware that he was making those internal shifts (thus the insistent "I'm am!!'s"), but he was either not aware that I did not know, or more likely, he assumed that I would not believe him or would not care.

By choosing to see Andre', I finally realized that I had choices in how to respond to him. Instead of arguing with him when he claimed, "I'm am!"... I could:

- Ask, "Are you, Andre'?"
- Say, "Okay, thanks."
- Say, "I need to see it—it helps me."
- Say, "Tell me when I can see it, Andre'."
- Ask, "How can you show me that you are?"
- Say, "Cool."

Looking more carefully and listening more clearly allowed me to see that I had a choice in how to respond to Andre'. I did not have to push against what I perceived as his pull. I did not have to punish him or nag him until he listened in a way that *I* could see it. I could trust in him and offer him two things: (a) my recognition of his efforts and difference, and (b) some lessons about ways to better respect others' needs in relationships.

Just as it had been when I visited Edwin George and held his tomahawk (from chapter 2), my vision was impaired, offering only an incomplete picture of Andre' and his ways. I did not see him fully and so allowed myself to base my responses on a limited reading of the moment. Looking—*really* looking—and really listening served to complicate my understanding.

As Pinar famously wrote: conversations should be complicated—"extraordinarily" so. There must be room for complexities and multiple realities in "complicated conversation across and within culture, class and place" (Pinar 2004, 157). And what could better serve to complicate than to contemplate Deleuze's (1987) "AND" logic: "Think with AND instead of thinking IS, instead of thinking for IS" (p. 57)? Rather than thinking what it IS (or IS NOT) that we see, and so how to react—one could think with AND—and action rather than reaction. When Deleuze (in 2001) discussed Nietzsche, he wrote, "Everywhere we see the victory of No over Yes, of reaction over action. Life becomes adaptive and regulative, reduced to its secondary forms; we no longer understand what it means to act" (p. 74–75). In the case of Andre', I had been thinking IS/IS NOT. I said, "Jump," and saw he IS NOT jumping. Instead, thinking with AND, I said "Jump," AND saw Andre' did not jump AND saw he did jump AND saw his knowing AND *not* knowing what I saw AND... Which led to my stuttered experience with our interactions—stuttered and full of possibilities in understanding one another in new ways.

The complicated sensibility of this conversation resonates with Lather's (2006) discussion of the value of "proliferation" as a good thing to think with in research. I would argue that the same "wild profusion" of aporia toward "estranging the basis of authority of the dominant" discourses is present in what is now called classroom management or discipline. As long as the dominant view perpetuates the ideal of good teachers as those who hold tight control over their students and of effective classrooms as those that enact the dominant order, there is little space left for these good teachers to meaningfully engage with the children in their own wild profusion of ways to be in the kindergarten classroom. Lather (2006) noted in her article that Deleuze calls for "'a thousand tiny sexes' rather than the binary categories of homosexual and heterosexual" (p. 43). In a similar fashion, we teachers might view children and their actions in "thousands of tiny qualities" rather than the binary categories of good or bad. In this way, one is compelled to consider multiple ways to respond, because "such nomadic rather than sedimentary conjunctions produce fluid subjects, ambivalent and polyvalent, open to change, continually being made, unmade and remade" (p. 43).

Consider Jacob—leaving his timeout to help Clark. In what ways might any adult respond to such a moment of disobedience? Would he or she prioritize the ordered behavioral structures of the kindergarten and so enforce a consequence? Wong and Wong (1998) claim that allowing children to get away with small infractions leads to chaos. This was echoed by Mr. Watts, the principal in the school studied in Jan Nespor's 1997 *Tangled up in School*, as he responded to parents' complaints about silent lunches: "When they [the kids] don't behave, I'm going to put them on silent lunch ...bad *is* bad, and *we've got to make them pay for it* [emphasis mine]" (p. 125). Given this, *do* teachers have choices?

In the episode, *Shoulder to Cry On*, Mrs. Krinkle made the choice *not* to make Jacob pay for it, and so let him get away with the infraction of leaving Time-Out. This led not to chaos, but to kindness. Might she have seen this moment as an opportunity to better know this child/these children? Might a teacher experience a moment of joy in seeing a child step up to comfort a child in need?

Mrs. Krinkle's and Mr. Scott's Choices

While observing the children's interactions and moments of disobedience in Mrs. Krinkle and Mr. Scott's classrooms, I also had the opportunity to note choices made by these teachers—choices that indicated some evidence of resistance to the norm. The following are moments of interactions that allow some experience with teacher disobedience—or at least a degree of resistance or defiance to the structured expectations of a particular situation, place or person.

In the following descriptions of Mrs. Krinkle and Mr. Scott's classroom choices, the two teachers seemed to be responding to what they *saw* as what the children involved *needed*. As Alfie Kohn has pointed out, in wondering which of two questions schools seek to answer (How can we get these kids to obey? or What do these children need?), the structured expectations of School are not generally responsive to children's needs. In this way, Mrs. Krinkle and Mr. Scott were disobedient.

Mrs. Krinkle's Choice: Touching Briona.

Briona was a child who entered Mrs. Krinkle's classroom as a new student early in the school year. Briona came from the kindergarten across the hall. I was aware of an escalating situation between Briona and her previous teacher due to my role as a university facilitator. I had biweekly interactions with Briona's former teacher related to one of my students who had been placed in the classroom as part of a practicum. My student had raised concerns in class regarding Briona and her disintegrating role in the classroom. Several times a day Briona was removed from individual children and from the classroom itself. The teacher had, herself, come to me about this "difficult" child only weeks before. She described a girl who was disruptive and unmanageable—so much trouble, in fact, that by the third week of school, the teacher had already called an intervention meeting that included Briona's parent, the school counselor, principal and a system psychologist. The teacher reported that Briona was "always too close": too close to other children, too close to the front of the carpet, and too close to the teacher. She annoyed everyone, the teacher said. Three weeks later, Briona had been transferred to Mrs. Krinkle's classroom.

Briona continued to be too close—for some children. The following is a transcript of the videotape of the children as they took part in a whole-group lesson on Mrs. Krinkle's carpet. Briona is seated in the back row (recall, Mrs. Krinkle's students sit in rows on the carpet and have assigned places), next to Princess and very close to her, shoulder-to shoulder in fact. No one is sitting on her right.

Princess: She's ...

Briona: No, I'm not

Princess: she is shhshhh... (0.2) she's touching me!

Briona: ((simultaneously)) only a little!

Teacher: Princess, what?

Princess: She IS touching me

Teacher: is she hurting you?

Briona: NO!

Princess: ((softly and slightly after Briona)) No...

Teacher: then what should we do about this?

Briona: // I'll scoot over ((she exaggerates her movement to her right and ends up off the carpet and on the linoleum floor))

Teacher: ((laughing a little)) what about you Briona, are you comfortable there?

Princess: She's good

Briona: ((simultaneously)) // I like it here

Teacher: Princess, is that good enough for you?

Princess: she's good

((The lesson goes on for about 4 more minutes—and in that four minutes Briona has gradually scooted over closer to Princess, although not as close as before—and the girls have been whispering now and then—when there is another outburst from Princess.))

Princess:	She's ( ) itting on me! ((Princess has a lisp which makes her sometimes hard to correctly understand))
Teacher:	where? How is she sitting on you?
Princess:	ssss(ss ...)) itting!! ssss(ss ...)) itting!!

((Briona looks at Princess with concern and looks at her body and the small space between them))

Princess:	She's (0.3) with her mouth...(0.2)... sshpiitting
Teacher:	oh! Spitting! Briona?
Briona:	((shrugs))
Teacher:	Were you talking to Princess?
Briona:	sure. Sure
Teacher:	Princess, Briona was talking to you. Sometimes when we talk, saliva can escape from our mouth. I am sure she would never spit on you on purpose
Princess:	((looks at Briona))
Briona:	I wouldn't!! ((hugs Princess enthusiastically while Princess cringes))
Teacher:	Princess, you can go to the washroom if you want.

Mrs. Krinkle did not ignore Princess's need for care. She acknowledged her complaint concerning Briona as valid; and yet, she also recognized that Briona's need for proximity was not "bad," and so Briona was not a problem for Mrs. Krinkle as she had been for her previous teacher. Briona's need and Princess's need were in conflict, and Mrs. Krinkle saw her responsibility to the two girls as helping them mediate the conflicting needs. In seeing the needs of both girls, Mrs. Krinkle made a choice with intentions to acknowledge Princess's need to be heard and Briona's need to be close.

Mrs. Krinkle's Choice: Jacob and the Paint Shirt.

Another instance that demonstrated Mrs. Krinkle's resistance to the norm in her role as teacher took place during my first taped observation of Mrs. Krinkle's kindergarten children. In mid-

September, Mrs. Krinkle had set the children to mix yellow and blue paint in the hallway with one of our university's field students. Into the room came Jacob, holding at arm's length in front of him his paint shirt, dripping with blue and yellow and looking to weigh at least ten pounds.

Teacher:	Jacob!
Jacob:	It got wet
Teacher:	Again?
Jacob:	Where's my other shirt?
Teacher:	Jacob, Jacob, Jacob
Jacob:	had another shirt?
Teacher:	Hmm. Yes. ((Takes the shirt from his hands and holds it up – showing me how wet it is and shakes her head while smiling))
Jacob:	oh yeah. //
Mrs. Krinkle:	oh yeah
Jacob:	.. get it?
Mrs. Krinkle:	do you think it's dry
Jacob:	*smiles slowly* okaaaaay... // should I clean this one?
Teacher:	go to it, sir
Teacher:	((shakes her head again, still smiling—and holds the shirt away from her body, using only her thumb and forefinger, as far as her arm will reach))
Jacob:	((backs up a few steps and runs in place, vmmmmm, trots toward Mrs. Krinkle, snatching the wet shirt from her hand and stiff-legged runs to the in-class-room restroom—holding the shirt outstretched in the same hold Mrs. Krinkle demonstrated earlier)).
Teacher:	((singsong to the field student in the hallway)): OH, Mr. Parker!!!
Peter:	Yes? ((faint--from the hallway))
Teacher:	Can you assist Jacob?
Peter:	((peers into classroom—with puzzled look))
Teacher:	He is cleaning his paint shirt
Peter:	((startled *OH!* Follows Jacob into the restroom))
Teacher:	He'll get it

I later asked Mrs. Krinkle whom she meant by "He'll get it": Jacob or Mr. Parker? She laughed and said, "I was talking about Jacob, but I guess it could apply to either one. Jacob has a lot of adjustments to make, and I am adjusting to him, too." She said these words in a way that communicated not exasperation or annoyance—but that she was looking forward to these mutual adjustments to this year's kindergarten.

Later I found out from Mr. Parker that when Jacob was holding his blue- and yellow-painted shirt under the water, he watched the paint run from his shirt: "Look!!! GREEN!!!"

Mrs. Krinkle's choice in responding to Jacob with humor and guidance rather than annoyance and punishment offered some insight into her relationship with him. She was his teacher and saw her responsibility as his teacher to allow latitude for mistakes, messiness, and humor—and so, acknowledged Jacob's energy and curiosity as valued.

Mr. Scott's Choice: Jonathan Pinched.

Mr. Scott described the following event from his afternoon kindergarten in his as-yet unpublished master's thesis:

> Today Jonathan pinched Andrew coming in from the playground. I removed Jonathan from the situation, asking him to wait for me in the beanbag chair in the book corner. I then apologized to Andrew that this had happened. (The only sincere apology that I could offer Andrew was my own)...I told him that it is not ok for anyone to do this to him and promised him that we would make it up to him and would not allow it to continue...My goal is not to even the score for Andrew. My primary objective is to care for the injured child and help Jonathan find his role in helping.
>
> I went to Jonathan and asked him what he was going to do to make it up to Andrew. Jonathan, now flustered and in tears, responded, 'I don't know how! What am I supposed to do? I wish I wouldn't have done it and I would make it up to Andrew if I knew what to do.'
>
> I asked, 'Do want suggestions from me or from the class?' Jonathan pointed to his classmates, who were working at their tables. I explained, 'It will be your job to make it up to Andrew, but I'm sure that they will give you many good ideas to choose from.'

I called to the room, 'Emergency meeting! Everyone to the carpet! Jonathan needs our help!'

...I asked Jonathan to tell them about his problem. He said, 'When we were outside, it was Andrew. I pinched him. I hurt him. I made him cry. Now I have to make it up to him and I don't know what to do.' ... Hands shot up with a variety of suggestions. The children suggested that Jonathan make Andrew a picture, write him a letter or make him a card...Some children advised that a hug or a gift would help put a smile on Andrew's face....The children then returned to their table-work, leaving Jonathan and I at the carpet. Now, Jonathan was held accountable for his behavior. He had hurt someone, received advice from the class and it was his job to take action to fix the problem. Jonathan asked me to write the words that he wanted to say to Andrew. His letter read:

> *Dear Andrew,*
>
> *I'm sorry Andrew when I pinched you. Tomorrow I am going to give you a present. If you don't like it; I'll give you another present.*
>
> *Jonathan L*

Next, Jonathan took the pen, signed his name and drew a truck on the apology letter because Andrew 'really likes trucks'...I asked him to wait at the carpet, while I took the rest of the class to gym. Then, I walked Jonathan to room 11. I waited in the doorway and watched as he approached Andrew, handed him the letter, said he was sorry, mentioned the possibility of a gift and gave him a hug. (np)

In this circumstance, Mr. Scott's thoughtful response to Jonathan's and Andrew's needs and his recognition that both children were in need offered a rich counterbalance to the ritualized and scripted "apology" as described by one of the premiere character experts. In contrast to Mr. Scott's efforts to offer guidance as Jonathan sought ways to make it up to Andrew, Lickona (1997) offered the following directed model as a "great way to teach conflict resolution skills": "When one child has hurt another, Ms. Skinner teaches a reconciliation ritual that fosters the virtue of forgiveness. She instructs the offending child to say 'I am sorry—will you please forgive me?' If the victim judges the apology sincere, that child is instructed to respond, 'I do forgive you'" (p. 57).

In direct contrast to Lickona's efficient and popular example of instructing regrets and forgiveness, Mr. Scott viewed the time and effort expended in teaching Jonathan that *he* can find ways to offer his regrets to another child as a moral responsibility. In the following, final example of his deep regard for children, Mr. Scott once again disobediently determines that time can be invested in the needs of children.

Mr. Scott's Choice: Flash's Neck

In late September, on one of my last visits to Michael Scott's classroom, I was happy to have been witness to an event that we both call "Flash's Neck." Happy because the children in this class were afforded the opportunity to act in generous and generative ways toward one another—especially to a child who was in need. The story began as the children were seated in a circle on the carpet for a morning meeting in which Mr. Scott provided time for the children to tell their classmates something interesting:

Teacher:	Anyone has something interesting to say, we're in a circle; we can see everyone and we're ready to listen. (0.3) Flash has something to say. Let's listen to Flash!
Flash:	My neck hurts
Teacher:	Flash says his neck hurts. Questions for Flash?

((And the children begin offering suggestions for why Flash's neck hurts.))

Billy Bob Joe:	Maybe his neck is more stronger. Up here when that hurts ((grasps his bicep with his left hand)) that means it's getting more muscle... it's because it's getting stronger
Flash:	No my arms are strong, it's my neck that's hurting
Cupcake:	( ) when you put your head back.. ( )..
Teacher:	Did you hurt it when you were sitting in your chair?
Flash:	I think I didn't
Fred:	I think it's just hurting because it hurts
Ariel:	Maybe his neck is hurting because he's coughing

Teacher:	Is it a sore throat, Flash? Ariel says you've been coughing
Flash:	Maybe I did have a frog throaty but that's not....
N'than:	One time I bumped my head when I was sleeping
Flash:	So did I
Eric:	This morning—probably he fell down and hurt his neck
Flash:	Not right now... I haven't fallen for a long time.
Emily:	We could trace his steps back
Teacher:	Hmmm
Emily:	So we can figure out what happened
Flash:	Maybe I did fall down
Teacher:	What can we do to help Flash?
Emily:	Call the doctor...tell his mom... so she can call the doctor
Teacher:	Is there anything we can do here today to help our friend, Flash?
Fred:	(indistinguishable)
Ariel:	Mr. Scott, my thing fell out of my earring
Teacher:	No worries, we can take care of that ((he places Ariel's earring and earring back behind him on the counter)) And now we're helping Flash.
Corn-on-the-Cob:	We can bring a blue chair over for him
Teacher:	Would that help Flash? Having a chair when we come to the carpet ((gets up and gets a beanbag chair to take to Flash on the carpet))—so when we're on the carpet, this seat right here can be for Flash
Cupcake:	( )
Teacher:	I can't hear Cupcake
Cupcake:	( ) pillow under his neck....
Teacher:	Here we go Flash; Cupcake has suggested this purple pillow might help you. Does that help? (2.0) Another suggestion that's making our friend feel better

Emily:	I can't see him
Eric:	( ).. some water so...( )... his neck
Teacher:	Eric, come here, bud... I have cups up here. ((he walks to the side of the room and reaches up for a large plastic storage container)) can you please go to the drinking fountain and get Flash a small little cup of cold water
Fred:	You're big. You're really big. ((this because the storage container was placed very high up))
Emily:	I can't see him
Teacher:	((to Eric)) Can you please go to the drinking fountain and get Flash a little small cup of cold water?
The Mummy:	If he has to go potty, and he's in the chair, ( ) ((could not hear, but it must have then segued into something regarding an ice pack))
Teacher:	Flash, do you need an ice pack?

((Eric returns with the little small cup of cold water))

Fred:	Eric is back. Eric is here

((The children are looking at Flash as he sits in the blue beanbag chair, with a pillow behind his head and drinking a cup of water.))

Teacher:	The Mummy, I have a job for you, friend come here ((T is writing on paper while calling over The Mummy))
Teacher:	Boys and girls, The Mummy suggested that maybe an ice pack might help... I wrote on this paper, "Can we please have an ice pack?" ((to The Mummy)) Do you know where the nurse's office is?
The Mummy:	((shakes head))
Teacher:	The Mummy needs a helper—I need a helper for The Mummy

Here, I ran out of tape, and by the time I retrieved a new tape from the car and loaded it, the children had moved into center time—where they took the opportunity to make pictures for Flash and to bring him books (some children read to him) and toys—and were in the process of transitioning into snack time. Flash was still in his beanbag chair, with the pillow behind his head, laying stretched out—legs crossed at the ankles in front of him—with his ice pack and not only the little small cup of water, but a dozen or so snacks from the other children, a stack of drawings they have made for him and two girls on either side of his "throne"—Sally reading a book to him and Ariel holding his water when he was not drinking it.

As the snack time progressed, the children moved to their own tables to eat, but Flash was never alone. Children, sometimes without a word, walked to him and handed him a snack, Sally moved her snack to sit beside him on the floor; and Emily brought him a jacket to cover his bare legs. (It was still very warm in September.) When it was time to clean up, Flash had to move a pretzel, a bag of gummies, two drink boxes, baggies of Cheetos, a chocolate chip cookie and a wrapped apple off his stomach before he could get up, which he did in order to use the restroom. While he was gone, Bravo, Cupcake and Mr. Johnson (this is a child—as described earlier, when choosing their pseudonyms, some children decided on names that might be confusing—like this one, Mr. Johnson), with no discussion, cleaned up Flash's significant mess.

This event of Flash's Neck consumed a good part of the morning—albeit with a great deal of problem solving, reading, writing, verbal communication and community-building involved. However, I have to wonder how the Wongs and other techne' experts would fit such an event into their ideal of the highly predictable and efficient classroom. In direct opposition to the expected order of the kindergarten, Mr. Scott chose to spend an entire morning (and since this was a half-day kindergarten—their *whole* day), making one child feel cared for, and *all* of the children feel important and proficient in caring for another.

Choices: Making the Familiar Strange.

Kimes-Myers (1997) engaged in considering the joyful and freeing quality of choices by sharing a description of the Sunday newspaper cartoon, *Calvin and Hobbes*, opening as the characters of Calvin and Hobbes set out to explore an old field from a new perspective:

> Calvin pushes his way through newly fallen snow on a bright January day. Snowdrifts almost reach his waist as he plows forward into a large, snow covered field. Faithful tiger Hobbes walks in Calvin's track, carrying a toboggan. Calvin exclaims, 'Wow! It

really snowed last night! Isn't it wonderful?' Waking to the excitement of the experience, Hobbes brightens. Catching snowflakes with his extended paws, he suggests, 'It's like having a big white sheet of paper to draw on!' [Like Mason's everyday new experience with the carpet. Perhaps he sees it as a big orange sheet of paper to draw on, using his body as the pen.] All that is familiar is covered with snow and the world appears 'brand new.' There is a freshness in the air as Calvin concludes, 'It's a magical world.'

Together Calvin and Hobbes climb on the toboggan and push off down the slope. The little cloud of words over Calvin's head reads, 'Let's go exploring!' There may be trees to dodge, drifts to stumble into, and hidden rocks that will slow [us] down, but like Watterson (and Calvin and Hobbes), we can make a conscious choice to explore old places in new ways. (p. 56–57)

Here Kimes-Myers calls on the wisdom of Calvin and Hobbes in seeing an opportunity for choice, and in this case, a conscious choice of exploring old places in new ways. I am likewise moved by Maxine Greene's sentiments in *Teacher as Stranger* (2000) in which she wondered if teachers might, in Calvin and Hobbes fashion, enter the schoolroom as if a stranger—seeing it for the very first time (like a child!) and wondering what's to be done there. I share her goal in wanting my work to "make teachers' lives 'harder,' not easier, not more ordinary" (Greene 2000, 88). It is apparent that for the standards by which methods and techniques are promoted for and by teachers, the words "easy" and "quick" would seem to represent a greater appeal than "complex" and "deeply-encountering." Perhaps we can imagine teachers as philosophers, engaged in the "conflict between the life one should live and the customs and conventions of daily life [in] an effort to love and think according to the norm of wisdom (a never-ending progression)" (Hadot 1995, 59).

This idea of engaging in conflict with custom and conventions is the reason I was so taken with Mason's fluid and flexible engagement with school as structured in dominance via the time and space divisions of Kindergarten. In a place already complicated with people, rules, structures and cross-purposes, Mason's fluidity served to make it even more complex—and so was dangerous to the dominant and oppressive structure. Schools are, in fact, far less transparent, far more complex, and far more subject to serious debate about both ends and means than they appear to their students or to the adults who remember their school days. New teachers routinely find, to their deep dismay, that teaching is much more difficult and complicated than they anticipated.... [T]hey are likely to be overwhelmed and to fall back on inadequate and idiosyncratic personal resources. (Metz 2006, vii–viii)

In resisting what is unquestioned and unassailable regarding the ways of school, we might engage in strategies of resistance—ones like Mason's and Jacob's, which were natural responses to the place and events—strategies with purpose and design that may cause us to abandon our current identities as the dominant and compliant in order to engage in the common good.

Democracy and Freedom

You measure a democracy by the freedom it gives its dissidents, not the freedom it gives its assimilated conformists.

~ Abbie Hoffmann (in Avni 1989, 16)

In considering the zeitgeist of schooling as represented in chapter 4, I would ask, as Macdonald (1995) did, "whether school essentially reflects service to democratic ideals and individuals," and offer in response McLuhan's (1968) words from *Education as War*, that the educators and schools are aggressors who "simply impose on them [children] the patterns we find convenient to ourselves and consistent with the available technologies" (in Macdonald 1995, 45).

Dewey has described democracy as a way of life guided by an ethical ideal and sustained by personal commitment. In a Deweyian world, each person would be best served by a democracy "created to maximize the common good." Such a condition would necessitate relatedness. In Kimes-Myers's (1997) words:

A spirituality of caring assumes the condition and process of interrelatedness as necessary for a whole approach to young children. This means that a spirituality of caring is political...We recognize such consequences in the ways children are stunted or invited into the world... and we are responsible for the political and social decisions that [in recognition of relationality] mediate the claims of the individual and the community. Ours is a humbling responsibility. (p. 98–99)

And a responsibility that requires not ease and convenience, but great "power of thought." In Dewey's (1910/1978) words, "Genuine freedom, in short, is intellectual; it rests in the trained power of thought, in an ability to 'turn things over' to look at matters deliberately, to judge whether the amount and kind of evidence are requisite for decisions at hand, and if not, to tell where and how to seek such evidence" (p. 232).

In examining Dewey's principles of democratic living, Henderson (2001) explained that we conduct our lives and make decisions based on the following: habit/tradition, coercion/force, or intellect. Dewey insists that in order to educate for democratic living, we must make every effort to nurture in our students dispositions and abilities in conducting their lives using their intellect for *generous* and *generative* purposes—generous, in being sensitive to others, and generative in being in love with life and a desire to learn and grow. And that as their teachers, we must do so ourselves, and not allow ourselves to be coerced, intimidated or seduced into falling into thoughtless patterns of living.

Dewey wrote, "Democracy means freeing intelligence for independent effectiveness—the emancipation of the mind ...[to be associated with]...freedom of action, but freedom of action without freed capacity of though behind it is only chaos. If external authority in action is given up [as I hope it *is*], it must be because internal authority of truth, discovered and known to reason, is substituted" (p. 193). He then asked, "How does the school stand with reference to this matter? Does the school...exhibit this trait of democracy as a spiritual force? Does it lead and direct...[or] does it lag behind at cross-purpose?" (p. 193).

In emancipating the mind, and freeing the heart, I wonder if by turning over Henderson and Kesson's (2004) Deweyian problem of how to "teach for Subject matter understanding while facilitating democratic Self and Social growth" one could make, instead, a problem of how to allow/create space in school for Self and Social growth and democratic participation—which then *requires* Subject matter understanding. Otherwise, I worry that school continues to lag behind at cross-purpose to generous and generative ways of thinking and being. If the self and social understanding that undergird democratic living become first in mind, and the schooled notions of content of disciplines are engaged in response to the common good, perhaps children and their teachers will feel less constrained, less swaddled in the traditions and forces of school life.

> The question I would raise concerns why we prefer democratic and humane arrangements to those which are autocratic and harsh. And by 'why,' I mean the reason for preferring them ....Can we find any reason that does not ultimately come down to the belief that democratic social arrangements promote a better quality of human experience? (Dewey 1969/1938, 34)

In contrasting democracy with fascism, one author noted, "If the major emotional sources of fascism are fear and destructiveness, Eros may be seen to represent the emotional currents of love that a democratic culture obviously requires" (Burch 2000, 182). These emotional currents of love are essential to the development of deep democracy and the quest for democratic goodness.

Where to Go from Here: Love, Comfort and Joy

> *Hello, babies. Welcome to Earth. It's hot in the summer and cold in the winter. It's round and wet and crowded. At the outside, babies, you've got about a hundred years here. There's only one rule that I know of, babies—'God damn it, you've got to be kind!'*

> ~ Vonnegut (1965, 129)

To the late Mr. Vonnegut, the only possible escape from the madness and apparent meaninglessness of existence was human kindness. The title character in his 1965 novel, *"God Bless You, Mr. Rosewater,"* summed up his philosophy: "God damn it, you've got to be kind!"

In considering my own choices in how to respond to this research, my readings of what I observed and learned lead me toward a pursuit of spaces in school for love, comfort and joy. I worry that the harshness of our culture is mirrored too accurately in the places where our children live. It matters to me that children are nurtured as our kin; that they have spaces to move, touch and connect with one another; and that they are cared for and have opportunities to care for others.

I have come full circle in this decision. In one of my very first doctoral classes, only three weeks or so into the course, my professor said to me, "Your problem is that you don't think there's enough joy in school." I was stunned at that time—a little taste of aporia again—and realized he was right. I had never thought of this, but found that when naming my issues with school, with teachers, with the system, most could be traced to a lack of joy.

At times, such lack of joy translates into a harshness that is uncalled for; into a humorlessness that would appear to be the least likely characteristic of a place in which children come to stay; and into yawning chasms separating those who share the space—distances larger than the "arm's length between" or the imaginary "bubble" that serves as a force fields to prevent touches. All of this, even while we likely know that "if we want to develop and deepen the capacity for connectedness at the heart of good teaching, we must understand—and resist—the perverse but powerful draw of the 'disconnected' life" (Palmer 1998, 35).

This brief comment early in my doctoral career shifted my lens toward a more sensuous, spiritual perspective on what happens in classrooms among the people and things that share the space. In this conclusion, I hope to make connections not only to instances of joy, but to instances of comfort (learned from Julian and from other children whose generosity was stunning), and of love.

Comfort

The opposite of freedom is not determinism, but hardness of heart. To be free is to be able to enjoy the fruits of life in a just, caring and compassionate community.

~ Rabbi Heschel (in Purpel 2001, 126)

Recently, James Lawson, a student of Gandhi and renowned civil rights activist who has worked tirelessly toward non-violent solutions and methods, spoke at my university. At the end of his talk, a member of the audience asked what he would have done if he had been the one to respond to the 2001 destruction of the Twin Towers. Lawson replied that he would have comforted those who experienced pain and loss and reflected on the way to heal.

Lawson's answer would find a home in a world where thought and deed spring from love and where we see one another's needs and respond in moral action to the messages sent—a world that resonates with the generous and generative ideals of a Deweyian democracy. His response also stands in stark contrast to the response made by those who *were* in the position to respond to this outrageous tragedy.

I have witnessed this sort of generous spirit in the children and in their teachers—acting with heart, with feeling, as they make room for one another's needs. I saw this spirit in Mrs. Krinkle as she worked with Briona and Princess to share the space on the carpet as one needed to touch and one needed not to be touched. I saw it in Jacob, rising from time-out to place his arm around Clark whose need was great, and even when Clark was inconsolable, Jacob remained generous in his care. And I saw it in Mr. Scott and his children as they tended to Flash's sore neck with attention and regard for his needs and feelings.

In acting with heart—comforting, in joy, with love—these children and their teachers resisted the dominant structures that are in place in school. Spending the entire kindergarten morning in comforting a child with a sore neck is not efficient; moving joyously through the classroom in one's own time is not orderly; seeking contact with another child through playful touches is not appropriate; and no permission was given to lovingly share an arm and some kind words with a crying child. In these inefficient, disordered, inappropriate and presumptuous moments, children and teachers gave and received comfort, joy and love.

In my last year of teaching in public school, my kindergarten children were naming the kinds of jobs they might do to contribute to the well-being of the classroom. After eighteen years of "hiring" board-washers, rabbit walkers, greeters, sharpeners of pencils, gardeners, and messengers, I was joyfully astounded when one child, Aisha, suggested the job of "comforter." In naming the job, she was required to explain what the job would entail and did so with words that approximate these:

> Sometimes people are sad. They come to school sad or they get sad once they are here. They don't always cry, but you can tell that they are sad anyway. If someone had the job of comforter, we could be sure that no one stays sad because the comforter's job would be to notice them.

Aisha, five years old, who, according to developmentalists, would be incapable of this kind of high-level moral thinking, said, *"It would be the comforter's job to notice them"*!! She, at five, understood *seeing* the moral opportunity in order to act on it!

Noddings might view Aisha's idea as an opportunity to support moral life: "We want schools to be places where it is both possible and attractive to be good ....And so it becomes part of our everyday moral obligation to develop and maintain an environment in which moral life can flourish" (Noddings 2002, 9).

In looking back on those sometimes comical, often touching moments of children learning to give and receive comfort, I wondered where they might have learnt it. Even in my classroom, where we bent, folded and mutilated many of the expected structures of school, giving and receiving care was merely incidental. Most classrooms are not places in which moral life can flourish, and as much of the comforting was physical, there is little experience in touch to be gained by spending time in sterile spaces of school. Even the teachers do not touch. As Alison Jones (2003) wrote, "The good teacher today 'touches without touching' (p. 103) [and removes themself] from any physical intimacy with children because of increased awareness of the risk, of the inappropriateness of touch" (p. 109).

I am torn, though—do children need us to "teach" them the moral life? To comfort? Or do we need them to teach us? It seems they do this in spite of how we distance ourselves from them. A pop culture reference may illustrate this point. The child characters on the ribald sitcom *My Name is Earl* demonstrated that moral life can flourish even on a dark-comedy sitcom. The two boys' father/stepfather Earl attempted to take them to Fun Land (he had broken a promise to do so, attending an AC/DC concert instead, and in a nod to Karma, sought to make it up to them), and on arriving at the spot, discovered that Fun Land had been closed down and demolished. He lamented that he could not cross them off his Karma list (they were number 98) and said, "I don't know what I am supposed to do. This has never happened before." And one of the children said, "What if we just forgive you?" Earl, shocked, asked, "What???" And the other son answered, "When someone tells the truth and says they are sorry, you just forgive them" (Buckland 2006). Earl was comforted, not only because his sons forgave him, but also because he re-learned from children that not every trespass and every mistake requires compensation or restitution.

Comfort can be given to those harmed, but also to those who do harm. This is a lesson that may be learned on a television show, but not in school where transgressions are measured, documented and assigned a consequence. If we educators wish for children to experience the feelings and skills necessary to comfort and be comforted, we must learn to engage in comforting the meek *and* the strong.

Joy

Divine laughter is helpless laughter. The recognition that all social constructions are but frail, weak, and finally ineffectual...calls forth an irrepressible belly laugh.

~ Gilbert (1996)

Small things—the morning, perspective—can be lost in the bowels of the earth,
in tunnels where trains convey bodies, human beings with purposes,
human beings surviving.

~ Wenner (2004, 3)

I've said it before and I'll say it again: I worry about small things being lost. Children are not just small things themselves—they are great appreciators of small things: a silly joke, a fly crawling on the window, a ray of sunlight, a tickle fight, a secret. Yet, in most early childhood classrooms, the lives of young children and their teachers "are made up of a series of moments that are missing not necessarily because they are disturbing but because they are too quiet for us to hear, too small for us to see, so apparently uneventful that they fall beneath our threshold of attention" (Tobin 1997, 13). But *are* these moments too quiet or too small? Or are adult's eyes and ears desensitized and misdirected?

Awareness sensing, value sensing, mystery sensing—all require something to be sensed. Children who are swaddled, who are put into classrooms, seated one foot apart and told to face front and "keep hands, feet and other objects to yourself" find little to encounter— or certainly not to encounter deeply—within those tight constraints. As Alice Miller, the Swiss psychiatrist who in some of her paintings has portrayed herself as an infant swaddled by an "evil mother" (1983/1990), and who is a champion of children—those who are children now and those who once were children—is saddened to remark how these attentive, lively and sensitive children who can, for example, remember exactly how they discovered the sunlight in bright grass at the age of four, yet at eight might be unable to 'notice anything' or to show any curiosity...it appears that over time and in the space of school...they have all developed the art of not experiencing feelings, for a child can only experience his feelings when there is somebody there who accepts him fully, understands and supports him. If that is missing, if the child must risk losing the mother's love, or that of her substitute, then he cannot experience these feelings secretly 'just for himself' but fails to experience them at all. (1983/1990, 25)

We tell children what they are feeling ("Oh, You're not hurt"), what's wrong with what they are feeling ("Don't be a baby"), that they are feeling too much ("It's not that funny!") and not to feel at all ("Suck it up!"). As Tobin (1997) wrote: "The core of the problem is not that we are civilized but that we have gone too far. In our contemporary educational settings, under the guise of helping children let their feelings out, we interrupt and then attempt to eliminate expressions of pleasure and desire that we find grotesque, silly, sexual, or sadistic" (p. 17).

In Mr. Scott's classroom, I recall the children in the library center—one of the "hidden" spaces—who were surreptitiously snickering over the pictures that revealed a butt-crack or even a whole "heinie"! I recall the teachers in my former schools who would not read or have in their classrooms a copy of Maurice Sendak's brilliant work *In the Night Kitchen* because on one page Mickey floats out of the milk bottle naked! They asked me how I could show it, knowing that the children would giggle when we came to that page. I told them that children's giggling was one of the reasons I used the book.

Now I teach college students. Mostly young women who are in school to prepare to become teachers and most of whom are in love with the idea of being a teacher, in love with the idea of school. But they worry. They worry about having control over the children in their classroom. They worry about what they're told: not to be so nice, not to be their friend, not to smile until Halloween, or Christmas, or January. They are taught techniques and strategies and are trained to draw a straight line of practice from book to plan to child, They come to believe that being a good teacher is defined by the quiet, orderly, well managed classrooms described by Wong and Wong—classrooms without surprises.

I tell them that with surprise comes joy. I tell them that the very best part of being a teacher is that you get to laugh every single day, and even better, you get to hear the laughter of children every day, too. I tell them what I always knew in my heart—that if the laughter stopped, there's something wrong.

Love

I vow to live fully in each moment and to look at all beings with eyes of compassion.
~ Hanh (1990, 3)

Look at things not with the eyes in your face but with the eyes in your heart.
~ Crow Dog and Erdoes (1995, 1)

Spirituality is what we do with the fire inside us, about how we channel our eros.
~ Rollheiser (1998, 11)

"Democratic living is a particular loving way of being—a celebration of the diversity and humanity underlying the complicated equality of an inclusive 'you and me' and transformative curriculum leaders understand that their responsibility is to cultivate this 'Eros'" (Burch, 2000). Jonathan Kozol took on the responsibility to cultivate this "loving way of being" while appearing on a panel of educators and politicians on PBS's *Children in America's Schools with Bill Moyers* (Hayden and Cauthen 1996). He challenged the other members of the panel and the audience to provide better places for children to attend school, not because it was "good for America," or "would get results," but because, as Americans, *we love our children.* I wonder about this. I think he did, too, really. And was, perhaps, trying to shame us all into thinking about whether we really *do* love *all* of our children. And, if so, in what ways do we demonstrate that love in the places we interact with nearly *all* children—school?

Sadly, the word "love" is rarely mentioned in educational circles. I think back to the teachers' conversations on *teachnet.com* in chapter 4—ones in which "it was worth it to see the shocked looks on their faces," and in which the children are "trying to get across the ocean safely without being disturbed by the sharks" of disrespect and bad behavior. One admired teacher was published in the front page of the town's newspaper saying that she is "killing herself trying to get them to where they should be." The teachers seem to be angry with the children, and not to be looking on them as what Jardine (1998) sadly lamented as "our kin, our kind."

One of my favorite treasured photographs from my teaching years is of my group of kindergartners on the carpet listening to Miss Pryor as she teaches them how to write a poem. Most of the children are seated cross-legged and looking at Miss Pryor or the chart she is using, but Eddie and Matthew are not. Instead, they are lying down—Eddie is facing the ceiling and rolling a pencil between his hands, and Matthew is sprawled on top of Eddie, his legs tangled in Eddie's and his head resting on Eddie's chest as he looks toward Miss Pryor's chart. I love the photo because of the ease the children show with one another. The children who are sitting "properly" are not bothered or concerned with the two boys who are not sitting at all. And Eddie and Matthew are happily engaged with the poem, and with the easy connection with one another. It is a loving picture,

Long ago, I read almost all of the Don Juan books written by Carlos Castaneda. Reading Castaneda was a rite of passage in the 60s and 70s, and one particular lesson in his tales made an impact that I never forgot. Don Juan told Castaneda to do the following toward the living of a good life:

> Look at every path closely and deliberately. Try it as many times as you think necessary. Then ask yourself, and yourself alone, one question: Does this path have a heart? All paths are the same: they lead nowhere...If it does have a heart, the path is good; if it doesn't, it is of no use. Both paths lead nowhere; but one has a heart, the other doesn't. One makes for a joyful journey; as long as you follow it, you are one with it. The other will make you curse your life. One makes you strong; the other weakens you. (Castaneda 1968, 75)

Surely the path with a heart is one in which we carefully and *lovingly* consider our choices and our actions with children, as if all children were our kin and our kind. For aren't they?

Conclusion

Martin Luther King's actions and activism were manifestations not only of his moral character and courage, but also of his frustration and his view of what was unjust—not right. He wrote of a kind of maladjustment, in which he refused to adjust to what was unjust (in Kohl 1994). I believe that moral emotions, such as empathy and moral indignation, may impel action where a more intellectual, even rational, attitude may not. In the passionate words of Mario Savio:

> There is a time when the operation of the machine becomes so odious, makes you so sick at heart, that you can't take part...and you've got to put your bodies on the gears and upon the wheels, upon the levers, upon all the apparatus and you've got to make it stop! (in Goines 1993, 361; a clip of Savio's speech was shown in the 2006 film, *Half Nelson*)

King and Kohl each wrote with passion of a maladjustment to what must be refused due to injustice; Mario Savio fervently exhorted that a time comes when "you've *got to* put your bodies on the gears." It's as simple as Badiou's (2001) statement, "Something must happen, in order for there to be something new" (p. 122). It is in response to the feeling of urgency for *something to happen* for children that my voices as a researcher, advocate, teacher, and teacher educator join together in one loud hue and cry—for in engaging in the "something new," one can (must!) act in any combination of roles and from any position. Beginning with the moment of Reuben's fall, something has happened, and it takes all of my selves—*our* selves— to respond to the call to make something new. To make it *stop*.

Poster (1989, in Lather 1991) writes, "We live amid a world of pain, [and] much can be done to alleviate that pain." This book is my act of putting a stick in the machine—in making something happen—to confront painful and poisonous pedagogy and disrupt the assumptions we make of children, of teachers, and of school.

I often think of what might have happened had Mrs. Buttercup realized she had a choice in how to respond—if she had realized that there was more to see in that moment than Julian's disobedience to the rules of the line. She might have seen Reuben's pain rather than Julian's rule-breaking, and as James Lawson would have done, acted to comfort rather than punish. She might have seen the goodness of Julian's act, and acknowledged it so that all the children could hear, rather than reacting only to the badness of the act. She might have seen the complicated nature of Julian's moment and engaged all of the children in a conversation about the moral dilemma of breaking a rule in the process of giving comfort and aid to another. She might have learned something about Julian that she did not know before— that his active engagement with the other could be considered a good thing. She might have learned that children act with goodness and kindness without threat or promise of punishment or reward. She might have experienced a moment of happiness in the pleasure of witnessing the kindness of a child.

The memory of Reuben's fall forever serves as a symbol of my resistance to order for the sake of order, valuing control over concern and sacrificing kindness to a keeping of the rules. Throughout my remaining teaching years, whenever I found myself leaning toward forcing order and compliance, I looked back on what happened in the hallway outside my classroom and considered whether I had lost my own generosity. For children do need us. They need us to see them, to listen, to care and look out for them. There are many ways to do this, and the cost is so small to us.

In the complicated event of Reuben's fall, I learned a great deal from that moment and from Julian. Julian taught me to *look*, to see what's really there, to recognize each child around me. Julian taught me it matters when the ones who see also share what they see. Julian taught me that the smallest kindness can make a difference. Julian taught me how important it can be to stand up for a child and how it feels when you don't. Julian taught me about strength of spirit and about hope. Julian taught me not to forget.

Appendix

Discipline and Management Plans

As described in earlier chapters in the book, much of the discussion surrounding children's behavior in classrooms is focused on *managing* those behaviors. An emphasis on *techne'*—the details of various methods, strategies and techniques of controlling children—becomes apparent through the quantity and pervasiveness of management plans such as the examples in this appendix, an infinitesimally small sampling of what might have been included.

Consistent among these plans are systems of reward and punishment for behaviors that will be determined by some static external reference for "good" and "bad." Each plan appears to respond to Alfie Kohn's fundamental questions to drive classroom practice, *How can we get these kids to obey*? and not the more generous *What do these children need*? Also consistent among the plans is evidence that teachers are desperately seeking some external means of authority and control.

This is perhaps an opportune time to share Parker Palmer's 1998 discussion of authority:

> In a culture of technique, we often confuse authority with power, but the two are not the same. Power works from the outside in, but the authority works from the inside out....External tools of power have occasional utility in teaching, but they are no substitute for authority, the authority that comes from the teacher's inner life. The clue is in the word itself, which has *author* at its core. Authority is granted to people who are perceived as *authoring* their own words, their own actions, their own lives, rather than playing a scripted role at great remove from their own heart. When teachers depend on the coercive powers of law or technique, they have no authority at all. (32–33)

Discipline Plan

The following rules have been established in my classroom to
ensure a productive learning environment for all students.

Rules:

1. Always follow directions and listen carefully.
2. Keep hands, feet, and objects to yourself.
3. Raise your hand and wait to be called on.
4. Remain in your seat until you have permission to get up.
5. While in the building use in-door voices.

Consequences:

The following will be used to reinforce positive behavior:
1. Positive remarks
2. Recognition
3. Stamps or Stickers
4. Treats

The following guidelines will be used if the student does not follow
rules or is displaying misconduct.

1. The child will receive an oral warning.
2. Each child will have a ticket with ten happy faces on it. The
   second warning will result in losing a happy face.
3. Additional warnings will result in a loss of a happy face.
4. All ten happy faces must be left to receive a blue ribbon and a
   treat and at least five happy faces must be left to receive a
   treat at the end of the week.
5. If a child consistently loses happy faces I will have them sit by
   themselves [sic] for five minutes, [will] notify the parents, and if
   the behavior continues, the student will be referred to the
   principal.

http://hs.sabetha441.k12.ks.us/ses/kindergarten.html

Dear Parent,

I am excited that your child is in my class this year. We can look forward to many fun educational experiences as the year progresses. In order to provide the best instructional environment, I need to insure that no child infringes upon the right of another child to learn. As I firmly believe that lifelong success depends on self-discipline and developing life skills (Effort, Responsibility, Cooperation, Friendship, Respect), I have developed rules and guidelines. These go along nicely with our Character Education Program here at Pleasant Grove Elementary. Daily Behavior Reports will be sent home in a folder for parent's initials.

CLASSROOM RULES:

- Respect others and their property.
- Following directions the 1st time given.
- Keep hands feet and objects to yourself.
- Raise your hand to speak.
- Stay in your work space.

CONSEQUENCES

- Verbal Warning
- Pull Green Card.
- Pull Blue Card and lose a privilege.
- Pull Yellow Card and have 10 minutes time out.
- Pull Orange Card and no ice cream for the week.
- Pull Red Card and removal of student to another classroom or office visit as appropriate to that child. Notice sent to parents.

Please review the above with your child and return the attached slip. Please feel free to contact me at any time.

http://www.henry.k12.ga.us/pges/ingram/Information/discipline.html

Kindergarten Discipline Plan

We firmly believe that life's successes depend on self-discipline.
We have developed a classroom discipline plan that affords every
child the opportunity to manage his or her own behavior. Your
child deserves the most positive learning environment that is
possible for academic growth. Therefore, this plan will be enforced
at all times.

Classroom Rules:

- We listen to each other
- Hands are for helping not hurting
- We use "I Care" Language
- We care about each other's feelings

Students are encouraged to follow class rules by the use of an
apple tree. Each child will begin each day with 3 apples (green,
yellow, red). These apples can be lost for misbehaving in school.

Rewards:

- A prize from the surprise box if five consecutive days of green
  apples
- Daily stickers
- Daily small candy or suckers
- Hold the Class Compliment Chain*
- When the Class Compliment Chain has ten links, the class will
  have a popcorn soda party

*When the class is complimented by an adult on their behavior,
they receive a link in the Class Complement Chain.

Consequences of Misbehavior:

No Violation		Green Apple
1st Violation	Student Receives a Warning; Name is Written on Chalkboard	Maintain Green Apple
2nd Violation	Student Receives a Warning; Student is Placed in Time-Out for 5 Minutes	Yellow Apple
3rd Violation	Student Receives a Warning; Student Loses Recess Privileges	Red Apple
4th Violation	Student Receives a Warning; Parents are Contacted by Note or Telephone	No Apple

Excessive behavior problems will not be tolerated. Each student will have a behavior folder, which will be marked with the above "apple code". We ask that you look at, and initial it each day. Help your child to manage his/her behavior by discussing any behavior problems with them. We discussed this plan with your child at the beginning of school, and will continue to discuss it with them throughout the year. We thank you for your support in helping us to enforce this plan.

http://www.hsv.k12.al.us/schools/elementary/MontES/
Kindergarten.htlm

Discipline Plan

In my class, every child has an apple on the apple tree pocket chart. Every apple begins each day on the tree. The goal is for each child to "keep" their apple on the tree throughout the day. However, if a child does not follow classroom rules, he or she may be asked to move his/her apple to the colored pockets on the trunk of the tree.

Green—   Sit out for 5 minutes
Yellow—   Sit out for 10 minutes of recess or centers (depending
                 on time of day)
Orange—   Miss Half of Recess and/ or Centers (depending on
                 time of day)
Blue—   Time Out—ALL of Recess and/or Centers
Red—   Office

The positive side of this behavior plan is that every child's apple starts out each day on the tree. At the end of each day, those children whose apples are still on the tree will receive a penny stamp in their piggy bank. On Fridays, the "class store" will be open, in which they can "purchase" prizes with their savings. This system uses positive reinforcement as well as introducing the concept of money.

http://asscmail.hayscisd.net/~boothm/Discipline%20Plan.htm

References

Althouse, R., Johnson, M., and Mitchell, S. (2003). *The colors of learning: Integrating the visual arts into the early childhood curriculum*. New York and Washington DC: Teachers College Press/NAEYC.

Alvermann, D. (2001). Researching libraries, literacies and lives: A rhizo-analysis. In E. S. Pierre and W. Pillow (eds.), *Working the ruins: Feminist poststructuralist theory and methods in education*, 114–129. London: Routledge.

Alvesson, M., and Skoldberg, K. (2000). *Reflexive methodology:New vistas for qualitative research*. London: Sage Publications.

Ambrose, R. (2005). Relational spirituality and the lived experiences of classroom community. *Journal of Curriculum and Pedagogy*, 2(2), 93–96.

Anvi, B. (1989). Abbie Hoffman: An interview. *Tikkun*, 4(4), 15-19.

Asmussen, P., von Trier, L., and Pirie, D. (writer) (1996). Breaking the waves [film]. In V. Windelov and P. A. Jensen (producer). Denmark, Netherlands, Sweden, and France: October Films.

Ayers, W. (2001a). *Fugitive days: A memoir*. Boston, MA: Beacon Press.

Ayers, W. (2001b). *To teach: The journey of a teacher*. New York: Teachers College Press.

Ayers, W. (2005). Who in the world am I? In L. Nucci (ed.), *Conflict, contradiction, and contrarian elements in moral development and education*. Mahwah, NJ: Lawrence Erlbaum Associates.

Badiou, A. (2000). *Deleuze: The clamor of being* (L. Burchill, trans.). Minneapolis: University of Minnesota Press.

Badiou, A. (2001). *Ethics: An essay on the understanding of evil* (P. Hallward, trans.). London: Verso.

Badiou, A. (2006). *Being and event*. London: Continuum.

Baker, B. (1998). The dangerous and the good?: Developmentalism, progress, and public schooling. *American Educational Research Journal*, 36, 797-834.

Bakhtin, M. (1968/1984). *Rabelais and his world* (H. Iswolsky, trans.). Bloomington, IN: Indiana University Press.

Bakhtin, M. (1981). *The dialogic imagination: Four essays* (C. Emerson and M. Holquist, trans.). Austin, TX: University of Texas Press.

Barell, J, (1991) *Teaching for thoughtfulness: Classroom strategies to enhance intellectual development.* New York: Longman.

Barbetta, P., Leong-Norona, K., and Bicard, D. (2005). Classroom behavior management: A dozen common mistakes and what to do instead. *Preventing School Failure, 49* (3), 11-19.

Barone, T. (2001). *Touching eternity: The enduring outcomes of teaching.* New York: Teacher's College Press.

Barone, T., and Eisner, E. (1997). Arts-based educational research. In R. Jaeger (ed.), *Complementary methods for research in education* (2nd ed., 75-116). Washington, DC: American Educational Research Association.

Baumrind, D. (2005). Taking a stand in a morally pluralistic society: Constructive obedience and responsible dissent in moral/character education. In L. Nucci (ed.), *Conflict, contradiction, and contrarian elements in moral development and education.* Mahwah, NJ: Lawrence Erlbaum, Associates.

Behar, R. (1996). *The vulnerable observer: Anthropology that breaks your heart.* Boston: Beacon Press.

Bennett, W. (1993). *The book of virtues: A treasury of great moral stories.* New York: Simon and Schuster.

Bentham, J. (1787/1995). *The Panopticon writings.* In M. Bozovic (ed.), 29-95. London: Verso.

Berliner, C. (2002). Educational research: The hardest science of all. *Educational Researcher, 31*(8), 18-20.

Best, S., and Kellner, D. (1991). *Postmodern theory: Critical interrogations.* New York: Guilford Press.

Bey, H. (1991). *T. A. Z. The temporary autonomous zone, ontological anarchy, poetic terrorism.* Brooklyn, NY: Autonomedia.

Bluestein, J. (2004). *Is obedience enough?* Retrieved September 30, 2005 11:36 PM, 2003

Borden, I. (2001). *Skateboarding, space and the city: Architecture and the body.* Oxford: Berg.

Bowd, A. (1982). *Quiet please: A practical guide to classroom discipline.* Toronto: Gage.

Bradley, B. (2001). *Skateboarding and the countermapping of city space.* Retrieved April 27, 2004

Bredekamp, S., and Copple, C. (eds.). (1997). *Developmentally appropriate practice in early childhood programs*. Washington DC: National Association for the Education of Young Children.

Broadway, F., Leafgren, S., and Gilbert, A. (2007). *Touch me! Touch me! Touch me! Pleasure, desire, and sexuality in early childhood*. Paper presented at the Curriculum and Pedagogy Conference.

Browning, F. (1998). *A queer geography. Journey towards a sexual self*. New York: The Noonday Press.

Buber, M. (1956). *The workings of Martin Buber*. In W. Herberg (ed.). New York: Meridian Books.

Buber, M. (1958/1970). *I and thou: A new translation with a prologue "I and you" and notes by Walter Kaufmann* (W. Kaufmann, trans.). New York: Scribner.

Buckland, M. (writer) (2006). Barn Burner. In J. H. Lange (producer), *My Name is Earl*. Los Angeles: Twentieth Century Fox.

Bunyard, D. (2005). Sticky fingers, or how to love a postmodern child. *Contemporary Issues in Early Childhood, 6*(3), 292-300.

Burbules, N. (1986). Tootle: A parable of schooling and destiny. *Harvard Educational Review, 56*(3), 239-256.

Burch, K. (2000). *Eros as the educational principle of democracy*. New York: Peter Lang.

Burnard, S. (1998). *Developing children's behaviour in the classroom: A practical guide for teachers and students*. London: The Falmer Press.

Butchart, R. (1995). Discipline, dignity and democracy: Reflections on the history of classroom management. *Educational Studies, 26*(3), 165-185.

Butler, M. (1998). Negotiating place: The importance of children's realities. In S. Steinberg and J. Kinchloe (eds.), *Students as researchers: Creating classrooms that matter*, 94-112. London: Falmer.

Buzzelli, C. (1993). Morality in context: A sociocultural approach to enhancing young children's moral development. *Child and Youth Care Forum, 22*(5), 375-386.

Cannella, G. (1999). The scientific discourse of education: Predetermining the lives of others—Foucault, education and children. *Critical Issues in Early Childhood Education, 1*(1), 36-44.

Canter, L., and Canter, M. (1992). *Assertive discipline: Positive behavior management for today's classroom*. Santa Monica, CA: Canter and Associates.

Capra, F. (1985). *The tao of physics: An exploration of the parallels between modern physics and eastern mysticism* (2nd ed.). Toronto: Bantam Books.

Castaneda, C. (1968). *The teachings of Don Juan: Yaqui way of knowledge.* Berkeley, CA: University of California Press.

Chomsky, N. (2004). *Chomsky on miseducation.* Lanham, MD: Rowman and Littlefield Publishers, Inc.

Church, E. (2007). *What makes a good kindergarten: See how to evaluate a program — and how to advocate for your child if his classroom doesn't measure up.* Retrieved May 24, 2007 from http://content.scholastic.com/browse/article.jsp?id=10189

Clarke, J. (2004). Picturing places in the assemblage of flexibility in further education. In R. Edwards and R. Usher (eds.), *Space, Curriculum and Learning.* Charlotte, NC: Information Age Publishers.

Coles, R. (1990). *The spiritual life of children.* Boston: Houghton Mifflin.

Colvin, G., Sugai, G., and Patching, B. (1993). Pre-correction: An instructional approach for managing predictable problem behaviors. *Intervention in School and Clinic, 28*(3), 143-150.

Corbett, S. (1991). Children and sexuality. *Young Children, 46,* 71-77.

Counts, G. (1932). *Dare the school build a new social order?* New York: John Day Company.

Crow Dog, L., and Erdoes, R. (1995). *Crow dog: Four generations of Sioux medicine men.* New York: Harper Perennial.

Daniels, G., and Groening, M. (writer). (1995). Lisa's wedding, *Simpsons*: Twentieth Century Fox.

Das, L. (1998). *Awakening the Buddha within: Tibetan wisdom for the western world.* New York: Doubleday Religion.

Davidson, L. (1998). *Wisdom at work: The awakening of consciousness in the workplace.* Burdett, NY: Larson Publications.

Debruyn, R., and Larson, J. (1984). *You can handle them all: A discipline model for handling over one hundred different misbehaviors at school and at home.* Manhattan, KS: The MASTER Teacher, Inc.

Deleuze, G. (1983). *Nietzsche and philosophy* (H. Tomlinson, trans.). New York: Columbia University Press.

Deleuze, G. (1987). *Dialogues.* New York: Columbia University Press.

Deleuze, G. (1995). *Negotiations* (M. Joughin, trans.). New York: Columbia University Press.

Deleuze, G. (2001). *Pure immanence:Essays on a life* (A. Boyman, trans.). New York: Zone Books.

Deleuze, G., and Guattari, F. (1972/1983). *Anti-Oedipus: Capitalism and schizophrenia.* Minneapolis, MN: University of Minnesota Press.

Deleuze, G., and Guattari, F. (1987). *A thousand plateaus: Capitalism and schizophrenia* (B. Massumi, trans.). Minneapolis, MN: University of Minnesota Press.

den Heyer, K. (email communication, 2007).

den Heyer, K. (2009). Education as affirmative invention. *Educational Theory,59*(4).

DeNoon, D., and Peterson, L. (writer). (2000). Baby Killer [television]. In D. J. Burke (producer), *Law and Order: Special Victims Unit.* New York: Wolf Films Production; NBC Universal Television Studio.

Derrida, J. (1967/1974). *Of grammatology* (G. Spivak, trans.). Baltimore: Johns Hopkins.

Dever, M., and Falconer, R. (2008). *Foundations and change in early childhood education.* Hoboken, NJ: John Wiley and Sons.

DeVries, R., and Zan, B. (1994). *Moral classrooms. moral children: Creating a constructivist atmosphere is early education.* New York: Teacher's College Press.

Dewey, J. (1902). *The educational situation.* Berkeley, CA: University of California Press.

Dewey, J. (1903). Democracy in Education. *The Elementary School Teacher, 4* (4), 193-204.

Dewey, J. (1910/1978). *Educational Essays.* London: Blackie and Son.

Dewey, J. (1916). *Democracy and education.* New York: Macmillan Co.

Dewey, J. (1929/1984). The quest for certainty. In H. F. Simon (ed.), *John Dewey: The later works, 1925-1953* (Vol. 4). Carbondale, IL: Southern Illinois University Press.

Dewey, J. (1932). The nature of moral theory. In J. Tufts (ed.), *Ethics,*171-176. New York: Holt, Rinehart and Winston.

Dewey, J. (1934). *Art as experience.* New York: Minton, Balch.

Dewey, J. (1937). Democracy and educational administration in school and society XLV. In J. Gouinlock (ed.), *The moral writings of Dewey,* 457-462.

Dewey, J. (1938/1969). *Experience and education.* London: Collier Books.

Dewey, J. (1960). *The quest for certainty.* New York: Capricorn Books.

Dewey, J. (1985). Ethics. In J. A. Boydston (ed.), *The later works of John Dewey, 1925-1953* (Vol. 7). Carbondale, IL: Southern Illinois University Press.

Dreikurs, R. (1982). *Maintaining sanity in the classroom* (2nd ed.). New York: HarperCollins.

Driscoll, A., and Nagel, N. (2002). *Early childhood education, birth-8: The world of children, families and educators* (2nd ed.). Boston, MA: Allyn and Bacon.

Duke, D., and Jones, V. (1984). Two decades of discipline: Assessing the development of an educational specialization. *Journal of Research and Development in Education 17*(4), 25-35.

Ehrensal, P. (2003). Constructing children in schools: Policies and the lessons they teach. *Journal of Curriculum Theorizing, 19*(2), 117-134.

Eisenberg, N., and Hand, M. (1979). The relationship of preschoolers' reasoning about prosocial moral conflicts to prosocial behavior. *Child Development, 50,* 356-363.

Eisner, E. (1998). *The enlightened eye: Qualitative inquiry and the enhancement of educational practice.* Upper Saddle River, NJ: Prentice Hall, Inc.

Eisner, E. (2002). *The arts and the creation of the mind.* New Haven, CT: Yale University Press.

Eisner, E.W. (1994). *Cognition and curriculum reconsidered* (2nd ed.). New York: Teachers College Press.

Elias, N. (1978). *The civilizing process: The history of manners.* Oxford: Basil Blackwell.

Ellsworth, E. (1992). Why doesn't this feel empowering? Working through the repressive myths of critical pedagogy. In C. Luke; and J. Gore (eds.), *Feminism and critical pedagogy,* 90-119. New York: Routledge.

Emerson, R. (1940). Self-reliance. In B. Atkinson (ed.), *The complete essays and other writings of Ralph Waldo Emerson,* 145-169. New York: Random House.

Emerson, R. (2001). *Contemporary field research: Perspectives and formulations* (2nd ed.). Long Grove, Illinois: Waveland Press, Inc.

Eminem. (2004). Mosh [CD]: Aftermath.

Erny, P. (1973). *Childhood and cosmos:The social psychology of the Black African child* (A. Mboukou, trans.). New York: New Perspectives.

Everston, C., and Harris, A. (1992). Synthesis of research: What we know about managing classrooms. *Educational Leadership 49,* 74-78.

Fifield, S. (2008). *Comments on "Touch me! Touch me!" Sexuality, pleasure and gender in early childhood.* Paper presented at the American Educational Research Association.

Foucault, M. (1979). *Discipline & punish: The birth of the prison* (A. Sheridan, trans.). New York: Vintage Books.

Foucault, M. (1980a). *Power/knowledge: Selected interviews and other writings, 1972-1977.* London: Harvester.

Foucault, M. (1980b). *The history of sexuality, volume 1: An introduction*. New York: Vintage.

Foucault, M. (1988). The ethic of care for the self as a practice of freedom: An interview with Michel Foucault on January 20, 1984. In J. Bernauer and D. Rasmussen (eds.), *The Final Foucault*. Cambridge, MA: MIT Press.

Frankl, V. (1984). *Man's search for meaning*. New York: Washington Square Press.

Freiberg, H. J. (ed.). (1999). *Beyond behaviorism: Changing classroom management paradigm*. Needham Heights, MA: Allyn and Bacon.

Freire, P. (1970). *Pedagogy of the oppressed*. New York: Herder and Herder.

Friedenberg, E. (1965). *The dignity of youth and other atavisms*. Boston: Beacon Press.

Gaines, E. (1993). *A lesson before dying*. New York: A. A. Knopf

Garrison, J. (1997). *Dewey and Eros: Wisdom and desire in the art of teaching*. New York: Teachers College Press.

Gatto, J. T. (1992). *Dumbing us down: The hidden curriculum of compulsory schooling*. Philadelphia, PA: New Society Publishers.

Gay, G. (1997). Connections between character education and multicultural education. In A. Molnar (ed.), *The construction of children's character: Ninety-sixth yearbook of the National Society for the Study of Education*. Chicago: National Society for the Study of Education/University of Chicago Press.

Geertz, C. (1973). *The interpretation of cultures*. New York: Basic Books.

Geisel, T. (1957). *The cat in the hat*. New York: Random House Books for Young Readers.

Gilbert, S. (1996). Etymologies of humor: Reflections on the humus pile. Retrieved January 8, 2007,   http://sincronia.cucsh.udg.mx./etymolog. htm

Giroux, H. (1983a). Theories of reproduction and resistance in the new sociology of education: A critical analysis. *Harvard Educational Review, 53*(3), 257-293.

Giroux, H. (1983b). *Theory and resistance in education: Toward a pedagogy for the opposition*. Massachusetts: Bergin and Garvey Publishers.

Giroux, H. (1996). *Fugitive cultures: Race, violence and youth*. New York: Routledge.

Giugni, M. (2006). Conceptualizing goodies and baddies through narratives of Jesus and Superman. *Contemporary Issues in Early Childhood, 7*(2), 97-108.

Glod, M. (2007, June 18). Va. school's no-contact rule is a touchy subject. *Washington Post*, B01.

Goffman, E. (1961). *Asylums*. New York: Anchor Books Doubleday and Company, Inc.

Goines, D. (1993). *The free speech movement: Coming of age in the 1960s*. Berkeley, CA: Ten Speed Press.

Goodman, J. (2001). Niceness and the limits of rules. *Journal of Moral Education, 30*(4), 349-360.

Gordon, A., and Browne, K. (2008). *Beginnings and beyond: Foundations in early childhood education* (7th ed.). Clifton Park, NY: Thompson Delmar Learning.

Gouinlock, J. (Ed.). (1994). *The moral writings of John Dewey*. Amherst, New York: Prometheus Books.

Gray, J. (1967). *The teacher's survival guide*. Palo Alto, CA: Fearon Publishers.

Greene, M. (1981). The humanities and emancipatory possibility. *Journal of Education, 163*(4), 287-305.

Greene, M. (1988). *The dialectic of freedom*. New York: Teachers College Press.

Greene, M. (1991). Teaching: The question of personal reality. In A. Lieberman and L. Miller (eds.), *Staff development for education in the '90s* (2nd ed.), 3-14. New York: Teachers College Press.

Greene, M. (2000). Reflections on *Teacher as Stranger*. *Journal of Curriculum Theorizing, 16*(3), 85-88.

Greene, M. (2001). Reflections on teaching. In V. Richardson (ed.), *Handbook of research on teaching* (4th ed.), 82-89. Washington, D.C.: American Educational Research Association.

Groening, M. (1988). *Childhood is hell: A cartoon book by Matt Groening*. New York: Pantheon.

Groening, M. (1997). *The huge book of hell*. New York: Penguin Books.

Grosz, E. (1994). *Volatile bodies: Toward a corporeal feminism*. Bloomington, IN: Indiana University Press.

Hadot, P. (1995). *Philosophy as a way of life: Spiritual exercises from Socrates to Foucault* (M. Chase, trans.). Malden, MA: Blackwell Publishing.

Hanh, T. (1990a). *Our appointment with life: Discourse on living happily in the present moment*. Berkeley, CA: Parallax Press.

Hanh, T. (1990b). *Present moment, wonderful moment: Mindfulness verses for daily living*. Berkeley, CA: Parallax Press.

Hanh, T. (1998). *Interbeing: Fourteen guidelines for engaged Buddhism.* Berkley, CA: Parallax Press.

Hansen, D. (1995). Teaching and the moral life of classrooms. *Journal for a Just and Caring Education, 2,* 59-74.

Hansen, D. (2001). *Exploring the moral heart of teaching: Toward a teacher's creed.* New York: Teachers College Press.

Harris, M. (1989). *Dance of the spirit: The seven stages of spirituality for women.* New York: Bantam Books.

Hart, T. (1999). The refinement of empathy. *Journal of Humanistic Psychology, 39*(4), 111-125.

Hart, T. (2003). *The secret spiritual world of children.* Makawao, Maui, HI: Inner Ocean.

Hart, T. (2006). Spiritual experiences and capacities of children and youth. In E. Roehlkepartain, P. Ebstyne-King, L. Wagener; and P. Benson (eds.), *The handbook of spiritual development in childhood and adolescence,* 163-177. Thousand Oaks, CA: Sage Publications.

Hawthorne, R., and Henderson, J. (2000). *Transformative curriculum leadership.* Upper Saddle River, NJ: Merrill-Prentice Hall.

Hay, D., and Nye, R. (1998). *The spirit of the child.* London: Harper Collins.

Hayden, J., and Cauthen, K. (1996). Children in America's schools with Bill Moyers [Video Recording]. South Carolina: The Saint/Hayden Company.

Henderson, J. (1999). Three personal reflections. In J. Henderson and K. Kesson (eds.), *Understanding democratic curriculum leadership.* New York: Teachers College Press.

Henderson, J. (2001a). Deepening democratic curriculum work. *Educational Researcher, 30*(9), 18-21.

Henderson, J. (2001b). *Reflective teaching: Professional artistry through inquiry* (3rd ed.). Upper Saddle River, NJ: Merrill Prentice Hall.

Henderson, J., and Kesson, K. (2004). *Curriculum wisdom: Educational decisions in democratic societies.* Upper Saddle River, NJ: Pearson/Merrill Prentice Hall.

Henderson, J., and Kesson, K. (eds.). (1999). *Understanding democratic curriculum leadership.* New York: Teachers College Press.

Henderson, J., and Slattery, P. (2006). Democracy, artistry, improvisation, and transformation: Curriculum and pedagogy in a new key. *Journal of Curriculum and Pedagogy, 3*(1), 1-9.

Henderson, J., and Slattery, P. (2007). Editor's Introduction. *Journal of Curriculum and Pedagogy, 3*(2).

Highsmith, P. (1941/2002). Miss Juste and the green rompers. In *Nothing that meets the eye: The uncollected stories of Patricia Highsmith*. New York: W.W. Norton and Company.

Holland, D., Lachicotte, W., Skinner, D., and Cain, C. (1998). *Identity and agency in cultural worlds*. Cambridge, MA: Harvard University Press.

hooks, b. (1993). A life in the spirit: Reflections on faith and politics. *ReVision, 1*(3).

hooks, b. (1994). *Teaching to transgress: Education as the practice of freedom*. New York: Routledge.

Hostetler, K. (2005). What is "good" educational research? *Educational Researcher, 34*(6), 16-21.

Hwu, W. (2004). Gilles Deleuze and Jacques Daignault: Understanding curriculum as difference and sense. In W. Reynolds and J. Webber (eds.), *Expanding curriculum theory: Dis/positions and lines of flight,*181-202. Mahwah, NJ: Lawrence Erlbaum Associates.

Infinito, J. (2003). Jane Elliot meets Foucault: The formation of ethical identities in the classroom. *Journal of Moral Education, 32*(1), 67-76.

Jackson, P. (1968). *Life in classrooms*. New York: Holt, Reinhart and Winston.

Jackson, P., Boostrom, R., and Hansen, D. (1993). *The moral life of schools*. San Francisco: Jossey-Bass Publishers.

Jardine, D. (1992). Reflections on education, hermeneutics, and ambiguity: Hermeneutics as a restoring of life to its original difficulty. In W. R. Pinar, W. (ed.), *Understanding curriculum as phenomenological and deconstructed text*. New York: Teachers College Press.

Jardine, D. (1998). *To dwell with a boundless heart: Essays in curriculum theory, hermeneutics, and the ecological imagination*. New York: Peter Lang.

Jardine, D., Clifford, P., and Friesen, S. (2003). *Back to the basics of teaching and learning: Thinking the world together*. Mahwah, New Jersey: Lawrence Erlbaum Associates, Inc.

Jeralyn. (2004). *Treating children like criminals*. Retrieved February 23, 2007, http://www.talkleft.com/story/2004/05/15/144/98415, posted on Sat May 15, 2004 at 01:00:16 PM EST

Johnston, B., and Buzzelli, C. (2002). Expressive morality in a collaborative learning activity: A case study in the creation of moral meaning. *Language and Education, 16*(1), 37-47.

Jones, A. (2003). Touching children: Policy, social anxiety, and the 'safe' teacher. *Journal of Curriculum Theorizing, 19*(2).

Jones, F. (1978). Instructor's guide to sanity-saving discipline. *Instructor, 64.*

Keleman, S. (1981). *Your body speaks its mind.* Berkeley: Center Press.

Kesson, K. (1999). Toward a curriculum of mythopoetic meaning. In J. Henderson and K. Kesson (eds.), *Understanding democratic curriculum leadership.* New York: Teachers College Press.

Kesson, K. (2005). On bumblebees and Pleiades: Schooling and the great journey of the soul. *Journal of Curriculum and Pedagogy, 2*(2), 42-44.

Kesson, K. (2006). *Response to Traveling the spiritual path toward social justice, activism and disobedience: Engaging in public moral leadership.* Paper presented at the American Educational Research Association, San Francisco.

Kimes-Myers, B. (1997). *Young children and spirituality.* New York: Routledge.

King, M. L. (1963). *Why we can't wait.* New York: Harper and Row.

Kohl, H. (1994). *I won't learn from you and other thoughts on creative maladjustment.* New York: The New Press.

Kohl, H. (1998). *The discipline of hope: Learning from a lifetime of teaching.* New York: Simon and Schuster.

Kohlberg, L. (1981). *Essays on moral development: Vol. 1. The philosophy of moral development: Moral stages and the idea of justice.* San Francisco: Harper and Row.

Kohlberg, L., Levine, C., and Hewer, A. (1983). Moral stages: A current formulation and a response to critics. In J. Meacham (ed.), *Contributions to human development* (Vol. 10). New York: Karger.

Kohlberg, L., and Lickona, T. (1987). Moral discussion and the class meeting. In R. DeVries, and Kohlberg, L (eds.), *Programs of early education: The constructivist view,* 143-181. New York: Longman.

Kohn, A. (1990). *The brighter side of human nature.* New York: Basic Books.

Kohn, A. (1993/1999). *Punished by rewards: the trouble with gold stars, incentive plans, A's, praise, and other bribes.* Boston: Houghton Mifflin.

Kornfield, J. (2007). Teachings of the Buddha. Boston, MA: Shambhala.

Kozol, J. (1967). *Death at an early age.* New York: Houghton Mifflin.

Krieg, S. (2006, November). *Working with unbelievable children: Troubling professional identities in contemporary early childhood education.* Paper presented at the The Center for Equity in Early Childhood International Early Childhood Conference: Honouring the Child; Honouring Equity 6, Melbourne, Australia.

Lather, P. (1991). *Getting smart: Feminist research and pedagogy with/in the postmodern*. New York: Routledge.

Lather, P. (1993). Fertile obsession: Validity after poststructuralism. *The Sociological Quarterly, 34*(4), 673-693.

Lather, P. (1997). Creating a multi-layered text: Women, AIDS, and angels. In W. Tierney and Y. Lincoln (eds.), *Representation and the text: Re-framing the narrative voice*, 233-258. Albany: State University of New York Press.

Lather, P. (2006). Paradigm proliferation as a good thing to think with: Teaching research in education as a wild profusion. *International Journal of Qualitative Studies in Education, 19*(1), 35-57.

Leafgren, S. (2004). A teacher's story. In J. Henderson and K. Kesson (eds.), *Curriculum wisdom: Educational decisions in democratic societies,*135-144. Upper Saddle River, NJ: Pearson/Merrill Prentice Hall.

Leafgren, S. (2006). *Joining the "spirited" child on the playful, uncertain and disobedient path toward wisdom.* Paper presented at the Annual Conference of the American Educational Research Association, San Francisco, CA.

Leafgren, S., and Ambrose, R. (2005). *Reuben's fall: Intellectualizing moral agency and power relationships.* Paper presented at the Reconceptualizing Early Childhood Conference, University of Wisconsin, Madison, WI.

Leander, K., and Rowe, D. (2006). Mapping literacy spaces in motion: A rhizomatic analysis of a classroom literacy performance. *Reading Research Quarterly, 41*(4), 428-460.

Leavitt, R., and Power, M. (1997). Civilizing bodies: Children in day care. In J. Tobin (ed.), *Making a place for pleasure in early childhood education*. New Haven: Yale University Press.

Lechte, J. (1994). *Fifty key contemporary thinkers: From structuralism to postmodernity*. London: Routledge.

Lennon, J. (1967). *Strawberry fields forever.* [LP] Parlophone/Capitol.

Letts, W., and Sears, J. (1999). *Queering elementary education: Advancing the dialogue about sexualities and schooling*. Lanham, MD: Rowman and Littlefield Publishers, Inc.

Lickona, T. (1991). *Educating for character: How our schools can teach respect and responsibility*. New York: Bantam Books.

Lickona, T. (1997). Educating for character: A comprehensive approach. In A. Molnar (ed.), *The construction of children's character: Ninety-sixth yearbook of the National Society for the Study of Education*. Chicago: NSSE/University of Chicago Press.

Lightfoot, C. (2000). On respect. *New Ideas in Psychology* (18), 177-185.

Lightfoot, C. (2005). Risk-taking, carnival, and the novelistic self. In L. Nucci (ed.), *Conflict, contradiction, and contrarian elements in moral development and education.* Mahwah, NJ: Lawrence Erbaum Associates.

Lincoln, Y., and Guba, E. (1985). *Naturalistic Inquiry.* Beverly Hills, CA: Sage.

Linn, R. (1989). *Not shooting and not crying: Psychological inquiry into moral disobedience.* Westport, CT: Greenwood Press.

Lorde, A. (1984). *Sister outsider: Essays and speeches.* Trumansburg, N.Y.: Crossing Press.

Lozinsky, M., and Collinson, I. (1999, June). *Epistemological shudder:The X-files, myths and mimetic capital.* Paper presented at the University of South Wales Post

Graduate Conference School of English and Modern Languages, South Wales.

Lundry, W. (2003). To classify is to control. *Thrasher* (267), 134-149.

Lynch, K. (1979). The spatial world of children. In *The child in the city: Today and tomorrow,* 102-127. Toronto: University of Toronto Press.

Macdonald, B. (ed.). (1995). *Theory as a prayerful act: The collected essays of James B. Macdonald* (Vol. 22). New York: Peter Lang.

Macdonald, J. (1974). *A transcendental developmental ideology of education.* Paper presented at the Rochester Conference, Berkeley, CA.

MacNaughton, G. (2003). Eclipsing voice in research with young children. *Australian Journal of Early Childhood, 28*(1), 36-42.

MacNaughton, G. (2004). The politics of logic in early childhood research: A case of the brain, hard facts, trees and rhizomes. *The Australian Educational Researcher, 31*(3), 87-104.

MacNaughton, G. (2005). *Doing Foucault in early childhood studies: Applying poststructural ideas.* New York: Routledge.

Makarushka, I. (1998). Transgressing goodness in Breaking the Waves. *Journal of Religion and Film, 2*(1), na.

Martinson, F. (1994). *The sexual life of children.* Westport, CN: Bergin and Garvey.

Massumi, B. (1992). *A user's guide to capitalism and schizophrenia. Deviations from Deleuze and Guattari.* Cambridge: Massachusetts Institute of Technology.

McCadden, B. (1996). Becoming a student: The moral significance of entry into kindergarten. *Educational Foundations, 10*(2), 23-36.

McCadden, B. (1998). *It's hard to be good: Moral complexity, construction, and connection in a kindergarten classroom*. New York: Peter Lang Publishing.

McDaniel, T. (1994). A back-to-basics approach to classroom discipline. *Clearing House, 67* (5).

McGoey, K., Prodan, T., and Condit, N. (2007). Examining the effects of teacher and self-evaluation of disruptive behavior via school-home notes for two young children in kindergarten. *Journal of Early & Intensive Behavior Intervention, 3-4*(4), 365-376.

McLuhan, M., and Fiore, Q. (1968). *War and peace in the global village*. New York: Bantam Books.

Mead, M. (1951). What makes Soviet character? *Natural History Magazine*.

Mehan, H. (1979). *Learning lessons: Social organization in the classroom*. Cambridge, MA: Harvard University Press.

Merriam, S., and Associates (eds.). (2002). *Qualitative research in practice: Examples for discussion and analysis*. San Francisco: Jossey-Bass.

Merrill, J. (1965). *The pushcart war*. New York: William R. Scott, Inc.

Metz, M. (2006). Foreword. In J. Pace, and A. Hemmings (eds.), *Classroom authority: Theory, research and practice*. Mahwah, NJ.: Lawrence Erlbaum Associates.

Milgram, S. (1974). The perils of obedience. In *Obedience to authority: An experimental view*. London: Tavistock Publication.

Miller, A. (1979/1990). *The drama of being a child* (R. Ward, trans.). New York: Vantage Point

Miller, A. (1983/1990). *For your own good: Hidden cruelty in child-rearing and the roots of violence* (H. and H. Hannum, trans.) (3rd ed.). New York: Noonday Press.

Miller, A. (1990). *Banished knowledge: Facing childhood injuries* (L. Vennewitz and A. Miller, trans.). New York: Anchor Book.

Miller, A. (2000). Mary and Joseph—Parents to emulate. A Message for Christmas 2000. Retrieved December 12, 2005, 2:03a.m.

Miller, J. (2000). *Education and the soul: Toward a spiritual curriculum*. New York: State University of New York Press.

Morrison, T., and Morrison, S. (1999). *The big box*. Boston: Hyperion.

Mullooly, J., and Varenne, H. (2006). Playing with pedagogical authority. In J. Pace and A. Hemmings (eds.), *Classroom authority: Theory, research and practice*. Mahwah, NJ: Lawrence Erlbaum Associates.

Murdoch, I. (1970/1985). *The sovereignty of good.* London: Ark.

Nelson, A. (2004). *The outlaw collective: Skateboarding and rhizomatic countermapping.* Pittsburgh, PA: Carnegie Mellon University.

Nespor, J. (1997). *Tangled up in school: Politics, space, bodies and signs in the educational process.* Mahwah, NJ: Lawrence Ehrlbaum Associates.

Nietzsche, F. (1883/1982). Thus spoke Zarathustra (W. Kaufman, trans.). In W. Kaufman (ed.), *The portable Nietzsche,* 103-440. New York: Penguin Books.

Nietzsche, F. (1966). *Beyond good and evil* (W. Kaufmann, trans.). New York: Random House.

Noddings, N. (1993). *Educating for intelligent belief or unbelief.* New York: Teachers College Press.

Noddings, N. (2002). *Educating moral people: A caring alternative to character education.* New York: Teachers College Press.

Noddings, N. (2003). *Happiness and education.* Cambridge: Cambridge University Press.

Nucci, L. (ed.). (2005). *Conflict, contradiction, and contrarian elements in moral development and education.* Mahwah, NJ: Lawrence Erlbaum Associates.

O'Donaghue, D. (2006). Situating space and place in the making of masculinities in schools. *Journal of Curriculum and Pedagogy, 3*(1), 15-33.

Oser, F. (2005). Negative morality and the goals of moral education. In L. Nucci (ed.), *Conflict, contradiction, and contrarian elements in moral development and education.* Mahwah NJ: Lawrence Erlbaum Associates.

Oser, F., and Spychiger, M. (2004). *Learning is painful. Towards a theory of negative knowledge and the praxis of mistake culture.* Freiburg, Germany: Universitat Freiburg, Departement Erziehungswissenchaften.

P!nk. (2006). Dear Mr. President. On *I'm Not Dead* [CD].

Pace, J., and Hemmings, A. (2007). Understanding authority in classrooms: A review of theory, ideology, and research. *Review of Educational Research, 77*(1), 4-27.

Paley, V. (1981). *Wally's stories: Conversations in the kindergarten.* Cambridge, MA: Harvard University Press.

Paley, V. (1999). *The kindness of children.* Cambridge, MA: Harvard University Press.

Palmer, P. (1998). *The courage to teach: Exploring the inner landscape of a teacher's life.* San Francisco: Jossey-Bass.

Patton, P. (1996). *Deleuze: A critical reader.* Oxford, UK: Blackwell Publishers Ltd.

Phelan, A. (1997). Classroom management and the erasure of teacher desire. In J. Tobin (ed.), *Making a place for pleasure in early childhood education.* New Haven: Yale University Press.

Phenix, P. (1974). Transcedence in the curriculum. In E. Eisner and E. Vallance (eds.), *Conflicting conception of curriculum.* Berkeley: McCutchan.

Piaget, J. (1932). *The moral judgment of the child.* New York: Free Press.

Piaget, J. (1995). *Sociological studies.* London: Routledge.

Pillow, W. (1997). Exposed methodology: The body as deconstructive practice. *International Journal of Qualitative Studies in Education, 10*(3), 349-363.

Pinar, W. (2004). *What is curriculum theory?* Mahwah, NJ: Lawrence Erlbaum.

Pinar, W., Ayers, W., and Schubert, W. (2007). *The future of curriculum studies and teacher education.* Paper presented at the 2007 Curriculum Summit: School of Teaching and Learning, Bowling Green University, Bowling Green, OH.

Pittman, S. (1985). A cognitive ethnography and quantification of a first-grade teacher's selection routines for classroom management. *Elementary School Journal, 85,* 541-557.

Purpel, D. (1989). *The moral and spiritual crises in education: A curriculum for justice and compassion in education.* Granby, MA: Bergin and Garvey.

Purpel, D. (2001). *Moral outrage in education.* New York: Peter Lang.

Quinn, D. (1992). *Ishmael.* New York: Bantam/Turner.

Quinn, M. (2001). *Going out, not knowing whither: Education, the upward journey and the faith of reason.* New York: Peter Lang.

Rendon, L. (2007, April 9). *Spirituality in teaching for diversity and equity in secular higher education settings: Interactive session.* Paper presented at the American Educational Research Association, Chicago, IL.

Rendon, L. (2008). *Sentipensante (sensing/thinking) pedagogy.* Sterling, VA: Stylus Press.

Reynolds, W. (2004). To touch the clouds standing on top of a Maytag refrigerator: Brand-name postmodernity and a Deleuzian "in-between". In W. Reynolds and J. Webber (eds.), *Expanding curriculum theory: Dis/positions and lines of flight,* 19-33). Mahwah, NJ: Lawrence Erlbaum Associates.

Rinne, C. (1997). *Excellent classroom management.* Belmont, CA: Wadsworth Publishing Co.

Roffey, S.and O'Reirdan, T. (2001). *Young children and classroom behavior: Needs, perspectives and strategies.* London: David Fulton Publishers.

Rogers, C. (1980). *A way of being.* New York: Houghton Mifflin Company.

Rogovin, P. (2004). *Why can't you behave? The teacher's guide to creative classroom management, K-3.* Portsmouth, NH: Heinemann.

Rollheiser, R. (1998). *Seeking spirituality.* London: Hodder and Stoughton.

Rorty, R. (1986). Foucault and epistemology. In D. C. Hoy (ed.), *Foucault: A critical reader,* 41-49. Cambridge, MA: Basil Blackwell.

Rosemond, J. (2006a, February 28). Pundits propogate problems with kids, self-esteem, discipline among exposed myths. *Akron Beacon Journal,* E1.

Rosemond, J. (2006b, September 19). "Shhhhhhh!' isn't enough for talkative 8-year-old. *Akron Beacon Journal.*

Rosenberg, M. (1994). Physics and hypertext: Liberation and complicity in art and pedagogy. In G. Landow (ed.), *Hyper/Text/Theory,* 268-298. Baltimore: John Hopkins University Press.

Rosenblatt, L. (1994). *The reader, the text, the poem : The transactional theory of the literary work.* Carbondale, IL: Southern Illinois University Press.

Rousseau, J. (1979). *Emile, or On Education* (A. Bloom, trans.). New York: Basic Books.

Saukko, P. (2001). *Doing research in cultural studies: An introduction to classical and new methodological approaches.* London: Sage.

Schwartz, B. P., J. (1981). *How to get your children to be good students; How to get your students to be good children.* Englewood Cliffs, NJ: Prentice-Hall, Inc.

Scott, M. (in progress). *The people who own the school.* Unpublished Master's Thesis, Kent State University, Kent, OH.

Sergiovanni, T. (1994). *Building community in schools.* San Franciso: Jossey-Bass.

Shahjahan, R. (2007, April 9). *Spirituality in teaching for diversity and equity in secular higher education settings: Interactive session.* Paper presented at the American Educational Research Association, Chicago, IL.

Shannon, D. (1999). *David goes to school.* New York: Blue Sky Press.

Shapiro, S. (2006). Elements of a Jewish Pedagogy. *Journal of Curriculum and Pedagogy,* 2(2), 23.

Sheets, R. (1996). Urban classroom conflict: Student-teacher perception: Ethnic integrity, solidarity, and resistance. *Urban Review, 28*(2), 165-183.

Sherblom, S. A. (1997). *Moral sensibility and experience in young children: A relational study in moral development.* Unpublished dissertation, Harvard University.

Sinclair, U. (1922). *The goose-step: A study of American education.* Pasadena, CA: Upton Sinclair.

Slattery, P. (1995). *Curriculum development in the postmodern era* (Vol. i). New York: Garland Publishing, Inc.

Smith, K. (2003, November). *The paper bag princess, Harry Potter, and Buffy the Vampire-Slayer: Exploring popular culture texts to create new co-ordinates for observation as a political practice for social justice.* Paper presented at the Honouring the Child Honouring Equity 3 Conference, Melbourne University.

Solomon, D., Watson, M., and Battistich, V. (2001). Teaching and schooling effects on moral/prosocial development. In V. Richardson (ed.), *Handbook of research on teaching.* Washington DC: American Educational Research Association.

St. Pierre, E. (1997). Methodology in the fold and the irruption of transgressive data. *International Journal of Qualitative Studies in Education, 10*(2), 175-189.

St. Pierre, E. (2000). The call for intelligibility in postmodern educational research. *Educational Researcher, 29*(5), 25-28.

St. Pierre, E. (2002). Troubling the categories of qualitative inquiry. In S. Merriam and Associates (eds.), *Qualitative research in practice: Examples for discussion and analysis.* San Francisco: Jossey-Bass.

Steiner, R. (1995). *The kingdom of childhood* (H. Fox, trans.). Hudson, NY.: Anthroposophic Press.

Strong, T., and Fuller, M. (2000, July). *"Alive" moments & "poetic" invitations to spiritual discourse.* Paper presented at the International Conference on Searching for Meaning, Vancouver, British Columbia.

Tanner, L. (1980). A model of school discipline. In E. H. Weiner (ed.), *Discipline in the classroom.* Washington, DC: National Education Association.

Thomas, S. (2002). The silence of the lambs: Construction of childhood in the public sphere. *Journal of Curriculum Theorizing, 18*(3), 91- 104.

Thoreau, H. (1848/1966). *Walden and civil disobedience.* New York: W.W. Norton and Co., Inc.

Thorpe, R. (writer). (1996). The right thing, *"ER".* USA.

Tobin, J. (ed.). (1997). *Making a place for pleasure in early childhood education.* New Haven: Yale University Press.

Trantino, T. (1972). *Lock the lock.* New York: Knopf.

Trantino, T. (2001). Part III Interview with Tommy Trantino. *moment: http://www.moment.gr.jp/4/special.html*

Turiel, E. (2005). Resistance and subversion in everyday life. In L. Nucci (ed.), *Conflict, contradiction and contrarian elements in moral development and education.* Mahwah, NJ: Lawrence Erlbaum Associates.

Turner, H.,and Watson, T. (1999). Consultant's guide for the use of time out in the preschool and elementary classroom. *Psychology in the Schools, 36*(2), 135-147.

Turteltaub, J. (writer) (1999). *Instinct.* B. Boyle (producer). USA: Buena Vista Productions.

Vonnegut, K. (1965). *God bless you, Mr. Rosewater.* New York: Dell Publishing.

Vonnegut, K. (1999). *God bless you Dr. Kevorkian.* New York: Seven Stories Press.

Wang, M., Haertel, G., and Walberg, H. (1993). Toward a knowledge base for school learning. *Review of Educational Research, 63*, 249-294.

Watson, M. (2003). *Learning to trust: Transforming difficult elementary classrooms through developmental discipline.* San Francisco, CA: Jossey-Bass.

Watts, A. (2007). *In my own way* (2nd ed.). Novato, CA: New World Library.

Weiner, E. H. (ed.). (1980). *Discipline in the classroom.* Washington DC: National Education Association.

Weinstein, C., Tomlinson-Clarke, S., and Curran, M. (2004). Toward a conception of culturally responsive classroom management. *Journal of Teacher Education, 55*(1), 25-38.

Weisberg, J. (2002). More George W. Bushisms: *More of Slate's accidental wit and wisdom of our 43rd president.* New York: Fireside Publications.

Welker, W. (1976). Discipline—A reality of teaching. *Education 76*(3), 238- 240.

Wells, H. G. (1895/1986). *The time machine.* New York: Tom Doherty Associates.

Wenner, K. (2004). *Dancing with Einstein.* New York: Scribner.

Wheldall, K. (ed.). (1992). *Discipline in schools: Psychological perspectives on the Elton Report.* London: Routledge.

White, P. (2007, April 13). Mrs. White's kindergarten class. Retrieved March 10, 2007, http://www.holyrosary.edu/TeacherWeb/WhiteWeb/White.htm#Rules

Whitelock, R. (2006). Queerly fundamental: Christian fundamentalism, southern queerness, and curriculum studies. *Journal of Curriculum and Pedagogy, 3*(165-186).

Wilber, K. (1996). *The Atman Project: A transpersonal view of human development.* Wheaton, IL: Quest Books: Theosophical Publishing House.

Wong, H., and Wong, R. (1998). *The first days of school: How to be an effective teacher.* Mountain View, CA: Harry K. Wong Publications, Inc.

Woolley, H., and Johns, R. (2001). Skateboarding: The city as playground. *Journal of Urban Design, 6*(2).

Wragg, E. (2001). *Class management in the primary school.* London: Routeledge.

Wynne, E.,and Ryan, K. (1993). *Reclaiming our schools: A handbook on teaching character, academics, and discipline.* New York: Macmillan.

Wynne, E. and Ryan, K. (1997). For-character education. In A. Molnar (ed.), *The construction of children's character,* 63-76). Chicago: University of Chicago Press.

Zahn-Waxler, C., Radke-Yarrow, M., and King, R. (1979). Child rearing and children's prosocial initiations toward victims of distress. *Child Development, 50*(2), 319-330.

Zinn, H. (1968). *Disobedience and democracy: Nine fallacies on law and order.* New York: Random House.

Zinn, H. (2001). Democracy isn't falling into line. *Socialist Worker Online, http://www.socialistworker.org/2001/379/379_09_HowardZinn.shtml,* 8-9.

Zinn, H. (2005). You can't be neutral on a moving train. On *You can't blow up a social relationship* [CD]. Chicago, IL: Thick Records.

Index

About the Author

Sheri L. Leafgren is an assistant professor in the Department of Teacher Education at Miami University in Oxford, Ohio. Her research interests include studying the possibilities within, and complexity of, children's disobedience; studying the role children's spirituality plays in the socio-moral opportunities within the classroom; applying Greene's "teacher as stranger" to teacher preparation and development; and studying the role of the "Elder" in African-centered education.

Prior to joining Miami University, she taught children in grades K-3 for nineteen years in the Akron Public Schools in Akron, Ohio. She continues to work with the Council of Elders associated with the African-centered school where she last taught, and has carried gifts of the Elder's wisdom to her new place of work and life.

Sheri holds a Ph.D. in Curriculum and Instruction from Kent State University. She currently serves as an assistant editor for the *Journal of Curriculum & Pedagogy,* as a research consultant with the Curriculum Leadership Institute, and as a university partner to the teachers, children and community of Middletown Ohio's Central Academy.

Mother to Monica, Aaron and Kerry, and grandmother to Alana, Kristopher, and Olan, Sheri lives in Oxford with her youngest daughter, Sylvia, and their dog Meryl.